THEOLOGY AND DIALOGUE

THEOLOGY AND DIALOGUE

Essays in Conversation with George Lindbeck

Edited by Bruce D. Marshall

Essay Index

Library of Congress Cataloging-in-Publication Data

Theology and dialogue : essays in conversation with George
Lindbeck / edited by Bruce D. Marshall.
    p. cm.
    Includes index.
    ISBN 0-268-01873-1 – ISBN 0-268-01874-X (pbk.)
    1. Theology. 2. Lindbeck, George A. I. Lindbeck, George A.
II. Marshall, Bruce, 1955–
BR50.T42955 1990
230–dc20   90-70847
                                                    CIP

Dedicated to
GEORGE A. LINDBECK
Pitkin Professor of Historical Theology
Yale University
with affection and esteem

CONTENTS

ACKNOWLEDGMENTS

I would like to thank all of the contributors to this volume, who responded so willingly to the invitation to write an original essay for it; all of their work is here published for the first time. The volume was originally planned by a group of four: Hans Frei, David Kelsey, Joe DiNoia, and myself. Without the ever-ready advice and encouragement of David and Joe, the book would simply not exist, and I am deeply grateful to them. John Bollier and Michael Root helped extensively with the bibliography; Rojean Fall-Vetsch and Joe DiNoia also provided emergency aid. Amidst her innumerable other duties, Jody Greenslade typed the original manuscript for the volume, made all the needed corrections, and responded to my numerous cries for help when confronted with the mysteries of the microcomputer.

Finally, I join the other contributors in expressing my gratitude and appreciation to, as David Burrell observes in his essay, "the work and person of George Lindbeck—for I have learned equally from both."

Bruce D. Marshall
Northfield, Minnesota

CONTRIBUTORS

DAVID B. BURRELL, C.S.C., is Theodore M. Hesburgh, C.S.C., Professor of Arts and Letters at the University of Notre Dame.

J. A. DINOIA, O.P., is Associate Professor of Theology and Editor of *The Thomist* at the Dominican House of Studies, Washington, D.C.

HANS W. FREI was until his death John A. Hoober Professor of Religious Studies at Yale University.

DAVID H. KELSEY is Professor of Theology at Yale Divinity School.

NICHOLAS LASH is Norris-Hulse Professor of Divinity at the University of Cambridge.

BRUCE D. MARSHALL is Assistant Professor of Religion at St. Olaf College.

PETER OCHS is Wallerstein Visiting Associate Professor of Jewish Studies at Drew University.

MICHAEL ROOT is Research Professor at the Institute for Ecumenical Research, Strasbourg, France.

The Right Reverend STEPHEN SYKES is Bishop of Ely and formerly Regius Professor of Divinity at the University of Cambridge.

DAVID TRACY is Andrew Thomas Greeley and Grace McNichols Greeley Distinguished Service Professor of Catholic Studies at the Divinity School, the University of Chicago.

INTRODUCTION

BRUCE D. MARSHALL

Contemporary Christian theology is markedly dialogical in character, even where dialogue is not an explicit preoccupation. Theologians routinely find that their own tasks naturally lead them into dialogue on at least three distinguishable fronts: with the ecumenical Christian community at large and the claims of other segments of that community and other theologians about the shape Christian belief and practice ought to take; with the claims to goodness and truth—political, philosophical, and otherwise—alive in their cultures; and with other religious traditions and the comprehensive ways of ordering life and understanding reality which they propose. Each of these types of conversation has a long history in Christian theology; no one of them, by its presence, distinguishes current theology from that of the past. The remarkable feature of the present situation is rather the far-reaching agreement among theologians—regardless of their differing convictions about the direction the dialogues should take—that all three types of dialogue insistently and simultaneously demand their constructive attention.

These dialogical imperatives have helped to engender much puzzlement and reflection about how theology now ought to proceed: how can theology best undertake its own distinctive tasks while honoring these urgent imperatives for dialogue? One of the most influential and controversial proposals about the path contemporary theology should take is that of George Lindbeck. The publication of *The Nature of Doctrine* in 1984 brought Lindbeck's vision of religion, Christian doctrine, ecumenical dialogue, and the tasks of theology to the attention of a wide audience of Christian theologians and other students of

1

religion. The book is the work of a theologian who, from the beginning of his career, has been oriented consistently toward theological questions where the imperatives for dialogue are most pressing. His early work focuses on the complex relation between theology and philosophy in the Western Middle Ages, particularly in Aquinas and Scotus. He was an observer from the Lutheran World Federation at the Second Vatican Council and was deeply engaged in the American and international Lutheran-Roman Catholic dialogues from their inception. Decades of reflection upon progress and problems in these ecumenical discussions lead Lindbeck to make, in *The Nature of Doctrine*, the "postliberal" proposals (as they have come to be called, using Lindbeck's own term) about religion, doctrine, and theology for which he has become widely known. And his recent work in ecclesiology suggests a pattern for the Christian church's self-understanding which is substantially informed by constructive dialogue between Christians and Jews.

Sharing his commitment to theological dialogue, and in gratitude for his contributions to it, the authors of this volume wish to honor George Lindbeck by themselves heeding the imperatives for dialogue to which he has so consistently attended. All of them have found their own reflection shaped by conversation with Lindbeck— and that not just of a purely literary kind, since all have known him as colleague and friend, and several have been his students. But the primary aim of this volume is not to debate Lindbeck's theological claims, even though they do, to be sure, receive significant attention. The chief aim is to chart new ground in each of the three areas of theological dialogue: to rethink established assumptions and lines of division and to open up new possibilities for constructive theology. The essays presented here seek to accomplish this aim by addressing two sets of issues to which Lindbeck's work has drawn especially powerful attention, however one assesses his own claims.

The three essays in Part One of the book deal with the question of how the present task of theology should be conceived, given a context in which, as the threefold imperative for dialogue suggests, it is especially important to clarify the relationship between what is distinctive to Christianity and the wider array of human belief and practice. Each of the essays approaches that basic question by focusing on a specific problem. David Kelsey analyzes the relationship between the Christian church's own discourse and the wider public realm by considering whether "culture" and "language," taken as master metaphors for the nature of religion and doctrine, imply a sectarian account of the church. David Tracy argues that the plain sense of the passion narrative is central to Christian theological interpretation of the Bible and at the same time that recognition of its centrality should fund theological receptivity to the widest possible range of interpretations of that narrative. The essay by Bruce Marshall focuses on the interaction between the beliefs of the Christian community and the array of truth claims the community encounters, proposing a strategy for the articulation of Christian truth claims which both ascribes criteriological primacy to Christian beliefs and entails an open-ended engagement with other claims to truth.

The essays in Part Two of the book all focus on historically specific and problem-specific cases of theological dialogue. David Burrell, Nicholas Lash, and Hans Frei attend to relationships between theology and its environing culture. Burrell and Lash both deal with the dialogue between relatively independent philosophical and scientific worldviews and Christian theology, and specifically with how this dialogue affects the ways theologians talk about God—Aquinas and Scotus for Burrell; several theologians at the dawn of modernity for Lash. Hans Frei develops a typology of contemporary ways of reading biblical narratives as these have emerged in a complex conversation between theology, hermeneutics, and literary theory.

With the essays by Michael Root and S. W. Sykes the focus shifts to dialogue within the Christian community. Root analyzes a key problem which has emerged after several decades of official dialogue between historically divided Christian confessions: how can a consensus sufficient for church unity reliably be identified? This problem might best be resolved, he suggests, by employing appropriate practical tests for doctrinal consensus and dissensus. Sykes's essay engages one of the most vexed areas of Christian ecumenical dialogue: the power of bishops. He argues that the issue is best understood, and the difficulties it poses best handled, by combining theological with sociological modes of analysis.

Dialogue between Christianity and other religious traditions is the focus of the final essays in Part Two. Peter Ochs shows how some of the key ideas in *The Nature of Doctrine* have deep affinities with those of an emerging group of "aftermodern" Jewish thinkers and suggests how an engagement with Lindbeck might prove fruitful for Jewish self-understanding. J. A. DiNoia proposes an alternative to problematic contemporary ways of constructing a Christian theology of religions by attending especially to the distinctive relationship between the ultimate goals at which different religious communities aim and the specific patterns of life they commend to their members.

The volume concludes with an Epilogue by Hans Frei in which Lindbeck's lifelong colleague offers his own reflections on Lindbeck's work and on their theological friendship. The essay was originally given as a talk at Yale Divinity School several years ago, at a gathering convened to celebrate the publication of *The Nature of Doctrine*. Hans Frei died suddenly while our volume was in preparation, and it seems especially fitting to leave the last word in it to him.

PART ONE:

Conceiving the Theological Task

CHURCH DISCOURSE
AND PUBLIC REALM

DAVID H. KELSEY

In *The Nature of Doctrine* George A. Lindbeck made the controversial proposals that a religion be looked at as "a kind of cultural and/or linguistic framework or medium that shapes the entirety of life and thought"[1] and that its doctrines (in contradistinction to theological remarks) are best construed as "communally authoritative rules of discourse, attitude, and action."[2] One of the major objections to this pair of theses[3] has been that, when applied to Christianity in particular, they somehow inescapably bring with them a "sectarian" view of the church according to which the churches and their discourse could not be genuinely engaged in the "public" realm.

Lindbeck has published three essays sketching programmatically a distinctive theological view of the church. It will be illuminating to play his theses about the nature of doctrine and his theses about the church off against each other. Do his proposals about the church tend to support the objection noted above to his theory of doctrine? If not, does that show that Lindbeck has simply been inconsistent? Or that he has been misread? I will argue that the objection is materially wrong but, in a manner of speaking, formally correct. That is, Lindbeck's two theses about doctrine do not entail any one material theological view of the church, "sectarian" or otherwise. However, the worry that they might do so is rooted in a genuine insight into the formal limits of the usefulness of the terms "linguistic framework," "cultural," and "language" as metaphors for the church and its discourse and action.

7

I. CULTURE AND LANGUAGE AS METAPHORS

The root of the problem, if there is one, may lie in Lindbeck's master metaphors for the nature of doctrine. More exactly, it may lie in a chain of metaphors and a final analogy: A religion (in this case Christianity) is (like) a culture; a culture is (like) a language; and as French grammar is to the French language, so is Christian doctrine to Christianity. The view of doctrine is intended to be purely formal; the objection is that nonetheless it somehow makes church life and discourse be *in principle* disengaged from, and logically incapable of engaging in, the public realm. It may be that the objection is rooted in an intuition about an inapplicability of the metaphor. After all, it is as important to a metaphor's force that the two things it compares be *un*like in some regards as it is that they be alike in others.

According to Lindbeck's celebrated "cultural-linguistic"[4] way of construing them, religions—in this case we consider Christianity only —"are thought of primarily as different idioms for construing reality, expressing experience, and ordering life."[5] In Christianity the "idiom" consists of a "comprehensive scheme or story used to structure all dimensions of existence . . ."; it is "not primarily a set of propositions to be believed, but rather the medium in which one moves, a set of skills that one employs in living one's life."[6] Thus Christianity is like a culture which taken as a whole involves both a rich complex of forms of life and ways of speaking. Following Clifford Geertz,[7] Lindbeck then proposes that cultures are best construed as ordinary languages, intelligible because the symbols that comprise them are used in accord with an implicit "grammar." So much for the chain of metaphors; on to the concluding analogy: As rules of grammar are to a language, so are doctrines to Christian discourse.

It is crucially important to discussion of Lindbeck's theses about the nature of Christian doctrines always to keep in mind that the theses are developed to resolve a particular problem. The chain of metaphors and the concluding analogy that fund the theses are not selected because of some sort of general, topic-neutral illuminating power they might have, but only because they are fruitful of a reso- lution of a particular problem: How can it be claimed both that (a) Christian teachings have profoundly changed through history, and that (b) through history Christianity remains the "same thing"? In Lindbeck's view, making truth-claims has been an essential aspect of

Christianity's unchanging identity. Hence it is inadequate to resolve this problem by proposing that changing teachings were not properly truth-claims in the first place but were rather symbolic "expressions" of unchanging religious "experience." Nor will it do to defend the truth-claimingness of Christianity by denying the reality of deep changes in Christian teaching and practice. Lindbeck proposes that the "abiding and doctrinally significant" aspect of Christianity lies "in the story it tells" (a story which functions as an "idiom" for Christians) "and in the grammar that informs the way the story is told and used." This story, as narrated in canonical Scriptures, is the source of "the core of lexical elements" in this language (symbols, concepts, rites, injunctions, stories); but it is the "grammar" of Christianity, not the lexicon, "which church doctrines chiefly reflect."[8] Hence Lindbeck's central thesis about church doctrines: "The function of church doctrines . . . in this perspective is their use . . . as communally authoritative rules of discourse, attitude, and action."[9]

This requires a distinction between doctrine and theology. "Church doctrines" are described as "communally authoritative teachings regarding beliefs and practices that are considered essential to the identity or welfare of the group in question."[10] In what way are they teachings *regarding* beliefs and practices? Doctrines are second-order teachings of the rules governing authentically Christian first-order formulations of beliefs and rules shaping practices. Doctrines are authoritative insofar as they function as "*rules* of discourse, attitude, and action."[11] Furthermore, doctrines are limited to teaching the rules relevant to those beliefs and actions that constitute the church's *identity*. Moreover, doctrines are rarely, if ever, straightforwardly formulated. Rather, they are taught, as aspects of an ordinary language's grammar often are, by "exemplary instantiations or paradigms of the application of rules."[12] Lindbeck suggests, for example, that Nicene and Chalcedonian formulations are best seen as "paradigmatically instantiating doctrinal rules"[13] which are held faithfully, not when they are simply replicated, but rather when the directives they illustrate are followed in making new first-order formulations. Paradigms are inevitably imperfect and often misleading. A competent speaker, who may have no talent for second-order reflection on the rules inherent in the speaking, is more likely to be a reliable guide.[14] In any case, in Lindbeck's theory of doctrine, church doctrine does not dictate *what* to say and do in novel circumstances, but rather what rules must be followed if what is said is to count as authentically Christian. As "rules," doctrines are in that sense formally and not materially significant.[15]

"Theology," by contrast, stands alongside a variety of kinds of first-order Christian discourse. Christianity's "vocabulary of symbols and its syntax may be used for many purposes, only one of which is the formulation of statements about reality."[16] Theology is distinguished as the discourse involved in the "explanation, communication, and defense of the faith within the framework of communal doctrinal agreement."[17] There is room in theology so conceived for an enormous range of topics and for deep disagreements.[18] The range follows from the fact that whereas doctrine deals only with what is communally essential, theological proposals "generally deal with everything that is desirable to teach...."[19] Because explanation, communication, and defense all involve the effort to construe reality in the idiom that *is* Christianity, and because that "reality" itself constantly changes, there will always be disagreements among theological proposals about what is desirable to teach and why. Lindbeck stresses that Christianity, like any religion, is inherently engaged in a dialogue with its social and cultural situation. As the situation changes, the idiom "develops anomalies in its application in new contexts."[20] This requires changes in first-order theological truth claims,[21] but just which changes is a question open to extensive disagreement. Where changes in the social and cultural situation generate theological disagreement, doctrines-as-rules are the condition of the possibility of significant disagreement. Disagreement is possible precisely when formulations of the remarks of all parties to the dispute are ruled by the same "framework of doctrinal agreement."

Doctrines-as-rules do not mandate any particular material content to changing theology. What they do require of theology is three types of testing. First, they must be tested as to their "faithfulness" or authentic Christianness. Lindbeck proposes that "[o]ne test of faithfulness ... is the degree to which [theological] descriptions correspond to the semiotic universe paradigmatically encoded in holy writ,"[22] and he sketches an "intratextual" hermeneutic as the way to do this. He stresses that in Christianity this criterion of faithfulness is formal, leaving open the possibility of intra-Christian disagreement not only in "theological descriptions of a religion"[23] (in this case Christianity) but even concerning the biblical norm itself.[24]

Second, theological proposals must also be tested as to their applicability in church praxis in the current situation. "All-embracing systems of interpretation possess their own internal criteria of applicability."[25] The criteria of applicability mandated by the grammar of Christianity surface in an "activity more like contemporary futurology than biblical prophecy." Drawing on empirical studies to help discern "the signs of the times," its aim is "not to foretell what is to come, but to shape present action to fit the anticipated and hoped-for future,"[26] thereby exhibiting the applicability of the Christian praxis to social reality.

Third, theological proposals must be tested as to their intelligibility and reasonableness. Lindbeck proposes that the criterion relevant here is "skill." To the degree that Christianity is like a language, the test of its intelligibility is its learnability. Its intelligibility cannot be exhibited by translating it into some other language (another "all-embracing system of interpretation"), but by being skillful at teaching it to people.[27] Lindbeck points out that this approach "need not confine . . . theological study . . . to an intellectual ghetto, but can free it for closer contact with other disciplines."[28] So too, the credibility of Christianity is best exhibited by the church's living it so skillfully that it strikes others as attractive—attractive, among other things, for "its assimilative powers . . . its ability to provide an intelligible interpretation in its own terms of the varied situations and realities adherents encounter."[29] Although it is not possible to decide between major alternative "interpretations" on the basis of reason alone, it is possible to subject a Christian theological proposal to "ad hoc apologetics," "rational testing procedures not wholly unlike those which apply to general scientific theories or paradigms (for which, unlike hypotheses, there are no crucial experiments)."[30]

Against this sketch of Lindbeck's theses about the nature of doctrine and the metaphors that govern them, let us turn to his theological remarks about the nature of the church. The purpose, of course, is to test the complaint that Lindbeck's theses about doctrine in fact privilege a sectarian ecclesiology according to which the church in principle cannot engage in the public realm. If true, Lindbeck's theses bear two grievous burdens: internal inconsistency in not being neutral as to possible alternative theological positions on every topic, in this case ecclesiology; and then favoring a particularly unattractive ecclesiology in the bargain!

II. ECUMENICAL SECTARIANISM

More than twenty years ago in "Ecumenism and the Future of Belief" (1968),[31] Lindbeck outlined some theological theses about the church which he subsequently elaborated and sometimes qualified in two other essays, "The Sectarian Future of the Church" (1971)[32] and "The Story-Shaped Church: Critical Exegesis and Theological Interpretation" (1987).[33] Both these theological theses and the ways in which Lindbeck argues for them are directly relevant to our project.

In the present social situation, he proposes, "church" is most appropriately understood as a sect that is ecumenical, exclusivist, and engaged. As Lindbeck repeatedly and vigorously points out, the sense in which the "church" is best understood as "sect" is a sociological and emphatically *not* a theological sense of "sect." Sociologically, a sect is a relatively small group of persons whose beliefs and behavior are sharply differentiated from the surrounding society. It is a cognitive minority living in some cognitive dissonance with its host society. Because it is a deviant minority in a larger society, a sect receives no support for its beliefs from the society at large and has to rely on the group's own inner life to provide that support. In 1971, Lindbeck amplified this point. Although construing "church" as "sect" does stress the importance of "tight-knit fellowship," it does not entail a negative attitude toward the institutionalization of "church." It does not celebrate "community" at the expense of "structure." It does imply "a deinstitutionalization of old structures and a reinstitutionalization of new forms."[34] Theologically, by contrast, a sect is a relatively small group of Christians who separate from other churches, declaring themselves the only genuine church and breaking fellowship with all other self-described Christians.[35] Lindbeck uses "sect" and "sectarian" in the sociological sense only.[36]

More particularly, a church is best understood as an "ecumenical" sect. This is the positive obverse of the negative rejection of the theological concept "sect." The ecumenicity of which Lindbeck writes has "little to do with much that passes under that name in present discussions where it often tends to refer to any blurring of the distinctions and differences" among Christian groups. "[T]he official ecumenism of the ecclesiastical bureaucracies is in part the product of pressures similar to those which produce price-fixing, mergers and monopolies in the business world."[37] In contrast, what Lindbeck has in mind are churches that, while sociologically sectarian in their relationships with their host cultures, are in fellowship with one another in a world-wide network ("a Christian internationale"!)[38] and, further, are "ecumenical—or, if you prefer, 'catholic'—in their inclusion of rich and poor, black and white, educated and uneducated, alien and native."[39] Note an important consequence: Sociologically speaking, although they are sects in the sense of being cognitive minorities, churches on this view are *not* sects in the sense of being groups whose members are drawn from some one specificable socioeconomic location, and churches' unity does not derive from their members sharing the material interests attendant on any such location. Their ecumenicity or catholicity makes them thoroughly pluralistic in those regards.

Furthermore, a church is best understood as an "exclusivist" ecumenical sect. This theme is developed in the 1971 essay. "Christian sectarianism would continue to be 'orthodox' in the sense of maintaining recognizable continuity with the absolute and exclusive claims of the mainstream Christian tradition." The exclusivity is highly particular: it has to do with claims about Jesus. "It would persist in affirming that Jesus is the Lord of lords . . . the criterion of all criteria for evaluating whatever purports to be knowledge or experience of the mystery which surrounds our beginnings and our end." At very least, Lindbeck thinks, this is a "logical necessity." "The affirmation of the Lordship of Christ is historically so thoroughly embedded in the very notion of Christian identity, that it is . . . cognitively dissonant to maintain one without the other."[40] It is important to ask just what it is that is "exclusive." Lindbeck stresses that its formulation and interpretation has changed often in the history of Christianity. Whatever "it" is, it cannot be identified with any particular theological formula. Hence Lindbeck's use of "orthodox" cannot be understood (as would otherwise be quite natural) as the conservative preservation of and adherence to some set of dogmatic "symbols." Moreover, whatever "it" is that is exclusive, it is entirely compatible with the conviction that God works redemptively outside of church as well as within. "Christians must therefore respect and be ready to learn from non-Christians and to adopt dialogue rather than proselytism as the appropriate form of witness." Hence Lindbeck's use of "exclusivist" must be understood in a way consistent with a certain kind of theological "universalism."[41]

Finally, Lindbeck stresses the "engagement" of these exclusivist and ecumenical sects in the public realm. The fundamental purpose of the church is to witness to the Kingdom of God "in the power of the cross as suffering servants" of humankind; hence "the Church must stand with the poor and oppressed against the rich and the oppressors. . . . It must side with the underdeveloped nations against the complacency and irresponsibility of the affluent, so-called Christian ones."[42] The church is thus a thoroughly "this-worldly" sect that can be a "creative minority" in the very society from which it is deviant.[43] Lindbeck's description of those engaged ecumenical sects sometimes sounds uncannily like a description of Latin American "base communities."

Clearly, while Lindbeck's theological theses about the church emphatically adopt one kind of sectarian view, they do not entail a disengagement of the church from the public realm. To the contrary, they make engagement in the shared public world essential to the life of a church. The way in which Lindbeck argues in support of his theological theses underscores this point. He argues for his theses on three fronts: to show that they are relevant to the real world; to show that they deserve credence; to show that they are Christianly authentic. Lindbeck's arguments that his picture of the church is relevant are an exercise in practical theology. They proceed, not by showing that his picture is a body of theory that could be applied to current social actuality like a blueprint for reconstruction, but rather by arguing that his picture of the church is rooted in and could grow out of the dynamics of concrete social reality. This is something like "futurology" in which a conversation is generated between theology on one side and sociology and history on the other.

Theology: The question is, what are the major changes American society is undergoing in regard to religion?

Sociology: There is a progressive secularization of the society which will leave the churches as cognitive minorities whose views are not supported by society at large. Nonetheless, religions have remarkable staying power, so at least vestigial religious groups will survive.[44] (Or, alternatively, three years later): There is a vigorous resurgence of religious interest and practice that views religiosity as a highly private matter and is marked by extreme pluralism and eclecticism.[45]

Theology: No matter. The sociological and historical evidence is that given the dynamics of either type of social change, religious groups will probably survive as sects. The sectarian character of the future church is simply rooted in social reality. However, the historical evidence has been that when a Christian group became sociologically sectarian it also became theologically sectarian.[46] In the present situation, could a church become sectarian sociologically while remaining "ecumenical" or "catholic"?

History: The connection between the two sorts of sectarianism depended on the "establishment" of Christianity. Under those circumstances, to be deviant from society in general was therewith also to break from the *corpus christianum*. However, before the Constantinian establishment, churches were both sectarian (sociologically) and ecumenical. Under those conditions the connection between the two sorts of sectarianism did not hold.

Theology: If what the sociologists say is true, then the dynamics of our society are moving us into a situation analogous to that of the early church, whether through progressive secularization or through the rise of privatized and pluralized religiosity. The roots of the future sectarianism of the church and of the possibility of its ecumenicity lie deep in current social reality.

The point of such a conversation, Lindbeck reminds us, is not to forecast the future so that one may ride its crest into the new age but (in Daniel Bell's phrase) "to widen the spheres of moral choice"[47]— in this case, choice about how best to understand the nature and purpose of the church in a particular society at a particular time. In

Lindbeck's hands the conversation looks like a variant of the "method of correlation"[48] in practical theology. Its purpose is to exhibit how this theological picture of the church is "relevant" to our situation precisely because it is rooted in the dynamics driving one of its deepest changes.

Lindbeck's arguments that his picture of the church is credible are exercises in *ad hoc* apologetics. Granted that the form in which Christian churches are likely to survive is sectarian and possibly ecumenical, and assuming for the moment that it is desirable theologically that they be not only ecumenical but exclusivist (we shall return to this assumption), is it credible that specifically exclusivist sects can or should survive? In these essays Lindbeck relies on functionalist sociological arguments to make the case that they both can and should. This is *ad hoc* apologetics in that it is not a fragment of a comprehensive, coherent, and religiously neutral systematic argument designed to exhibit the credibility of belief in God in general and the Christian symbol system in particular. Rather, it is *apologia* undertaken in regard to the credibility of isolated proposals (the church as sect, not Christianity as such) and drawing on a body of theory (sociological in this case) which might not be adduced in regard to any other topic for which one might also want to make a case.

In this case sociological arguments are advanced to show that a sectarian church both can and should be highly "exclusivist" because that is good both for the church and for society. It is good for the church because it strengthens its capacity to support its members in their socially deviant belief system. The clearer they are about what is decisively different in their reading of the world, the easier it is for them to engage others in the public realm while remaining faithful to their own identity.[49] The ecumenicity of such an exclusivist sect would give it a further "competitive advantage" because it introduces into its common life a greater range and richness "social-psychologically."[50] The church as sect both can and should stress its exclusivity, secondly, because that would work for the well-being of society at large: "every society needs nonconformists, protestors and marginal groups in order to test and define its own standards of normality."[51] Moreover, a highly impersonal mass society needs stable "intermediate communities" of face-to-face encounter which are its "primary socializing agencies."[52] Furthermore, a highly pluralized society, lacking any one dominant "legitimation system," tends to be guided "in terms of short-range, rational-pragmatic considerations" and lacks any arena in which "questions of high principle and ultimate goals" can be considered.[53] The presence of ecumenical and exclusivist Christian sects can nurture society's well being by helping to satisfy exactly those needs.

The force of these arguments is situation relative. Granted their sociological cogency, they have the apologetic force in the present situation (in which virtually no churches fit Lindbeck's description) of persuading his skeptical audience that in a different situation it would indeed be good for both church and society for churches to be ecumenical, exclusivist, and engaged sects. However, in the changed situation in which churches did fit Lindbeck's description these arguments would not be sufficient. In that situation, the skeptical would need an additional kind of argument: evidence that these sects do function effectively in society as confrontational minorities, conduct their common life in such a way as to be attractive intermediary communities for socialization, and are also attractive arenas for exploring overarching human questions of purposes and values. In that setting, apologetics would have to involve the skilled *praxis* of the church's common life.

Note that in different ways both the "practical theology" and the *apologia* strands in Lindbeck's essays underscore the public character of churchly life. The apologetic argument that a sectarian church is good for society entails that such a sect would not withdraw its life into a ghetto[54] but would rather engage it in the society's common life. And as the arguments in both "practical theology" and apologetics show, that aspect of churchly life which is discourse can engage nontheological disciplines in a shared arena of public discourse without losing its standing as church discourse.

Lindbeck's argument that his picture of the church is Christianly authentic is an exercise in dogmatic or systematic theology. The Christianness of the proposal is established by its faithfulness to a christologically centered narrative reading of the New Testament. Most fully developed in his third essay, this argument assumes the view that for Christians what is centrally significant in the New Testament are narratives that "unsubstitutably identify and characterize a particular person," Jesus.[55] Because they identify and characterize him "as the summation of Israel's history and as the unsurpassable and irreplaceable clue to who and what the God of Israel and the universe is" those narratives involve an interpretation of "the Hebrew Bible in terms of christological anticipation, preparations, and promissory types."[56] That is how the communities for whom those narratives were written understood them and how they ordered the Hebrew Bible and the New Testament into one canonical "whole." Accordingly, for "the early Christians . . . Israel's history was their only history."[57] The narratives that identify and characterize who Israel is as God's people also identify who the early Christians are as church: Hence in discussion of the nature of the church, biblical story is logically prior to concepts like "unity, holiness, catholicity, and apostolicity." That is how it was.

Lindbeck is emphatic that it is an open question whether the early church's self-identification by Israel's story ought to be normative for theological description of the church today. The authority for ecclesiology of Israel's story is derivative from the authority of Jesus' story. It is possible that under certain circumstances faithfulness to the identity of the Lord of the church may involve departure from the New Testament's own picture of the church. Lindbeck notes several moments in the history of Christianity when the church's self-description departed entirely from Israel's self-description in story. Each is an enormously ambiguous change; but each is arguably mandated by novel situations and is Christianly authentic in its own way.[58]

Lindbeck stresses that the church's situation in contemporary society comes closer to approximating that of the New Testament churches than it has at any point in the intervening history.[59] This calls "for a return to Israel's story as the template by which the church shapes its own history."[60] What that template authorizes is a picture of the church as a deviant minority, with a strong self-identity rooted in high exclusivism, that is thereby empowered to be so engaged in society as to be a significant force in its history. The picture of the church as an ecumenical, exclusivist, engaged sect is, by this scriptural standard, authentically Christian.

III. CHURCH AND THE PUBLIC REALM

In his theological remarks about the nature of the church Lind-beck does what his theory of doctrine says theological remarks ought to do. He tests their Christian faithfulness against an intratextual narrative reading of Scripture that construes the narratives christo-centrically. In that way he seeks to show his remarks to be formulated in accord with the relevant features of the "grammar" of the biblical story, as grammar paradigmatically instantiated in church doctrines. He tests his theological remarks' applicability in church *praxis* through a futurological exercise. He tests their intelligibility and credibility in *ad hoc* apologetics relying on sociological arguments. And then he says half of what the critics worried he would say: Church *is* best understood in a sectarian way.

The rest of the objection to his theory of doctrine is that it entails a view of the church as not only a sect but a sect that is in principle disengaged from the public realm. As we have seen, his theological remarks about the church do not in fact propose such dis-engagement. To the contrary, they call for an ecumenical sectarianism that is deeply engaged in "the world." If the objection to his theses about the nature of doctrine are well founded, that would suggest that Lindbeck's theological remarks about the church are inconsistent with the implications of his own theory of doctrine. I hope to show that there is no such inconsistency. Lindbeck's theses about doctrine do not entail any particular theology of the church, certainly not the view that the church is a sect in principle disengaged from the public realm. The suspicion that his theses about doctrine do entail such a theology of the church does, however, bring out another kind of problem. It is a more formal than material problem. It is created by the limits of the governing metaphors "culture" and "language."

Showing all of this depends on sorting out several different senses of "public." That can be done by noting four different ways in which the contrast between "public" and "private" is often drawn. Each gives a significantly different force to the objection to Lindbeck's view of Christian doctrine.

(a) The public/private contrast might be drawn by reference to our emotional needs. "Public" would then be the realm of imper-sonal, institutionally structured social relationships in which we are subjected to the pressures of social duty and obligation. Emotional needs cannot be entirely satisfied in that realm and drive us to seek "emotional space" in intimate relationships (e.g., in families) which constitute the "private" realm.[61] Here "public" and "private" are mutually exclusive realms. They can be brought together if one adopts an assumption about human nature: Human beings are characterized by a corresponding antithesis between "outer life" or "exteriority," which takes place in the public realm, and "inner life" or "interiority" which takes place in the private realm. If churches were understood as essentially intimate communities in contrast to social institutions, they would be in the "private" realm and could not consistently be seen as part of the "public" realm. That would be a thoroughgoing privatizing of church life and discourse of the sort noted, analyzed, and lamented by Robert Bellah et al. in *Habits of the Heart*.[62] If Lindbeck's cultural-linguistic metaphors for Christianity entailed this view, they would indeed be privileging one of several possible views of the church and a very dubious one at that. However, as we have seen, in his theological remarks about the church Lindbeck rejects any view that pits "community" against "institution" or calls for "deinstitutionalization" of the church. Furthermore the theory of doctrine he builds on the basis of those metaphors explicitly rejects any systematic "inside vs. outside" picture of human being.[63] So his own theology is congruent with his theory of doctrine. In this sense of "public," the charges of favoring sectarian disengagement or of internal inconsistency in the theory do not hold.

(b) The public/private contrast might be drawn by reference to the conditions of access to knowledge. This way of drawing the contrast rests on assumptions about rationality that stress its independence and universality. The intellectual capacities for understanding discourse and the criteria by which to assess its truth-claims must be available to every normal person, independent to their affective or moral condition. That is what makes it "public" discourse and "public" knowledge. Whatever requires privileged conditions for comprehension or assessment, say a miraculous gift of faith or an ineffable experience, is "private" and cannot be brought into dialectical engagement with "public" discourse. If church discourse were "private" in this sense of the term, it in principle could not engage the realm of "public" discourse. It would be wholly esoteric discourse, logically invulnerable to critique from outside itself. If Lindbeck's metaphors for church and analogy for doctrine entailed this view of church discourse, it would indeed amount to fideism. Doubtless, some versions of the objection to his theses about doctrine charge Lindbeck with exactly that. However, as we have seen, Lindbeck's theological proposals about the church test its applicability by a method of correlation that involves conversation with the social sciences and assumes that first-order Christian discourse is as learnable, and hence as intelligible, as any ordinary language. And his tests of its credibility involve *ad hoc* apologetics employing sociological theory. No claim for theology's "private language" status is implied there. This is entirely consistent with his theory of doctrine. As William Placher[64] has shown in his admirable refutation of them, the objections resting on this sense of "public" beg the issues by assuming the validity of notions of rationality that Lindbeck's metaphors are, in part, designed to displace. On this sense of "public," then, the charges that Lindbeck's theses about doctrine entail a view of church discourse in principle disengaged from the realm of "public" discourse do not hold.

In these first two senses of "public" it cannot be objected that Lindbeck's theses about doctrine entail a view of church as disengaged from the "public" realm. Nor can inconsistency be shown between Lindbeck's own theological remarks about the church and his theory of doctrine. In two other senses of "public," however, the objection has a *prima facie* plausibility. In neither case will the objection survive a closer look. However, these two senses of "public" together do bring out an important limitation to the usefulness of "culture" and "language" used metaphorically of Christian churches. Use of these metaphors beyond this limitation would create serious material theological problems.

(c) The public/private contrast might be drawn by reference to two different kinds of ends for human action. "Public" would then be the realm of social goods, *res publica*; and public action would be action aimed at whatever makes for society's flourishing. "Social good" ought not to be thought of as something, say economic prosperity, such that its flourishing means that every individual life in the society is to some degree enhanced as individual, e.g., it enjoys a higher standard of living. Rather, a "social good" is whatever makes for the flourishing of society as such, as a complex network of inter-personal relations. By contrast, "private" is the realm of individual goods; and private action is action aimed at whatever makes for an individual person's flourishing without necessary reference to society and its flourishing. In general this way (rather than either of the previous senses of the contrast) was the way the public/private contrast was drawn in ancient Athens from the time of Pericles up through Aristotle's day, when the political conditions for it had given way to Macedonian rule.[65] This way of drawing the contrast rests on the assumption that there is some one most excellent social good, one truly highest mode of social flourishing, and that it can be ascertained by a group of intelligent persons (historically, by a group of intelligent *men*) engaged in rational political debate. On this construal the public realm is inherently a political realm, the realm of rational social self-governance. Moreover, because the public good is one, and all public action is ordered to discerning and realizing it, the public realm is by definition singular.

Given this sense of "public" the charge against Lindbeck's theses about the nature of doctrine is plausible. It would look like this. Cultures are always the cultures of some society. A society is in some respects by definition a "public realm," an arena of political action aimed at the society's flourishing. Lindbeck's metaphors liken church to a culture. That suggests that church is a society and as such itself a public realm. It is also essential to Lindbeck's thesis to stress that church is necessarily in dialogue with a constantly changing host culture in which it is located. That suggests that church's host is a society, itself a public realm. But there can be but one public realm. To which does "public realm" properly apply? Church or host society? Lindbeck selected culture and language as metaphors for church because they promised to resolve an apparent antinomy about the church's self-identity through radical historical change. Hence the theory of the nature of doctrine governed by those metaphors focuses on the church and preserving its internal identity against erosion by the host society's non-churchly culture and language. The logic of the theory of doctrine requires that "public realm" be applied to church and not to society. In that case, one can imagine the objection continuing, out of all the possible theological views of church's proper relation to its host culture the theory of doctrine favors two. Church must overcome society's corrosive effects either by wholly disengaging from it or by somehow absorbing society into itself so that the two are one culture on the church's terms.

Rebuttal to this objection is not hard to find. The entire objection rests on a failure to note that culture and language are used as metaphors for church. It is as important to the force of a metaphor that the two things likened to one another are in some respects *un*like as that they are alike. The master metaphors in Lindbeck's theory of doctrine do not amount to the claim that church is *a* culture or *a* language, let alone that it *is* the "public realm," but that it is culturelike in certain respects. It is entirely consistent with the theory to insist that properly speaking it is the host society alone that *is* the public realm. The ways in which church is culturelike do not entail any particular theological judgment about how church ought to be related to that realm.

However the objection does draw attention to a major limitation to the usefulness of culture and language as metaphors for church life and discourse. The metaphors were adopted because of their fruitfulness in resolving a particular problem: the apparent antinomy between affirmation of radical changes through history in church teaching and practice and affirmation of the preservation of church self-identity through time. They can confuse and mislead when used in relation to the quite different problem raised by this third sense of "public," namely, the apparent antinomy between "the church must be in the public realm" and "the church must not be of the public realm."

As we have seen, Lindbeck's own theological remarks include the view that the church as sect must be engaged in the public realm on behalf of the poor and disempowered. Presumably that engagement involves both an ongoing critique within the public realm of the power arrangements of the public realm by which some are made poor and are oppressed. And, presumably, engagement involves continuing action in the public realm aimed at the flourishing of society as such. When one presses for content to such engagement, however, there is room for a wide variety of theological judgment about what is Christianly appropriate and mandated. The variety ranges from the view that church should entirely disengage from the public realm *as* political realm so that critique of the public realm (expressed in symbolic, nonpolitical action) is not compromised by churchly complicity in it, at one pole, to the view at the opposite pole that church should fully identify with those parties in the public realm that seem to share parts of churchly vision of social flourishing.[66] Lindbeck's theory of doctrine sketches the conditions of the possibility of debate among these contrasting theological opinions and is neutral in regard to the material outcome of the debate. All of this is entirely consistent with a theory of doctrine governed by the metaphor "church is (like) a cultural-linguistic system." But the apparent antinomy that generates this particular theological debate is not much illuminated by that family of metaphors.

Used as the master metaphors for church life and discourse, "culture" and "language" tend to obscure the political character of both church and its host society and the complex dialectic marking their interrelationships. True, "language" suggests that "church" is to "host society" as a dialect is to the language of which it is a dialect. As a dialect can be powerful in shaping a language and generating new ways to construe both one's society and one's situation and life within that society, so church discourse may shape the host culture's ordinary language and generate fresh ways to construe that society and one's life within it. So too, "culture" suggests that "church" is to "host culture" as a subculture is to its dominant culture. As a subculture involves a repertoire of forms of life that can, especially in a time of rapid social change, empower one to cope more creatively with the challenges and ills of human life than more traditional cultural forms of life seem to allow, so churchly life may more powerfully empower human life to flourish than can the forms of life traditional to its host culture. The metaphors "culture" and "language" provide terms in which these points can be made both fruitfully and persuasively, without thereby committing one to any particular material theological view of the optimal concrete character of these relationships between church and society.

But churchly discourse and life are the discourse and life of concrete churchly communities. And they are themselves as truly political arenas as are their host societies. Internally, they are arrangements of social, economic, and political power and, however modestly, they are also centers of such power within their host societies. Fruitful *theological* analysis and debate of the best modes of churchly engagement in a host society requires attention to the organization and dynamics of power in both the host society as a public realm and in church as a "public realm"—even when church is, sociologically speaking, a sect. Indeed, it might be argued that for its own cogency a cultural-linguistic theory of doctrine requires just such attention to power analysis precisely because the theory partly rests on the assumption that a church is constantly engaged with a constantly changing host society. But that is a point at which the metaphors funding the theory of doctrine reach a limit to their illuminating power. Although they do powerfully illuminate the logical conditions of the possibility of profound theological disagreement and even radical theological change regarding churchly discourse and life while nonetheless remaining genuinely *churchly* discourse and life, they do not provide analogous illumination of the conditions of the possibility of various and even contrary types of churchly engagement in society, which are all modes of engagement in which church preserves its identity as church. They do not illuminate the conditions of the possibility of church being politically *in* but not *of* its host society.

(d) The "public/private" contrast might be drawn by reference to different kinds of material interests that shape perceptions of what count as "social goods" and "individual goods." A group of persons' "material interests" are the interests it has in preserving various powers it already possesses or in overcoming various forms of relative disempowerment it already suffers. These interests are "material" or concretely actual in contrast to "formal" or purely ideal interests. They are rooted in the realities of economic, social, and political power arrangements. "Public," in this case, is the realm of social goods that are shared ends for action because those who hold them to be social goods share the same material interests. The assumption here is that persons' location in a society's power arrangements deeply shapes what they judge to count as genuine social and individual flourishing.

On this view the concept "public" in (c) above is inadequate by reason of abstractness. It is abstracted from the material realities of the power arrangements that obtain among groups of persons. This abstractness tends to obscure important features of social reality. For example, in the case of ancient Athens it obscured the fact that only free propertied males were entitled to participate in the rational dialectic through which social goods were clarified. Judgments about what counted as social good were biased in favor of what was good for the dominant group in Athenian society, not necessarily what was good for women, slaves, or freedmen.

This more concrete way of construing "public" undercuts the implication of the more abstract sense of the term that the public realm is singular. To the contrary, there is an apparently irreducible plurality of "publics" in any society, each defined by a group's set of material interests rooted in its socioeconomic location in the society. Indeed, the idea of "society as a whole" is weakened. Who is in a position to define what ends would constitute its "wholeness"? Every proposal would reflect the material interests of the group proposing it. In this view "private" comes to have a new force. In addition to referring to the realm of purely individual goods, it now becomes a pejorative term for other groups' definitions of "social goods" and their pursuit of them. (*We* pursue public good; *they* merely pursue their—group—private interest.)

Given this sense of "public" the charge against Lindbeck's theses about doctrine gains a different kind of plausibility. It would look like this: a society constituted by a multiplicity of publics is deeply threatened with disintegration. There is no view of social and individual flourishing that is widely enough shared to unite it into some one thing, a single public. There may not even be shared rules to govern the struggle among groups as they each pursue their several perceptions of the social good. To liken the church to a culture and its language is to take it as one more public. On that view, any church engagement with other publics would only be action aimed at actualizing the church's own vision of social flourishing at whatever expense to other groups' actualization of their visions. And that would be deeply shaped by the church's own material interests. This is only underscored, the objection would continue, by the fact that the entire theory is ordered to the celebration and preservation of the church's identity in the face of threats from other competing "cultures" and "languages." A theory of doctrine rooted in such metaphors would inescapably favor theologies of the church that locate its ends within itself. Understood that way, churches in principle could not be a resource against society's disintegration. Church could not be construed as an agent for the common good.

Rebuttal to this objection is close at hand. Once again the objection rests on a failure to note the force of the metaphorical use of "culture" and "language." The theory of doctrine proposes only that for purposes of clarifying the problem of Christian identity through change it is illuminating to see ways in which church discourse and church life are like a culture or a language. However, Christianity is not *a* culture or *a* language, and in some important ways it is unlike them. In particular, nothing in the theory of doctrine rests on the supposition that Christianity's identity is rooted in a set of shared material interests. Lindbeck's insistence in his theological remarks about the church that an ecumenical sect would embrace people from every socioeconomic location is wholly consistent with his theory of doctrine.

However this objection does draw attention to a second major limitation to the usefulness of "culture" and "language" as metaphors for church. The objection points out that a church is likely to be ideologically captive, so that its teachings and practice are in some ways in support of its own material interests, a state of affairs that the church's very identity requires it to name and repent as idolatry. Used as metaphors "culture" and "language" bring out the ways in which doctrine as the implicit rules of grammar for churchly discourse and life may be seen as the unchanging condition of the possibility of diversity, disagreement, and consensual change in theology and practice. But the same metaphors tend to obscure a third apparent antinomy: "churchly discourse and action cannot escape some sort of ideological captivity" and "churchly discourse and action must be not only ecumenical (or 'catholic') and authentically Christian (or 'evangelical') but also constantly self-reforming." Does the deep grammar of Christian discourse ever become ideologically deformed and itself stand in need of reform? Since that grammar could not logically be its own principle of reform and change, traditional theology relied on doctrines of revelation according to which it is God who, through new acts of fresh illumination of human minds or new acts of self-disclosure, brings judgment and reform on some aspect of the implicit rules governing churchly speech or action. Paul Tillich identified this question with the Protestant Reformation. In his view the "Protestant principle" was that nothing whatever is to be absolutized other than God, including, presumably, the grammar ruling Christian life and speech. Even that may need reform. Recent emphasis on the community's own current "religious experience" or "experience of grace" reflects a concern to keep the same possibility open. Used as metaphors, however, "language" and "culture" do not even permit *formulation* of this possibility. While they illuminate the relation between constancy and change in churchly discourse and action, they make it impossible to propose that church itself, as a "public" in this fourth sense, *may* need reform precisely in regard to some feature(s) of its principle of constancy, "doctrine as grammar." Nor do these metaphors illuminate the conditions of the possibility of church being brought so radically into judgment and being so radically reformed.

The issues surfaced by these last two senses of "public" may be brought together this way. H. Richard Niebuhr once proposed that the principle opponent to trust in and loyalty to the One beyond the many, or "radical monotheism," was not atheism outside Christianity but "henotheism" within Christianity. In henotheism we place our trust in and give our loyalty exclusively to one *among* the many (usually a closed society) as the ground of the value and meaning of life. Henotheism in Christianity may take a church-centered form, Niebuhr pointed out: "In church-centered faith the community of those who hold common beliefs, practice common rites, and submit to a common rule becomes the immediate object of trust and the cause of loyalty."[67] Critics seem to have worried that Lindbeck's theory of doctrine presupposes just such henotheistic valuing of the church. As we have seen the worry turns out to be misplaced. Lindbeck's own theological remarks characterize the church as an ecumenical, exclusivist sect deeply engaged in its host society for society's well-being, rather than centering on its own well-being. In this he is consistent with his own theory of the nature of doctrine and its relation to theology. Far from entailing a view of church as disengaged in principle from the public realm, Lindbeck's theory of doctrine presupposes that the church is in continuous dialogue with a constantly changing host culture and it calls for theological proposals to be in conversation with nontheological disciplines.

However, Niebuhr developed a second theme in the same essay. Faith in the One beyond the many never exists in pure form. Radical monotheism is never lived purely in its own right. It is always lived in some host society. Precisely as *radical* monotheism, it calls those who live that way to continuing conversion regarding all aspects of the society, cultural, political, *and* religious.[68] Radical monotheism is usually lived out in terms of some religion. "Radical monotheism" is thus not one more religious option we might select in preference to polytheisms or henotheisms. Radical monotheism does not introduce us to true religion as such or to a new religion. It does not introduce us to the experience of the holy or the practice of prayer. Rather, it calls for repeated conversion and re-form of our apparently endemic religious reverences and praying—and quite particularly our *Christian* religious discourse and practice.[69]

Now, as objections to a theory, the critics' worries about a cultural-linguistic theory of doctrine may be misplaced. But they are rooted in sound intuition about the limits of the usefulness of the master metaphors funding the theory. "Culture" and "language," as metaphors for churchly discourse and action, are powerfully illuminating and fruitful in the task for which they were selected: resolving the apparent antinomy between "church teachings and practice have changed radically through history" and "churchly identity, including its truth-claims, persist through historical change." But the same metaphors obscure rather than illuminate two other apparent antinomies, whose force may be brought out in Niebuhrian terms: (a) "Faith in the One beyond the many requires churches to be engaged in their host societies deeply enough to give significant calls to conversion, and engaged deeply enough to act for meaningful reform," (to be in the world) and "Faith in the One beyond the many requires churches not to slip into henotheism focused on their host societies" (not to be of the world); (b) "Faith in the One beyond the many is only lived in and as an organic part of societies that are themselves not the One but merely organizations of (some of) the many," and "Faith in the One beyond the many is always lived as a relation to the One and the One's judgment upon and gracious sustenance of the many, including society and, within it, churchly communities of radical monotheists."

"Language" and "culture" obscure these apparent antinomies when used as metaphors for churchly discourse and action because, in the nature of the case, they are not metaphors for the God-church relationship. Churches most certainly are concrete sociocultural realities. Understanding them requires the resource of the "social sciences" or "human sciences." Indeed, it requires help not only from "interpretive" social science like cultural anthropology (at least as practiced by Clifford Geertz) in which "culture" and "language" are fruitful metaphors, but also from more "explanatory" social sciences. We saw, for example, that when the "public realm" is understood as the realm of social goods, church's relation to its host culture requires analysis of the arrangement and dynamics of political, economic, and social power within it. However, by self-description churches are also constituted by relationships with God marked by "calling" and "sending," "vocation" and "mission." That relation is the condition of the possibility of churches not simply being "of" the societies "in" which they are engaged; and the God-relation is the condition of the possibility of churches being both judged for ideological captivity and radically reformed. Here we hit the boundary of the usefulness of "culture" and "language" in understanding Christian churches' action and speech. It is precisely anything having to do with this God-relatedness that falls outside the circle of light thrown by metaphorical use of "culture" and "language." It is no objection to the cultural-linguistic theory of the nature of doctrine to point out the limits to the usefulness of its governing metaphors and the danger of relying on them beyond their capacity to illumine. It is rather to test and exhibit its genuine power by feeling for its boundaries. Had it no determinate limits, it would be vacuous.

NOTES

1. George A. Lindbeck, *The Nature of Doctrine* (Philadelphia: Westminster, 1984), 33.

2. Ibid., 18.

3. See William C. Placher, "Revisionist and Postliberal Theologies and the Public Character of Theology," *The Thomist* 49 (1985): 392–417; Gordon E. Michalson, Jr., "The Response to Lindbeck," *Modern Theology* 4 (1988): 107–21.

4. It is important to note that Lindbeck develops his "cultural-linguistic" construal of religions to deal with a particular problem in Christianity in particular: how to reconcile the apparent antinomy between affirmation of real changes in Christian teaching and practices through history and affirmation of Christianity's abiding self-identity through time.

5. Lindbeck, *The Nature of Doctrine*, 47–48.

6. Ibid., 35.

7. E.g., ibid., 115.

8. Ibid., 81.

9. Ibid., 18.

10. Ibid., 74. The difference in wording between Lindbeck's description of doctrines in his chapter on "Theories of Doctrine" as "communally authoritative *teaching*" (p. 74) and his description of them in his opening chapter as "communally authoritative *rules*" (p. 18; emphasis added both times) reflects an unnecessary unclarity encountered elsewhere. In the opening chapter we are told that "the only job that doctrines do in their role as church teachings" is that of rules (p. 19). In the fourth chapter it is pointed out that doctrines as rules do involve propositions; but they are second-order propositions about how to act or speak correctly. But then it is also noted that "a doctrinal sentence may also function . . . as a first-order proposition"; however, when it is employed in this way "it either cannot or need not be construed as a norm of communal belief or practice: it is not being used as a church doctrine" (p. 80). The "paradigmatic" status of doctrinal sentences indicates the way to reconcile these remarks. The "sentence" may function in several ways. Used *as* a way to make an assertion, it is used as a first-order proposition. Why could one not use some sentence both ways at once?

11. Ibid., 18; emphasis added.

12. Ibid., 81.

13. Ibid., 95.

14. See ibid., 81–82.

15. See Lindbeck's discussion of doctrines as the condition of the possibility of genuine theological disagreements; ibid., 113, 121–122.

16. Ibid., 35.

17. Ibid., 76.

18. See ibid., 113.

19. Ibid., 76.

20. Ibid., 39.

21. See ibid., 82.

22. Ibid., 116.

23. Ibid., 121.

24. See ibid., 122.

25. Ibid., 124.

26. Ibid., 125.

27. See ibid., 129, 132.

28. Ibid., 129.

29. Ibid., 131.

30. Ibid.

31. George A. Lindbeck, "Ecumenism and the Future of Belief," *Una Sancta* (1968): 3–17.

32. George A. Lindbeck, "The Sectarian Future of the Church," *The God Experience*, ed. Joseph P. Whelen (New York: Newman Press, 1971), 226–43.

33. George A. Lindbeck, "The Story-Shaped Church," *Scriptural Authority and Narrative Interpretation*, ed. Garrett Green (Philadelphia: Fortress, 1987), 161–79.

34. Lindbeck, "The Sectarian Future of the Church," 227.

35. Lindbeck rejects any version of the theologically sectarian motto, "No salvation outside (our!) church"; ibid., 231.

36. For this paragraph, cf. Lindbeck, "Ecumenism and the Future of Belief," 4, 8, 12; "The Sectarian Future of the Church," 227–28.

37. Lindbeck, "Ecumenism and the Future of Belief," 12.

38. Ibid., 16.

39. Ibid., 12. Lindbeck points out strong parallels between his proposal and Karl Rahner's picture of a "diaspora" church; "The Sectarian Future of the Church," 227.

40. Lindbeck, "The Sectarian Future of the Church," 232.

41. Ibid., 230.

42. Lindbeck, "Ecumenism and the Future of Belief," 14–15.

43. Ibid., 14, 8–9.

44. Ibid., 5–6; Lindbeck, "The Sectarian Future of the Church," 227.

45. Lindbeck, "The Sectarian Future of the Church," 233–34.

46. Ibid., 227–28.

47. Ibid., 227.

48. Cf. David Tracy, *The Analogical Imagination* (New York: Crossroad, 1981), 24–27, for the most influential account of the method of critical correlation.

49. Cf. Lindbeck, "Ecumenism and the Future of Belief," 4–5; "The Sectarian Future of the Church," 231–32.

50. Lindbeck, "The Sectarian Future of the Church," 237–38.

51. Lindbeck, "Ecumenism and the Future of Belief," 5.

52. Lindbeck, "The Sectarian Future of the Church," 235–36.

53. Lindbeck, "Ecumenism and the Future of Belief," 11.

54. Lindbeck explicitly rejects a "ghetto" existence for such a sect; "The Sectarian Future of the Church," 231.

55. Lindbeck, "The Story-Shaped Church," 164. Here Lindbeck is explicitly indebted to the work of Hans W. Frei, especially *The Identity of Jesus Christ* (Philadelphia: Fortress, 1975).

56. Lindbeck, "The Story-Shaped Church," 164.

57. Ibid., 165.

58. Ibid., 170–74.

59. Ibid., 174; cf. "Ecumenism and the Future of Belief," 6, and "The Sectarian Future of the Church," 227, 238–39.

60. Lindbeck, "The Story-Shaped Church," 175.

61. Barrington Moore's survey of an extensive body of literature in cultural anthropology shows this to be one of the two most common ways in which the public/private contrast is drawn in the human sciences. The other way the contrast is commonly drawn turns on the question of control of human behavior: whatever society controls is the "public" realm; whatever individuals or smaller groups within the society control so as to exclude the intrusion of society is the "private" realm. Cf. Barrington Moore, Jr., *Privacy: Studies in Social and Cultural History* (Armonk, N.Y.: Sharpe, 1984), 3–81.

62. Robert Bellah, et al. *Habits of the Heart* (Berkeley: University of California, 1985), 219–50.

63. Lindbeck, *The Nature of Doctrine*, 33–34, 62.

64. William C. Placher, "Revisionist and Postliberal Theologies and the Public Character of Theology," *The Thomist* 49 (1985): 407–16.

65. Cf. Hannah Arendt, *The Human Condition* (Garden City, N.Y.: Doubleday Anchor, 1959), 1–72; Nicholas Lobkowicz, *Theory and Practice* (Notre Dame, Ind.: University of Notre Dame Press, 1967), 1–59; Barrington Moore, *Privacy*, 81–168.

66. This spectrum of theological positions about the proper relation between church and its host society parallels the spectrum of theological views of the proper relation of Christ to culture that H. Richard Niebuhr typologized in *Christ and Culture* (New York: Harper & Row, 1951); perhaps the shift of focus from "Christ" to "church" increases critics' wariness of the hidden implications of Lindbeck's proposal.

67. H. Richard Niebuhr, *Radical Monotheism* (New York: Harper & Row, 1960), 58.

68. See the sequence of chapter titles in *Radical Monotheism*: "Radical Monotheism and Western Religion," "Radical Faith in Political Community," "Radical Faith in Western Science."

69. Ibid., 50–63.

ON READING THE
SCRIPTURES THEOLOGICALLY

David Tracy

I. THE PLAIN SENSE OF SCRIPTURE

George Lindbeck has contributed so much to ecumenical Christian theology that it seems fitting, in a volume on theological dialogue dedicated to him, to reflect further on the ecumenicity of Christianity. To be faithful to Lindbeck's intentions and achievements, it also seems proper to reflect in theological terms which George Lindbeck can, in principle, and may, in fact, accept. I have stated elsewhere my criticism of Lindbeck's 'cultural-linguistic' model for theology and will not rehearse that criticism here.[1] Rather in this essay I wish to show my deep gratitude to Lindbeck and his community of colleagues at Yale and elsewhere by articulating what their joint work has taught me as well as by suggesting how their work, in its own terms, might also move in a yet more explicitly ecumenical, even Christian pluralistic direction. I have, therefore, chosen to write on one major aspect of Lindbeck's theology. As it turns out, it is an aspect he shares with Hans Frei.

Indeed, Lindbeck's own theological program, as he makes clear, is dependent on Frei's work at exactly this point: the plain sense of the common passion narratives as *the* common ground of all properly Christian self-understanding.[2] With Lindbeck and many others, I too have learned from the incomparable Hans Frei just how central that 'plain sense' should be for all Christian theology. My reservations on Frei's proposal (as on Lindbeck's) are on other theological and philosophical questions than those I shall discuss here: for example, Frei's, for me, unpersuasive reading of the nature and claims of the use of general hermeneutical theory in theology.[3] Although those reservations are important for other central theological and philosophical questions, they are relatively unimportant for the present question.

That question is the need to know how to read the Scriptures theologically. On this issue (an issue central for any theology that purports to be Christian) the work of Frei, Lindbeck, and their many colleagues has much to teach all theologians—even unrepentant correlational theologians like myself. The present paper, therefore, will state what has persuaded me in the Frei-Lindbeck proposal (section I) and then argue (sections II and III) on some further implications of possible plural readings of the plain sense. These implications, as far as I can see, might even turn out to be persuasive to Lindbeck himself in his continuing reflections on the diversity of readings encouraged by the 'plain sense' of the passion narratives. If there could be agreement on this controverted issue, then all theologians, despite their other crucial differences, would at least possess enough commonality of purpose and conviction on how to read the Scriptures to allow the further controverted questions (e.g., on correlational or intratextual theology) to be focussed more clearly. Such, at least, is my hope. This hope is reinforced by the generous ecumenicity of Lindbeck's entire theology: an ecumenical theology that might, in principle, also become what I shall name a prophetic-mystical theology without in any way losing its grounding in the plain sense of the passion narratives.

In any theological method which remains distinctively Christian, there logically must be criteria to assess the appropriateness of any particular theological proposal as Christian. For some theologians (including myself) there must also be criteria of intelligibility or credibility for a full theological method.[4] Although I continue to believe that the so-called 'mediating theologies' or 'correlational theologies' are correct to include this second set of criteria of credibility (even on the strictly intratextual grounds of the logic of God-language), it is possible to bracket that concern in order to consider only criteria of appropriateness. Such, at least, is my intent for the present analysis of the value of the Frei-Lindbeck insistence upon the 'plain reading' of the common passion narrative.

For whatever one's conclusions on the inner-theological debate on 'correlational' or 'intratextual' methods for Christian theology, the fact remains that every Christian theology, insofar as it claims to be Christian, must also possess criteria of appropriateness. The exemplary work of David Kelsey on different theological 'uses' of Scripture, as well as the seemingly endless debates in modern theology on a 'canon within the canon', or a 'working canon', or the 'whole canon' demonstrates the need for such criteria by all Christian theologians as Christian.[5]

The signal value of the work of Hans Frei is precisely on this issue of what Schubert Ogden has nicely named theological "criteria of appropriateness."[6] Both in his magisterial work on the eclipse of narrative understanding in modern historical-critical biblical interpretation and in his constructive christological work on the identity and presence of Jesus Christ as rendered in and through a 'literal' or 'plain' reading of the passion narratives of the gospels,[7] Frei's work has proved a breakthrough for all theology. The fruits of that breakthrough can be seen in many works, including George Lindbeck's incisive study of the ecclesiological implications of this narrative reading.[8]

By way of preface to my interpretation of the 'plain sense' position, I should admit at the outset that my own affirmation of this narrative proposal is more 'piecemeal' than 'wholesale'. I should also admit that my own affirmation is based more on Catholic than on Frei's and Lindbeck's properly Reformed theological grounds. My affirmation is 'piecemeal' insofar as, I shall argue below, the centrality of the 'plain sense' of the narrative can and should be open both to further questioning of its coherence with the 'Jesus-kerygma' of the original apostolic witness as well as to further reflections on the theological implications of the diversity of readings of that plain sense in the New Testament itself and, indeed, in all biblically sound readings of the common narrative in the great Christian tradition. My affirmation is more Catholic in theological orientation than Reformed insofar as an emphasis on the 'plain sense' of Scripture also further clarifies the Catholic sense of how the Scripture is the church's book. In sum, for myself as for many (but not all) modern Catholic theologians, as indeed, for many modern Protestant theologians (possibly including George Lindbeck), the central theological principle is 'Scripture in tradition', not either the older Roman Catholic 'Scripture *and* tradition', nor the Reformation's 'Scripture alone'.[9] This 'Scripture in tradition' principle continues, I believe, to be the most fruitful theological one for assessing the central role of Scripture for Christian theology as the plain *ecclesial* sense.

The principal, but not sole, meaning of 'plain sense' is the "obvious or direct sense of the text for the Christian community."[10] The secondary meaning of 'plain sense' (related to, indeed dependent on, the first) clarifies, through a modest use of literary-critical methods,[11] how to read the passion narratives as 'history-like, realistic' narratives. In Frei's persuasive reading, the identity of Jesus Christ and through that identity (and thereby presence), the further identities of both God and the Christian (both individually and communally) are rendered through close attention to the narrative interactions of an unsubstitutable character (Jesus) and the highly specific circumstances of all the events constituting the gospel accounts of the passion and resurrection.[12] These narrative interactions, as Frei shows, allow both for an identity-clarification of the agent's (Jesus) intentions and actions and, through that narrative identification, a manifestation of the agent as present to the Christian community as Jesus Christ.

This is not the place to review the details of Frei's brilliant and well-known (and curiously Anselmian) constructive theological proposal on how both identity and presence (and in that order) of Jesus Christ are fully rendered only in the passion narratives.[13] This is the place, however, to insist, with Frei, that the 'plain sense' of these narratives, with or without the aid of literary criticism or the specific narrative interactions of character and circumstance in the passion narratives, has traditionally been, is, and should be both realistic and history-like. In sum, the obvious and direct sense (i.e., the first meaning of 'plain sense'—their sense for the Christian community who affirms them as *Scripture*) of the common passion narratives is exactly what Frei insists: history-like and realistic. As Lindbeck might nicely formulate it, the grammar of these narratives as Scripture is realistic and history-like.[14] It is difficult to exaggerate the importance of this narrative insight for Christian theology.[15] For even those, like myself, who have found little theological fruit in 'quests for the historical Jesus', much less in further debates on textual 'inerrancy' or interpretative 'infallibility', or debates on unbroken and unambiguous 'tradition', have, nevertheless, often been hampered by a relative inability (before Frei's work) to show how the realistic and history-like character of these narratives *is* the plain sense of the Christian community. My difficulties here, I believe, were not, *pace* Frei, the result of a use of a 'general hermeneutical theory', much less of idealist or existentialist yearnings.[16]

Rather my own task was to emphasize the proclamatory aspect of these narratives as gospel (i.e., proclamation narratives). I was tempted thereby not to engage in the further task: an analysis of how the highly particular narrative interactions of the passion accounts actually render the identity and presence of Jesus Christ in order further to clarify my affirmation (then and now) of the ecclesial 'plain sense' of these narratives.[17] Instead, like so many other theologians, I made two distinct and still valuable but incomplete genre moves. First, I highlighted the proclamatory or kerygmatic character of the gospel by speaking of the ecclesial Christian affirmation of the 'event and person' (not only the 'event') of Jesus Christ.[18] Second, I attempted to reflect on the implications of the common Christian *confession* that "I (we) believe in Jesus Christ with the apostles."[19] I continue to believe that these strategic theological moves are fruitful ones: for, together, they do provide a theological defense of the plain ecclesial sense of the Scriptures. However, the limitation of this position, as Frei's work has helped me to see, is that even the implicitly narrative genre of confession ("I [we] believe in Jesus Christ with the apostles") and the kerygmatically helpful and also implicitly narrative categories 'event' and 'person' remain merely implicit.[20] The confessional genre and the kerygmatic categories do defend the first and dominant ecclesial and theological meaning of the 'plain sense' of Scriptures and thereby are appropriately Christian. However, the confessional genre and the kerygmatic categories state but fail to show what can only be shown in explicitly narrative terms (the second meaning of Frei's 'literal' or 'plain sense'): just how and why the identity and presence of Jesus as Jesus the Christ is indeed confessed in the common Christian confession, but is rendered in its fullness only in and through the details of the interaction of the unsubstitutable character of Jesus and the specific circumstances of his passion and resurrection.[21]

In fact, the common confession logically leads to that passion narrative. This, for me at least, is Frei's great contribution: to show, in narrative terms, how the Christian confesses not merely through the genre of confession but through affirming the passion narrative as the full meaning of that confession. The passion narrative shows us how and why the Christian community "believes *in* Jesus Christ *with* the apostles." For who Jesus Christ is when Christians confess that Jesus Christ is present to them ("we believe *in* Jesus Christ"), they find fully only through the narrative rendering in the passion accounts. That narrative rendering, moreover, Christians also acknowledge as the plain ecclesial (apostolic) sense of the passion accounts ("we believe with the apostles"). The common confession and the common narrative cohere in both affirming that plain sense. But only the narrative can show, and not merely state (confess), who this Jesus Christ, present to us in word and sacrament, really is for the Christian. This emphasis on narrative can also encourage a reappraisal of all the other New Testament genres—doctrine, confession, symbol, letter, commentary, mediative theological thinking (John) or dialectical theological thinking (Paul).[22]

I continue to defend the need and fruitfulness of these and other 'genres' for Christian theological use. But all the other genres are helpfully related to both the common confession and the plain sense of the common passion narrative in order to affirm (or, in principle, to deny, i.e., *Sach-Kritik*)[23] their Christian appropriateness. This, for me, is the substantive discovery of Frei and Lindbeck in their development of fuller criteria of Christian appropriateness beyond (but in harmony with) the common confession. Their position is not narratologically dependent on any particular theory of narrative for human life and thought.[24] It is theologically dependent solely on the plain meaning of the passion narrative as that meaning is clarified by being analyzed as narrative. The plain sense has and should define the Christian community's obvious and direct reading of its own common confession. That plain, ecclesial reading, moreover, is further clarified by the use of such general (and relatively nontheoretical) analyses of 'history-like' realistic narratives as that of Erich Auerbach and, sometimes but not always, Karl Barth.[25]

A theologically informed narrative (plain) reading can also clarify how these gospel narratives, as gospel and not merely 'story', are also proclamatory narratives of apostolic witness to the proclamation

of God's initiative in the event and person of Jesus Christ. Moreover, much could be gained and little lost by showing how these
relatively late passion narratives with their 'Jesus Christ kerygma' relate to the earliest apostolic witness of the historically reconstructed
'Jesus-kerygma'. Theologically this is the case insofar as the theologian
also wishes to clarify, beyond Frei's narrative analysis, the proclamatory (or kerygmatic) character of the passion narratives *as* gospel,
i.e., proclamatory narrative. Proclamation is, of course, already entailed by the church's 'plain reading' of these narratives. However,
this kerygmatic aspect of the narrative could be further clarified so
that the exact kerygmatic nature of the 'manifestation' of Jesus as Jesus
Christ in the passion narrative is clearer than a purely narrative account displays. Then one could show, through a modest genre analysis
of kerygma, how the Jesus Christ kerygma of the passion narratives,
i.e., the identity and presence of Jesus the Christ to the Christian
community, is in direct kerygmatic relationship to the relatively non-
narrative, but clearly kerygmatic, character of the Jesus kerygma of
the original apostolic witness.[26]

At the same time, it is indeed the 'plain meaning' of the passion
narratives that not merely makes explicit the implicit christology of
the Jesus kerygma but also renders in necessary narrative detail how
and why the identity and presence of Jesus Christ is experienced as
present to the Christian community then and now.[27] If the Christian
community means that 'Christ' and the 'Spirit' are present through
proclamatory word and manifesting sacrament as well as through various Christian spiritualities of 'presence', then the Christian community should try to clarify how Christ is present as none other than
this narratively identified *Jesus* the Christ and the Spirit is present as
the Spirit released by Jesus Christ.[28] The kerygma (including the original Jesus kerygma) is not merely the proclamation-manifestation of
the kerygmatic event of Christ's presence. Rather the kerygma is the
proclamation-manifestation of the event and person of *Jesus* Christ:[29]
as the one whose presence is experienced and known in knowing his
identity as the non-substitutable Jesus of Nazareth. That identity is affirmed in both the original Jesus kerygma, the Christ kerygma, and the
Jesus Christ kerygma of the passion narratives as traditionally read by
the Christian community and as confessed in the common Christian

confession. That identity is rendered through the interactions of character and circumstance in the narrative of the passion-resurrection of this one Jesus who is the Christ of God.

In sum, any Christian theology which confesses its faith in the presence of Jesus Christ (and the Spirit released by Christ) 'with the apostles' will always need the plain sense of these narratives to achieve what neither symbol *alone*, nor doctrine *alone*, nor historical-critical reconstruction of the original apostolic witness *alone*, nor conceptual theology *alone*, nor confession *alone*, can achieve: a theological clarification of how the reality of Christ's presence is manifested through the identity of that Jesus rendered in the realistic, history-like narrative of the passion and resurrection, a narrative-confession of this one unsubstitutable Jesus of Nazareth who is the Christ of God.[30]

The centrality of the plain sense of the passion narratives, moreover, should reopen rather than close Christian theological attention to many other theological readings. As long as the plain sense reading of the passion narratives is understood as the fullest rendering of the common Christian confession, then a diversity of readings of both confession and narrative will inevitably occur. Each of these further readings should be related to the plain reading (which, as suggested above, could profitably be related to the original apostolic witness of the Jesus kerygma and the various Christ kerygmas) in order to assure the Christian appropriateness of any particular new reading. This applies to all theologies, whether ancient or contemporary, as well as to all other New Testament genres and texts. This principle assumes that the church's 'plain sense' of the passion narratives does more fully articulate the church's central confession: "we believe in Jesus Christ with the apostles." If there could be agreement on this material christological principle[31] for all claims to *Christian* theological appropriateness, then there would also be a fuller substantive ecumenical theological criterion than previously available. At the same time, the contemporary Christian church, no less than its predecessors in the New Testament communities, need not confine itself to only one reading. There is no need for all theology to be narrative theology, as distinct from the need for all theology to cohere with the plain sense of the passion narrative.[32] Here, once again, the New Testament may provide our surest guide. For Frei's rendering of the passion narrative (like Lindbeck's reading of the New Testament church's relationship to Israel) is a reading which harmonizes the different passion narratives into something like a common passion narrative. Frei's sensitive use of the common elements in the distinct narratives seems most in harmony with the obviously realistic, history-like account of Luke.[33] However, this affinity of Frei's reading to Luke's Gospel is not merely Lukan. Rather, it simply reinforces the common elements in all the passion narratives as those narratives were read and are read in their plain sense by the Christian community. For Frei clearly is neither Tatian nor Marcion. Unlike Tatian, Frei does not eliminate differences as distinct from stressing commonalities in the synoptic passion narratives. Unlike Marcion, Frei may naturally prefer aspects of Luke's account (and, possibly, Paul's), but in no way does he eliminate either the Old Testament or the rest of the New Testament. In sum, Frei's understanding of the plain sense of the Scriptures, however harmonizing, is, in fact, the plain sense of the Scriptures in their obvious and direct sense as read by the Christian community over the centuries. This same plain sense, now on intratextual grounds, is also recognizably Lukan but without confining itself to Luke alone.

II. THE DIFFERENT READINGS OF THE COMMON NARRATIVE: A PLEA FOR ECUMENICAL PLURALISM

If one grants the importance of the plain sense of the passion narratives, then a further question occurs. Should the theologian also affirm: first, all the differences in the individual passion narratives; second, all the differences in all the other parts of the gospels (the ministry and sayings); third, all the differences in all the other genres of the New Testament? One possibility is ruled out: these differences cannot become the occasion simply to dwell in a finally empty pluralism of sheer differences in the mistaken belief that thereby one honors the 'whole canon'. The whole canon of the Scriptures is theologically the church's book. And yet, the church has made clear through the centuries how it fundamentally reads all the canonical books: through their harmony with the common Christian confession as that confession is more fully articulated in the plain sense of the passion narratives.

Nevertheless, the entire canon already bespeaks so remarkable a diversity of readings of the common confession and narrative that the diversity should also be theologically affirmed as long as the plain sense of the common passion narrative is not disowned.[34] For there is a danger in remaining solely with the plain sense of the common narrative. Today that danger is best seen by many over-claims for 'narrative theology'.[35] In the past (starting with Luke in the New Testament and with the Yahwist in the Hebrew Scriptures), the ecclesial danger was the move to too general a narrative of 'salvation-history'. However valuable such a generalized and abstract Lukan 'history of salvation' narrative may have been for some ecclesial and theological purposes, it is impoverishing for many other purposes.[36] An example of such possible impoverishment is the effective elimination of the theological significance of the important differences in the New Testament on how to read the history of Christianity.

The different readings begin in the New Testament itself. It is, of course, an exaggeration to say (with Martin Kähler) that the gospels are passion narratives with different introductions. The truth in this famous saying is its insistence on the common passion narrative as the heart of the matter. The exaggeration is the seeming downplaying of the differences in the individual gospels. To understand the theological importance of these differences, I will note some examples of distinct modern readings of the gospels. In each case, I shall cite a reading that seems plausible to me—with all the difficulties that such a choice entails for a non-biblical specialist like myself.[37] In each case I cite, however, if the reader finds my own readings implausible, she or he need only replace it with another presumably more adequate one in order to see how important the differences are. In every case (both mine and yours) the differences among the four gospels are significant enough to demand a theological affirmation of real, i.e., Christian ecumenical, diversity. If one also includes not only the gospels but also the other parts and genres of the New Testament (as one should if one honors the canon) then the question of Christian diversity becomes unavoidable.

An opening to the individual gospels is also an opening to the fuller story of Jesus: his ministry, his characteristic actions, and his typical speech. It is true, as Frei argues, that only in the passion narratives is the full identity and unique presence of Jesus the Christ adequately rendered. But it is also true that the synoptic accounts of Jesus' ministry, his actions and sayings, display to the alert reader how to understand a crucial presupposition of the passion narratives: the importance of the developing relationship through word and action of Jesus to the Reign of God and, thereby, to God. The gospel accounts of the ministry, moreover, provide the narrative details needed to assure that the relationship of Jesus and the Reign of God is embedded in the Christian consciousness while reading any of the passion narratives.[38]

Consider, for example, the notable differences between Mark's interruptive, indeed, apocalyptic account of Jesus and the Reign of God and Luke's more temporally continuous, even 'history of salvation', account. Since these redactional and theological differences also inform the differences in Mark and Luke in their distinct readings of the passion narrative itself, they theologically call for further close readings of the entire gospels. Moreover, the same kind of differences have erupted through the centuries in the Christian consciousness in different pieties or spiritualities. It is hardly surprising that Mark's Gospel (so little influential in the early church) now resonates so well with the kind of modern apocalyptic spirituality which informs certain contemporary theological readings of the plain sense of Scripture—for example, the Walter Benjamin-like *and* Markan 'political theology' of J. B. Metz.[39] It is also not surprising that Matthew's portrait of Jesus as the new Moses and his portrait of the church as the new Israel with a new Torah should have proved so influential in the early church—an emerging community concerned to develop its own institutional, doctrinal, and legal forms.[40] Matthew has also proven deeply influential on the community-forming Christian descendants of the Radical Reformation—Mennonites, Amish, Church of the Brethren. Nor is it unusual that the Gospel of Luke (in its full narrative of both the ministry and the passion) allows for quite different Christian readings. Consider the appeals to Luke of the Charismatic and Pentecostal Christians focusing on the central role of 'Spirit' in Luke. Consider, by way of contrast, how social justice oriented Christians tend to move instinctively to Luke with his clear 'preference for the poor' (rather than Matthew's 'poor in spirit').

Moreover, the Gospel of John has always been the favorite gospel of Christian meditative thinkers—whether they be mystics or metaphysical theologians from Origen through Schleiermacher and Rahner. And Paul's rendering of the common gospel in the genre of letter and the conceptual forms appropriate to a profoundly dialectical theology of the cross has rightly been central to many Christians from Luther to Bultmann. Nor do the pastoral epistles deserve Käsemann's pejorative dismissal of them as "Early Catholicism."[41] Rather, the pastoral epistles (as well as aspects of Luke and Matthew) describe a clearly Catholic sensibility where doctrine, institution, and tradition are prominent.[42] The Book of Revelation, with its wondrous genius at excess, will always appeal to two different kinds of Christians: either those with a historical sense of persecution and present apocalypse, or those apophatic mystic (and, today, postmodern) Christians with natural instincts for excess, intensity, and non-closure.[43]

These brief examples of legitimately different Christian readings of the common confession and the common narrative may illustrate that there is no necessity to suspect[44] that either the original Christian communities or the redactors who produced new readings abandoned the 'plain sense' of the passion narratives. Should we really doubt that these different spiritualities, pieties, and theologies manifest a finally radical diversity of Christian readings of the common narrative? If the theologian is to honor that diversity, then he or she should do so by showing the harmony or, in principle, disharmony (Sach-Kritik) of the foundational plain sense of the common narrative and common confession and the often non-plain, seemingly centrifugal, diverse readings of that common narrative and confession.[45] In sum, the common Christian confession and, more fully, the 'plain sense' of the passion narrative should define but should not confine the possible range of Christian construals of the common narrative and confession.

The too often underplayed literary aspects of both form criticism and redaction criticism also merit a new look.[46] The productive, not merely taxonomic, nature of the genres analyzed by form critics suggest the need for further literary-critical and theological attention to how a particular text is formed through its genre and not merely how a particular historical context may be reconstructed by placing it taxonomically in a genre.[47] In redaction criticism, furthermore, the particularities of the differences also involved in the distinct gospel accounts of the passion narratives have been further clarified by exegetes like Norman Perrin who are not reluctant to use modern literary-critical methods of analysis.[48] Recall, for example, Perrin's brilliant contrast of Mark as an 'apocalyptic drama' with Luke and Matthew as distinct 'foundation myths'.[49] These same kinds of redactional skills can allow biblical theologians to attend to the full gospel narrative of the ministry of Jesus in direct and dependent relationship on the plain sense of the passion narratives. Here exegetical and hermeneutical work on the characteristic language of the Jesus of the synoptic gospels—his proverbs, his eschatological sayings, and especially his parables—bears theological fruit.[50] For example, if the parables of Jesus are not explicitly related to the passion narratives (as they are in the plain sense of Scripture), then it is true that the parables may begin to play too solitary and too prominent a theological role for Christian self-understanding.[51] For the full theological meaning of Jesus' parables of the Reign of God is only clarified when the interpreter, through careful readings of the passion narrative, shows how Jesus is fully manifested in the passion narratives, and not earlier, as the enacted parable of God.

At the same time, it is theologically impoverishing to fail to pay attention to how the parables also display new Christian readings of the common narrative and confession: possibly even the theologically apophatic and culturally postmodern readings of the parables by Funk and Crossan; and surely the dialectical Reformed readings of the parables by Ricoeur and McFague.[52] Besides the parables, every element in the full gospel narrative, if related to the plain meaning of the passion narrative, may also show yet another authentically Christian way by means of which the passion narrative may be read anew. As far as I can see, Luke (or Luke-Acts) is the gospel that maintains the closest affinity to the plain sense of the common passion narrative. This is both the great advantage of Luke and its possible limitation. The advantage is obvious. The hermeneutical and theological disadvantage less so. Is it so wrong to sense that Luke's relatively sanguine and sometimes all-too-continuous salvation-history narrative (as well as Luke's muted theology of the salvific power of the cross) can lend itself too easily to an undesirable degree of abstraction from the painful negativities, interruptions, and sufferings of history as viewed in the light of the cross?

Even a more concretely 'realistic' (i.e., not generalizing, salvation-history) reading of either Luke or the common passion narrative has its own dangers and its own peculiar temptations. Consider, for example, a possible cultural problem.[53] There is the danger (not the necessity) that a theological emphasis on an exclusively 'realistic' reading of the common narrative will not merely disown alternative readings, which however 'unrealistic' in form, maintain hermeneutical fidelity to the common 'realistic, history-like' passion narratives, but may also accord all too well with a culturally Anglo-Saxon reading of Christianity: clear, reasonable, moral, firm, and realistic. There is much to honor in this Anglo-Saxon tradition of moral realism. But there are alternative cultures, alternative spiritualities and theologies that also honor the realistic narrative in other and (for the Anglo-Saxon sensibility) often disturbing ways: apocalyptical and mystical readings, for example. A resting in 'realistic narrative' alone may occasion a refusal to take those other ways with full theological seriousness. The 'realism' of the passion narrative includes, of course, the stark realism of the cross and the realistic vindication of the resurrection: theological affirmations kept alive both in Luke and in the usual theological forms of Anglo-Saxon moral realism.[54] But we should take pains to assure that this Anglo-Saxon penchant for moral realism does not become synonymous, albeit unconsciously, with the truly disturbing realism of the passion narrative itself.

Anglo-Saxon (including North American) proponents of the plain sense of the common passion narrative can help to fight this characteristic Anglo-Saxon temptation (which also takes theological forms!) by making sure that Anglo-Saxon theologians take seriously the remarkable cultural, spiritual, and theological diversity which the 'plain sense' of Scripture not merely allows but encourages. For example, a careful reading of the stunning African-American readings of the passion narratives (e.g., James Cone and Cornell West, or the readings in the blues and spirituals) shows the limits of Anglo-Saxon moral realism.[55] So do French mystical readings, German metaphysical readings, Latin American liberationist readings and almost all feminist readings. Each of these alternative readings has its own way of assuring fidelity to the plain sense of the passion narratives:[56] ways accounted for by the stark realism of the passion narrative itself but too often unaccounted for by the dominant (and usually male) Anglo-Saxon taste for moral realism.

One initial way to assure this Anglo-Saxon self-critique in an emerging world church is to take the next step: keep grounded in the plain sense but also move beyond the common passion narrative and even Luke to all the New Testament gospels and all other New Testament genres. The Gospel of Mark, for example (as read in distinct but related ways by Perrin, Kermode, and Ricoeur),[57] can be legitimately read more like a modernist than a realistic text. The non-closure of Mark 16:8 reveals the fear, uncertainty, and hesitation that Mark's gospel forces upon the attention of all careful readers—an uncertainty which modernists and postmodernists do not hesitate to embrace. The uncanny interruptions that disturb the Markan narrative consistently reveal both the apocalyptic sensibility and the strong spirituality of suffering as endurance of radical negativity. The disturbing inability of the Markan disciples to grasp the point of Jesus' words and actions at crucial points in the narrative as well as the pervasive motif of betrayal (Judas) and failure (Peter) should allow any sensitive reader to become hesitant to claim to understand too quickly this disturbing text through purely realistic terms. This remains the case even for those readers who accept the plain sense of the common history-like, realistic narrative as foundational even for the reading of the 'modernist' Mark. Notice, for example, how Perrin and Ricoeur, with their Christian sensibilities, can in principle learn from a secular literary modernist reading like Kermode's without embracing Kermode's exaggerations on the overwhelming secrecy and nonrealism of Mark's Gospel.

As Ronald Thiemann argues,[58] the Gospel of Matthew can also lend itself to a common narrative reading. But Matthew also seems to be something more like a manual for the new leaders of the new community—a manual now curiously rendered into narrative form. The Matthean Jesus as the New Moses proclaiming the new Torah to the new Israel displays the profoundly Jewish character of Matthean Christianity. Matthew's forceful (and Jewish) emphasis on community-formation also shows how both the early church and the Radical Reformers were not wrong to appeal to Matthew:

above all, for ordering the forms of the new community's life in the light of the passion and resurrection of Jesus Christ. These peculiarly Matthean emphases are allowed for, but are not accounted for, in Thiemann's exclusively 'plain sense' reading. And that can only be considered a loss of another distinctively Christian reading of the common narrative.

Amos Wilder seems exactly right on the Gospel of John: It is a narrative that is more like an oratorio.[59] For to read John attentively is more like listening to Handel's Messiah than it is like reading a realistic novel. The rhythmic character of this oratorio-like narrative with its brilliant use of signs and images (light-darkness, truth-falsehood, etc.), with its strange and pervasive irony, and with its meditative, disclosive, and iconic power, releases an attentive reader to meditate even while following the narrative. And was Luther so wrong to sense his own affinity to the powerfully dialectical nature of Paul's theology of the Crucified Christ? The tensive Pauline language of "so much more," "not yet," "and yet" released in Paul's relentless and unresolved dialectic, is, of course, Jewish (Sanders, Davies, Stendahl, et al.).[60] Nevertheless, Paul, through his unique conceptual power at dialectically rendering the searing centrality of Christ's cross into the Christian consciousness, is also entirely faithful to the common Christian passion narrative. Augustine and Luther, with their 'troubled introspective consciences', were right to sense that the very modes of dialectical intensification and negation in Paul's forms of theological reflection on the passion and resurrection encouraged their theologies.

As theological attention to the narratives and all the other genres of the New Testament (always in the light of the common narrative) expands, moreover, Christian theologians may learn further ways of reading the Hebrew Scriptures as now, for the Christian, the Old Testament: witness Lindbeck's sensitive reading of the relationship of church and Israel.[61] Or consider Preus's illuminating analysis of the use of typology (that halfway house between literal and allegorical readings) in the early church.[62] Or note the illumination cast upon the liberation implications of the passion narrative when those narratives are read alongside the Exodus narrative—as in African-American spirituality and theology, or Latin American theologies of liberation. Or consider how Westermann's Christian theological reading of Genesis can inform the implications of the passion narrative for a new theology of nature.[63] Or observe, with Eliade, how even the cross may be construed, without loss of Christian specificity, as also both the 'cosmic tree' of a cosmic Christianity and the 'tree of knowledge of good and evil' in Genesis. All these familiar examples show how attention to the common passion narrative may also illuminate how Christians can learn to read the Old Testament with greater genre sensitivity, whether those readings be typological or even allegorical.[64] Recall, for example, how Paul Ricoeur's sensitive hermeneutical attention to the interplay of the genres of narrative and law, prophecy, wisdom, and praise in the Old Testament can be employed exactly as Ricoeur employs it:[65] to clarify, on intertextual grounds, how Christians learn to 'name God' more adequately by attending to the naming of God in the interplay of all the Old Testament genres in the light of the common passion narrative.

III. CONCLUSION: THE PLAIN SENSE AND THE PROPHETIC-MYSTICAL DIALECTIC

Any full Christian reading of the communal Scriptures would demand a collaborative enterprise among all those theologians and biblical scholars who accept, in principle, the rediscovery of the 'plain sense' of the passion narrative united to the common confession as the 'working canon' for fuller theological criteria of Christian appropriateness.[66] This theological decision, rather than any confused appeal to 'narrative theology', is the central fruit of the Frei-Lindbeck position.[67] It is important to repeat that even theologians, like myself, who do not agree with the 'cultural-linguistic' model as adequate for a full Christian theology can still find the intratextual rediscovery of the plain sense of the Scriptures immensely promising for fuller criteria of appropriateness in correlational (not 'experiential-expressive') theologies.[68] But, as I have urged above, any genuine affirmation of the 'plain sense' also opens one to a remarkable diversity of readings. The readings cited above (all faithful to the New Testament itself) indicate some, but by no means all, of those possible readings.

A more general model for the basic kinds of further Christian readings of the plain sense of the common narrative may prove helpful. In the most general terms, that basic model may be named the dialectic of prophetic and mystical readings. In one sense, this description is simply a reformulation, in contemporary theological terms, of the traditional Christian theological insistence on both word and sacrament.[69] The prophetic and mystical dialectic also coheres with the more general history and philosophy of religion distinction between manifestation and proclamation. In another sense, this prophetic-mystical dialectic suggests that the attempts of many contemporary theologians (especially political, feminist, African-American, and liberation theologians) are correct to try to develop an encompassing 'mystical-political' theology.[70] In terms of contemporary Christian piety, this attempt often occurs by trying to relate dialectically prophetic social justice concerns to the many classic Christian spiritualities. In terms of the kinds of philosophy now developed by those correlational theologies which also employ a 'mystical-political' model, the new alliances being forged between philosophical hermeneutics and a revised pragmatism continue to seem the most hopeful analogy in contemporary philosophy to the prophetic-mystical dialectic.

The dialectic of prophetic-mystical readings is not confined, of course, to correlational theologies. Indeed, the openness to ecumenical diversity in 'intratextual' theologies through their recovery of the 'plain sense' of the passion narrative as endorsing diversity can employ the basic model of prophetic and mystical readings on their own terms. They can do so in order to understand and help to order the diversity of readings released by the foundational plain sense. The prophetic reading encompasses the kerygmatic-as-proclamatory elements of the original apostolic witness of the Jesus kerygma, as well as, of course, the Christ kerygmas and the Jesus and Christ kerygma of the passion narrative itself.[71] The prophetic reading, moreover, also opens to apocalyptic readings with their radically interruptive construals of history in the light of a theology of the cross in Mark, as well as, on the conceptual level, in Paul's apocalyptically informed dialectical reflections on Jesus Christ and Him Crucified.[72] When prophecy fails, apocalyptic takes over: as surely it does, not only in the dominantly apocalyptic matrix of the early New Testament (Käsemann), but also in the many explicitly apocalyptic passages throughout the New Testament (e.g., Mark 13) culminating in the tensive symbols and language of the Book of Revelation.[73]

The 'mystical' reading is classically represented in John's gospel and letters. Indeed, John's letters may be read as further meditative commentaries ("God is love") on John's gospel. The same mystical and cosmic emphases pervade the letters of Colossians and Ephesians. Unlike the Gnostics, to whom John is so often compared, John's med-itations (indeed, I do not hesitate to say his mysticism) remain rooted in the passion narrative and thereby in none other than this Jesus the Christ who is, for John, the very *Logos* of God. The liberation and political theologians are right to find the most natural New Testament warrants for their readings in the prophetic and apocalyptic texts and Exodus narratives of the Old Testament read in the light of the dis-tinct prophetic, apocalyptic, and dialectical readings of the common passion narrative. So too, Christian mystics and metaphysicians find the most natural warrants for their readings in the Wisdom literature (*Sophia*) of the Old Testament and in the *Logos* of John.[74]

Louis Dupré is profoundly right, I believe, to insist upon the Christian appropriateness of the classical Christian mystical tradi-tions in the characteristic motifs and meditative tendencies of John and the entire Wisdom tradition:[75] the Image mystics (and the Johan-nine *Logos*); the love mystics (God is love and we are commanded and empowered to love); the Trinitarian mystics (the Father, Son and Paraclete relationships in John). Even the radically apophatic mystics might, perhaps, be interpreted as intensifying the pervasive irony of John's meditative narrative into the full radicality of their own apophatic language. So too, Hans Urs von Balthasar's theology of the 'visible form' can justly appeal to John, as surely as Teilhard de Chardin can appeal to Colossians and Ephesians for his portrayal of the cosmic Christ.

Moreover, as Gershom Scholem's and Moshe Idel's researches into Jewish kabbalistic readings of biblical and classical Judaism[76] show, whenever mystical readings of narrative texts and prophetic traditions of reading occur, the power of the great archaic traditions of reading will eventually reemerge. Here Mircea Eliade,[77] in fidelity to the non-Augustinian genius of his own Orthodox 'cosmic Chris-tianity', can help all Christians recover their archaic roots by new readings of the archaic elements concealed in the passion narratives, the prophetic and apocalyptic texts, and the parables of Jesus.

Nor need one fear that this prophetic-mystical model (or, more expansively, this prophetic-apocalyptic and mystical-archaic model)[78] will disallow the doctrinal and institutional emphases of the pastoral epistles, parts of Luke-Acts, and the community-formation emphasis of Matthew. 'Doctrine', for example, can also be read in both a prophetic-apocalyptic way (e.g., Johann Baptist Metz and Gustavo Gutiérrez) and meditative, often mystical and sometimes even archaic, ways (e.g., Paul Tillich and Karl Rahner). The advantage of the basic prophetic-mystical model for clarifying the two basic kinds of reading of the plain sense is that it shows one way to order an otherwise overwhelming diversity of readings in the New Testament. If the intricate dialectical relationships between the prophetic and mystical readings were theologically clarified, moreover, the resultant fully theological model would encourage contemporary ecumenical Christian theology to reunite what have too long been kept asunder: manifestation and proclamation; word and sacrament; social justice and traditional spiritualities; the prophetic and the mystical. All the prophetic-apocalyptic and mystical-archaic readings, in principle, can be faithful to the plain sense of the passion narrative. Several forms of these two basic kinds of readings, in fact, are present in the New Testament itself (and the Old Testament read Christianly) as well as in the entire history of Christianity.

A final note: the 'intention-action' agency model for understanding the self in Christian terms so well delineated by Frei as entailed in the history-like, realistic passion narratives and so well developed by David Kelsey in its implications for theological anthropology, should continue to be *the* principal Christian model for the Christian agent as a responsible self before God and the neighbor.[79] But, even here, as further prophetic-mystical readings suggest, there is ample room for more theological reflection on different Christian construals of the self, as long as those construals do not eliminate the Christian responsible agent of the passion narrative. The 'self-understanding' models for the self employed in Christian understandings of the 'true self' in the great neo-Platonists, the idealists, and the existentialists should not be dismissed unless and until one shows how they effectively deny responsible agency to the understanding of the self. In fact, as far as I can see, they do not: even the most radical of them, Meister Eckhart, ultimately affirms agency—as is demonstrated by his 'return' to ethical-political agential responsibility for the world, even after his journey to the true self disclosed by the "birth of the Son in the soul." For the Christian, a fear of the loss of agency must be a real fear. However, Christian reflections on the 'true self' in the classic neo-Platonic mystical traditions and even the reflections, in some of the radically apophatic mystics, on Buddhist-like models of 'no-self' do not necessarily demonstrate a loss of agency. At their characteristic best, the neo-Platonic mystics are no more Gnostic than John.[80] They provide further meditations on the self-understanding of the 'true self' of the Christian agent first meditatively disclosed by John.

Moreover, the model of the 'alienated' self in the 'introspective conscience' tradition of Christian reflection (as Bultmann was right to insist) also need not be read as denying true Christian agency to the self. To wish to deny the disturbing insights into the realities of human agency manifested in Augustine's model of the self '*curvatus in se*' (as Elaine Pagels seems to wish to do)[81] is analogous to wanting to return to an untroubled pre-Freudian view of the constitution of the self and its agency. Notice, for example, how the view of the self in some French Freudian feminist thinkers (such as Julia Kristeva with her model of the 'self-in-process-on-trial') can resonate with (as Kristeva insists), but is clearly not equivalent to, the complex view of the self (including its self-alienations) in the classic Christian love mystics.[82] In sum, there is too much to be lost if an insistence on the model of the intention-action agent entailed by the plain sense of the passion narratives becomes an occasion to forget the further (and not alien) reflections on the self of the later Christian meditative models of the theological tradition: the '*simul iustus, simul peccator*' model of the self; the 'true self' of the image-mystics; the agential self always in-process-on-trial of the love mystics. Such further reflections on the self can be as *ad hoc* as Lindbeck desires or as systematic and correlational as I admit I desire. In neither case need they be foresworn.

All such further Christian theological reflections—again in either an *ad hoc* or a systematic manner—can also open Christian theology to dialogues with other traditions, both secular and religious, on every issue relevant to Christian self-understanding. Is it so surprising that the agential emphasis of so many 'plain sense' theological positions finds its most natural philosophical partner in certain reflections of contemporary analytical philosophy of agency?

Surely no more surprising than the natural affinity of these plain sense positions, culturally, to an Anglo-Saxon culture of moral realism. Theologically the plain sense position finds its most natural dialogue partner in the realistic and moral emphases of classical and contemporary rabbinic Judaism. But there are also other philosophies, other cultures, other religions, and even other forms of Judaism (e.g., kabbalistic mysticism).

Further readings of the plain sense will encourage those other dialogues, again on either an *ad hoc* or a systematic basis. Prophetic and apocalyptic readings will inevitably find much to discuss with Marxism—as political and liberation theologians show. Mystical and, more widely, meditative traditions will find much to discuss dialogically with neo-Platonism, with idealism and existentialism, with Buddhism and Hinduism, with Jewish kabbala and Islamic Sufi traditions.

Those same readings will encourage further theological dialogue with historians of religion like Eliade (and not only anthropologists like Geertz) to disclose the archaic-manifestation elements also present in the Christian narratives. This may help Christian theologians rethink the often tragic, even sinful, relationships of Christianity to the great indigenous traditions across the globe. Both the 'Jew' and those archaic traditions misnamed the 'pagans' have too often proved the 'projected other' of Christian identity. Our clear need is for a Christian theology to engage in genuine dialogue with real, not projected, others. Here, as in so many questions, Christian feminist theologies by their just suspicion of the 'maleness' possibly concealed in many dominant Western models of the self-as-agent, and by their retrieval of often repressed Christian models of radical relationality to genuine (not projected) others, have much to teach all Christian theology.

If Christian theology can find its true ground again in the common confession expanded to the plain sense of the common narratives, then all these interreligious dialogues will reopen with new resources for fuller criteria of Christian appropriateness and new and more promising inner-Christian arguments on the need and character (*ad hoc* or systematic) for criteria of credibility. As we learn anew as a community of theologians how to appropriate both the common confession and the common narrative, there is reason to hope that we may also relearn how to encourage the explosive diversity of the prophetic-mystical readings released by the plain sense of the common passion narrative itself. That, at least, is my hope for a communal Christian theology. It is also, perhaps, the kind of hope intratextually implicit in the deeply ecumenical Christian theology of George Lindbeck.

NOTES

1. David Tracy, "Lindbeck's New Program for Theology: A Reflection," *The Thomist* 49 (1985): 460–72; idem, "The Uneasy Alliance Reconceived: Catholic Theological Method, Modernity, and Postmodernity," *Theological Studies* 50 (1989): 548–70.

2. George Lindbeck, "The Story-Shaped Church: Critical Exegesis and Theological Interpretation," in Garrett Green, ed., *Scriptural Authority and Narrative Interpretation* (Philadelphia: Fortress, 1987), 161; idem, "Scripture, Consensus and Community," in Richard John Neuhaus, ed., *Biblical Interpretation in Crisis: The Ratzinger Conference on Bible and Church* (Grand Rapids, Mich.: Eerdmans, 1989), 74–101.

3. See Hans Frei, "The 'Literal Reading' of Biblical Narrative in the Christian Tradition: Does It Stretch or Will It Break?" in Frank McConnell, ed., *The Bible and the Narrative Tradition* (New York: Oxford University Press, 1986), 36–78, esp. 43–59.

4. For a clear exposition of these criteria see Schubert M. Ogden, *On Theology* (San Francisco: Harper & Row, 1986).

5. David Kelsey, *The Uses of Scripture in Recent Theology* (Philadelphia: Fortress Press, 1975); Ernst Käsemann, "The Canon of the New Testament and the Unity of the Church," in *Essays on New Testament Themes* (London: SCM, 1964); Hans Küng, " 'Early Catholicism' in the New Testament as a Problem in Controversial Theology" in *The Council in Action: Theological Reflections on the Second Vatican Council* (New York: Sheed & Ward, 1963), 159–95; Willi Marxsen, *The New Testament as the Church's Book* (Philadelphia: Fortress Press, 1972); idem, "Das Problem des neutestamentlichen Kanons aus der Sicht des Exegeten," in *Der Exeget als Theologe* (Gütersloh: Mohns, 1968), 137–50.

6. Besides the work cited in note 4, see also Schubert M. Ogden, *The Point of Christology* (San Francisco: Harper & Row, 1982), esp. 96–105.

7. Hans Frei, *The Eclipse of Biblical Narrative: A Study in Eighteenth and Nineteenth Century Hermeneutics* (New Haven, Conn.: Yale University Press, 1974); idem, *The Identity of Jesus Christ: The Hermeneutical Bases of Dogmatic Theology* (Philadelphia: Fortress Press, 1975).

8. George Lindbeck, "The Story-Shaped Church."

9. All three of these formulations would need, of course, at least a further essay to clarify their meanings. Although Lindbeck, to my knowledge, does not use the phrase 'Scripture in tradition', his position and my own here are not mutually contradictory and may possibly coincide. See his reflections in "Scripture, Consensus, and Community," (note 2 above) and his recorded further reflections in the same volume, pp. 167–76. For my own formulations, see *The Analogical Imagination: Christian Theology and the Culture of Pluralism* (New York: Crossroad, 1981), 233–339; Robert M. Grant with David Tracy, *A Short History of the Interpretation of the Bible* (London: SCM, 1984), 174–87; and my reflections on the distinct positions of Hans Küng and Edward Schillebeeckx, "Particular Questions within General Consensus," in *Consensus in Theology? A Dialogue with Hans Küng and Edward Schillebeeckx*, L. Swidler, ed. (Philadelphia: Westminster, 1980).

10. See Kathryn E. Tanner, "Theology and the Plain Sense," in Green, ed., *Scriptural Authority and Narrative Interpretation*, 76, note 4. Tanner's article is the clearest and most analytical account I have read of both the primary meaning of 'plain sense', its related meanings, and the openness to diversity that 'plain sense' position allows.

11. Hans Frei, *The Identity of Jesus Christ*, esp. 86–154.

12. Ibid., for Frei's important reflections on the logical priority of identity to presence, see esp. 1–9; 154–68.

13. The notion of 'rendering' is borrowed from Henry James. In the German philosophical and theological traditions, the discussion of the distinction between *Vorstellung* and *Darstellung* is relevant here: see Eric Crump, *Imagination, Representation and Faith: Foundations for a Revised Representational Christology* (Ph.D. diss.: University of Chicago, 1989).

14. George Lindbeck, *The Nature of Doctrine: Religion and Theology in a Postliberal Age* (Philadelphia: Westminster, 1984). The notion of 'grammar' is that of Wittgenstein. Lindbeck uses it in that work to illuminate 'doctrine' rather than 'realistic narrative'—but it seems faithful to his position (and Wittgenstein's) to also apply it as I have here.

15. This is distinct from suggesting, as some theologians (unlike Frei and Lindbeck) do, that all theology should be 'narrative theology': see the judicious analysis of these issues in William C. Placher, *Unapologetic Theology: A Christian Voice in a Pluralistic Conversation* (Louisville: Westminster/John Knox Press, 1989), 123–38.

16. Hans Frei, "The 'Literal Reading' of Biblical Narrative." A general hermeneutical theory, like a 'modest' use of Auerbach on 'realistic narrative', can inform without 'taking over' a theological analysis of scriptural

texts: as I try to show in *The Analogical Imagination*, 233–305. It is important to observe that the use of hermeneutical analysis and genre (including narrative) analysis in that chapter is coherent with but not logically dependent upon the use of general hermeneutics in the earlier chapters' analysis of 'the classic' (pp. 99–154) or the 'religious classic' (pp. 154–231). Moreover, philosophically, 'general hermeneutical theory' (Gadamer and Ricoeur) is not dependent on a Husserlian 'transcendental subject' as Frei seems to believe (p. 52). Indeed, Heidegger's later philosophy and Gadamer's hermeneutics have as one of their main arguments the need to move away from the 'transcendental subject' of (Husserlian) phenomenology. The central theological question, however, is the logical independence of my clarificatory (not foundationalist) use of hermeneutics and genre analysis in interpreting the New Testament. That hermeneutical analysis, to be sure, is also 'correlated' with, but is not logically nor theologically dependent upon, the earlier hermeneutical analyses of the 'classic' and the 'religious classic'. This kind of interpretive failure to observe distinctions is, regrettably, not merely confined to Frei's subtle article but is continued, in a far less nuanced way, in Garrett Green's interpretation of my position on scriptural authority and interpretation in Garrett Green, *Imagining God: Theology and the Religious Imagination* (San Francisco: Harper & Row, 1989), 118–23. The logic of the moves from 'classic' to 'religious classic' to 'Christian classic', therefore, does not make the former analysis 'foundational' to the latter. The logic (like Schleiermacher's in the *Glaubenslehre*) is from the abstract to the concrete, not, as too often interpreted, from the concrete (foundationalist) to the specific. I do not deny, however (indeed am thankful for the criticism), that my hermeneutically informed particular interpretations of some particular New Testament texts (especially the parables) are sometimes either too general or abstract (see, here, Gary Comstock, "Two Types of Narrative Theology," *Journal of the American Academy of Religion* 55 [1987]: 687–717) or that they are not explicitly enough related to the passion narratives (see Frei, "The 'Literal Reading' of Biblical Narrative").

17. It is, perhaps, important to emphasize that I understand Frei to provide 'fuller' not 'different' criteria of appropriateness than those I have previously employed in the works cited in note 9.

18. See *The Analogical Imagination*, 249–59, 281–87, 329–32.

19. See Robert M. Grant with David Tracy, *A Short History of the Interpretation of the Bible*, 174–87.

20. For this reason, thanks to Frei's work, I would not change the basic categories and genres of my own attempt at an analysis of the New

Testament. But I would reorder them so that the 'realistic narratives' played a yet more central role: see *The Analogical Imagination*, 269–81.

21. In realistic narratives, as Frei shows, the character is an agent with intentions (rather than a self-consciousness as in many modernist texts). The agent interacts with circumstances in such manner that one can understand the wisdom of Henry James's insistence: "What is character but the determination of incident? What is incident but the illustration of character?" (quoted in Hans Frei, "Theological Reflections on the Accounts of Jesus' Death and Resurrection," *Christian Scholar* 49 [1966]: 279.)

22. See the valuable studies on genre in Mary Gerhart and James G. Williams, eds., *Genre, Narrativity and Theology: Semeia* 43 (Atlanta: Scholars Press, 1988) and the forthcoming book of Mary Gerhart on genre. As genre analysis becomes more widely available for theological interpretation (as in Gerhart's work and the work of her colleagues), the possibilities of rendering a more refined analysis of the principal New Testament genres than the one I propose in *The Analogical Imagination* (pp. 259–87) could be used for further theological reflection on the relationship of the 'passion narrative' to the other New Testament genres. Consider, for example, the clarifications of Paul's use of ancient rhetorical models for the genre 'letter' by Hans Dieter Betz in "Second Corinthians 6:14–7:1: An Anti-Pauline Fragment?" in *Journal of Biblical Literature* 92 (1973): 88–108; idem, *Galatians* (Philadelphia: Hermeneia-Fortress, 1979).

23. The classic theological example of *Sach-Kritik* remains Luther's dismissal of the Epistle of James (the 'right strawy epistle') as theologically inadequate on the relationship of 'faith' and 'works'. Even if one disagrees with Luther's reading of James (as I do), one can and should affirm his use of the christological principle to criticize what a scriptural text says in terms of what it should mean. For a good analysis and use of Luther here (as well as a criticism of Luther's reading of James) see Schubert M. Ogden, *Faith and Freedom: Toward a Theology of Liberation* (Nashville: Abingdon, 1989), 37–56. Although I do not hold to Ogden's (in his revision of Marxsen) own insistence on the 'original apostolic witness of the Jesus kerygma' as, in effect, the 'canon within the canon', I do hold to the need for a christological material principle for *Sach-Kritik* of the Scriptures themselves. This need for such a christological principle for interpreting Scripture remains a need even for those theologians (e.g., Lindbeck and Frei) who do not accept, as Ogden and I both do, the need for criteria of credibility along with criteria of appropriateness. Lindbeck's own material christological principle, if I understand him correctly, is "a Christ-centered narrationally and typologically unified whole in conformity to a Trinitarian rule of faith" ("Scripture, Consensus and Community," 77).

24. This does not deny, of course, the possibility of understanding the biblical narratives in literary-critical rather than theological ways—e.g., Robert Alter, *The Art of Biblical Narrative* (New York: Basic Books, 1981); Wesley A. Kort, *Story, Text and Scripture: Literary Interests in Biblical Narrative* (University Park: Pennsylvania State University Press, 1988); and the authors in the *Semeia* volume cited in note 22. The Bible can be interpreted with different interests: e.g., *as* history or *as* literature. The concern of the present essay, as of Frei and Lindbeck, is to interpret the Bible theologically as Scripture. All other relevant methods (including narratological theories) can illuminate and refine but cannot replace the strictly theological interpretation of the Bible as Scripture. For a careful analysis here of the 'as' structure in different readings of the Bible, see Garrett Green, "The Bible As . . .: Fictional Narrative and Scriptural Truth," in *Scriptural Authority and Narrative Interpretation*, 79–96; idem, *Imagining God*, 139–42.

25. On Barth, see Hans Frei, "Karl Barth: Theologian," *Reflection* (Yale Divinity School) 66/4 (1969): 5–9; for an illuminating rhetorical analysis of Barth (especially his Romans commentary), see Stephen Webb, *Re-Figuring Theology: The Rhetoric of Karl Barth* (Ph.D. diss., University of Chicago, 1989). For Auerbach, see Erich Auerbach, *Mimesis: The Representation of Reality in Western Literature* (Princeton, N.J.: Princeton University Press, 1953).

26. I might note that my proposal here is to clarify further the kerygmatic character of the passion narrative rather than (as with Marxsen and Ogden) to provide a theological argument for the Jesus kerygma as, in effect, the 'canon within the canon'.

27. In one sense, the narrative rendering is merely one example of the wider logical type of "making explicit the implicit." In another sense, however, the narrative rendering of the identity and presence of Jesus Christ in the passion narratives can only be construed as unique—as Frei argues in his Anselm-like constructive theological (and not merely literary-critical) proposal in the full argument of *The Identity of Jesus Christ*.

28. The doctrine of the Holy Spirit is, on inner-Christian terms, dependent on the doctrine of Jesus Christ—as the fascinating and important debates among Quaker theologians suggest.

29. For the proclamation-manifestation dialectic which *may* prove helpful for clarifying further Frei's analysis of how the proclamatory narratives' (i.e., gospels') rendering of Jesus' identity thereby also manifests his presence as Jesus Christ, see Paul Ricoeur, "Manifestation and Proclamation," *The Journal of the Blaisdell Institute* 12 (Winter 1978) and my analysis in *The Analogical Imagination*, 193–229.

30. The common confession may logically imply the common passion narrative; the common narrative (as gospel, i.e., proclamatory narrative) logically entails the common confession.

31. The discussions in Neuhaus, ed., *Biblical Interpretation in Crisis*, are representative here of the need for a christological material principle for interpreting Scripture: e.g., Josef Cardinal Ratzinger's foundation of a 'Christus totus' principle (as cited, pp. 166–67). I cannot but mention here that the *animus* indulged in against 'liberationist' and 'feminist' interpretations of Scripture by several of the participants in the account of the encounter (pp. 103–90) without supporting evidence or argument or even an interpretation of a single feminist or liberationist interpretion is shocking.

32. Hans Frei's reluctance to call his position a 'narrative theology' is a happy exception to this temptation among too many construals of the importance of narrative. Another notable exception here is Stanley Hauerwas when he provocatively states: "In itself, recognition of the theological significance of narrative is not very important. After all, stories do not save. God saves." (In Green, ed., *Scriptural Authority and Narrative Interpretation*, 179.)

33. Note how Frei, of course, cites all the gospels, not only Luke, in *The Identity of Jesus Christ*.

34. This principle is clearly honored in Frei's use of all the gospels as well as several other New Testament passages.

35. See the Jewish critique of some Christian narrative theologies of Michael Goldberg, "God, Action, and Narrative: Which Narrative? Which Action? Which God?" *Journal of Religion* 68 (1988): 39–56.

36. On the debates on Luke-Acts, see Charles H. Talbert, "Luke-Acts," in Eldon Jay Epp and George W. MacRae, S.J., eds., *The New Testament and Its Modern Interpreters* (Philadelphia: Fortress Press, 1989): 297–321.

37. It is one of the plagues of theology in our day that theologians, justly aware of their limitations in biblical exegesis, retreat from biblical commentary in their theologies. As many forms of biblical scholarship, in the meantime, become more and more nontheological (even antitheological), the theological situation worsens. For a recent analysis of some of these problems, see Robert Morgan with John Barton, *Biblical Interpretation* (Oxford: Oxford University Press, 1988) and Reginald H. Fuller, "New Testament Theology", in Epp and MacRae, eds., *The New Testament and Its Modern Interpreters*, 565–86, and the essays and discussions in Neuhaus, ed., *Biblical Interpretation in Crisis*.

38. See Hans W. Frei, *The Identity of Jesus Christ*, 126–38.

39. Johann Baptist Metz, *Faith in History and Society: Toward a Prac-*

tical Fundamental Theology (New York: Crossroad, 1980). The description of Metz's theology as 'Markan' is mine, not his.

40. See G. Bornkamm, G. Barth, and H. J. Held, *Tradition and Interpretation in Matthew* (Philadelphia: Westminster, 1963); Jack Dean Kingsbury, *Matthew: Structure, Christology, Kingdom* (Philadelphia: Fortress, 1975); John Meier, *The Vision of Matthew: Christ, Church and Morality in the First Gospel* (New York: Paulist, 1979).

41. Note the Käsemann-Küng exchange noted in note 5. It is time, I believe, to retire the category 'early Catholicism'.

42. For a good, modern example of this 'Catholic' sensibility recall the theology of John Henry Newman—in both his Anglican and his Roman Catholic writings.

43. The first kind of reader includes not only fundamentalist readings but also sophisticated exegetical studies of the Book of Revelation like the several studies (with several methods) of Elisabeth Schüssler-Fiorenza: e.g., 'Revelation' in Epp and MacRae, eds., *The New Testament and Its Modern Interpreters*, 407–27; idem, "The Revelation to John," in G. Krodel, ed., *Hebrews, James I and II, Peter, Jude, Revelation* (Philadelphia: Fortress, 1977), 99–120.

44. There is 'no necessity', i.e., it is, of course, possible to do so in any particular case through various forms of *Sach-Kritik*. A more hermeneutical way to express this principle is that one has good reason to *trust* fundamentally the tradition which mediates and witnesses to the event of Jesus Christ. This does not preclude (as in friendship) either critique (internal and, when appropriate, external) or suspicion (e.g., of the patriarchy also present in the scriptural and later ecclesial mediations and disallowed on the basis of the fundamental material christological principle which the common confession and common narrative alike render). For some reflections on these principles: for general hermeneutical terms, see my *Plurality and Ambiguity* (San Francisco: Harper & Row, 1987), esp. chapters 3 and 4; for an example of the Christian's fundamental trust of the mediating tradition and church, see my exchange with Thomas Sheehan, 'Levels of Liberal Consensus," *Commonweal* 111, August 10, 1984, 426–31. For the more extensive theological criteria, see the works cited in note 9.

45. Lindbeck affirms his formulation of this principle in "Scripture, Consensus, and Community."

46. Note, for example, how Gunkel's form criticism highlights literary-critical factors more than many of his form-critical successors in, e.g., Herman Gunkel, *The Folktale in the Old Testament* (London: Decatur and Sheffield, 1987). A suggestive analysis on this issue may be found in the chapter

64 / David Tracy

entitled "The Literary Study of the Bible," in Robert Morgan with John Barton, Biblical Interpretation, 203–68, and in the studies in John H. Hayes, ed., Old Testament Form Criticism (San Antonio: Trinity University Press, 1977), esp. 1–57.

47. Analyses of the productive, not merely taxonomic, nature of genre and the Bible may be found in Mary Gerhart and James G. Williams, Genre, Narrativity and Theology.

48. See Norman Perrin, The New Testament: An Introduction (New York: Harcourt, Brace, Jovanovich, 1974); idem, Jesus and the Language of the Kingdom (Philadelphia: Fortress, 1978).

49. Norman Perrin, The New Testament, 143–221.

50. Norman Perrin, Jesus and the Language of the Kingdom, and Paul Ricoeur in Semeia 4, ed. John Dominic Crossan: Paul Ricoeur on Biblical Hermeneutics (Missoula: Scholars Press, 1975), esp. 107–45.

51. This is the case, I believe, in, for example, John Dominic Crossan, even in his earlier, less radical and less postmodern work, e.g., In Parables (New York: Harper & Row, 1973) and Robert Funk, even in his earlier, less radical work in Language, Hermeneutics and Word of God (New York: Harper & Row, 1966). It is also true, I fear, of my own analysis in Blessed Rage for Order, 124–46 but not in The Analogical Imagination. This is not to deny, of course, the value of these parabolic et al. analyses. It is, rather, to insist that if the parables are to play their full theological role they should be related to the common confession and to the diversity of genres (as in The Analogical Imagination) or the common narrative (as in Frei).

52. The qualifier 'possibly' relates to the more radical and postmodern turn in Crossan's analyses, starting with his Cliffs of Fall: Paradox and Polyvalence in the Parables of Jesus (New York: Seabury, 1980) as well as in Funk's work, starting with his Jesus as Precursor (Philadelphia: Fortress, 1975). The qualifier 'surely' refers to the clearly Christian (indeed Reformed) analyses of Paul Ricoeur in Semeia (see note 50) and Sallie McFague TeSelle, Speaking in Parables (Philadelphia: Fortress, 1975) and Sallie McFague, Metaphorical Theology (Philadelphia: Fortress, 1982), 42–67.

53. It is important to emphasize that this is a cultural, not a properly theological problem, except when Anglo-Saxon 'moral realism' unduly influences (usually unconsciously) theological proposals. The problem is not, of course, confined to Anglo-Saxon culture. Every culture has its strengths and limitations. The contemporary movement of Christianity from a Eurocentric to a 'world church' perspective fortunately heightens theological consciousness of the dangers of not merely Anglo-Saxon but, more widely, all European and North American theologies.

54. It is, perhaps, helpful to admit that I share here the Anglo-Saxon 'realism' on Jesus' resurrection as his vindication by God. This realistic interpretation seems to me more faithful to the New Testament than the Bultmannian interpretations.

55. See James Cone and Gayraud Wilmore, *Black Theology: A Documentary History, 1966–1979* (Maryknoll, N.Y.: Orbis, 1980); James Cone, *God of the Oppressed* (New York: Seabury, 1975); Cone, *The Spirituals and the Blues* (San Francisco: Harper & Row, 1974); Cornell West, *Prophecy Deliverance* (Louisville: Westminster/John Knox, 1982).

56. For example, see Elisabeth Schüssler-Fiorenza, *In Memory of Her: A Feminist Reconstruction of Christian Origins* (New York: Crossroad, 1983).

57. Frank Kermode, *The Genesis of Secrecy: On the Interpretation of Narrative* (Cambridge, Mass.: Harvard University Press, 1979); Norman Perrin, *Jesus and the Language of the Kingdom*; Paul Ricoeur, "Interpretative Narrative," originally published in *Recherches de Science Religieuse* 73 (1985): 17–38.

58. Ronald F. Thiemann, *Revelation and Theology: The Gospel as Narrated Promise* (Notre Dame, Ind.: University of Notre Dame Press, 1985), esp. 112–56; idem, "Radiance and Obscurity in Biblical Narrative," in *Scriptural Authority and Narrative Interpretation*, 33–39.

59. Amos Wilder, *The Language of the Gospel: Early Christian Rhetoric* (New York: Harper & Row, 1964), 120.

60. W. D. Davies, *Paul and Rabbinic Judaism: Some Rabbinic Elements in Pauline Theology* (Philadelphia: Fortress, 1980); E. P. Sanders, *Paul and Palestinian Judaism: A Comparison of Patterns of Religion* (Philadelphia: Fortress, 1977); idem, *Paul, the Law and the Jewish People* (Philadelphia: Fortress, 1983); Krister Stendahl, *Paul Among Jews and Gentiles and Other Essays* (Philadelphia: Fortress, 1976).

61. George Lindbeck, "The Story-Shaped Church, " in Green, ed., *Scriptural Authority and Narrative Interpretation*.

62. James Samuel Preus, *From Shadow to Promise: Old Testament Interpretation from Augustine to the Young Luther* (Cambridge, Mass.: Belknap Press of Harvard University Press, 1969).

63. Claus Westermann, *Genesis* (Grand Rapids, Mich.: Eerdmans, 1987).

64. On typology, see James Samuel Preus, *From Shadow to Promise*. Both Frei and Lindbeck consistently defend typological analysis. It takes nothing away from the centrality of typological interpretation and the 'literal sense' to defend, as well, the kind of controlled allegorical exegesis and the 'fourfold' sense of interpretation employed in both the patristic and medieval periods:

see, especially, the great work of Henri de Lubac, *Exégèse médiévale: le quatre sens de l'écriture* (Paris: Aubier, 1959–64).

65. Paul Ricoeur, "Toward a Hermeneutic of the Idea of Revelation," in Lewis L. Mudge, ed., *Essays on Biblical Interpretation* (Philadelphia: Fortress, 1980), 73–119. The interpretation of Ricoeur's position here as Christian, i.e., in light of the common passion narrative, is my interpretation, not his—but one with which his article clearly accords.

66. In terms of biblical scholars, this applies to all those who accept theological interpretation of the texts; in terms of theologians, this refers to the necessity of criteria of Christian appropriateness. For a good example of the application of theological criteria of appropriateness to theological proposals, see Schubert M. Ogden, "Problems in the Case for a Pluralistic Theology of Religions," in *Journal of Religion* 68 (1988): 493–508.

67. Both Frei and Lindbeck are consistently clear on this principle. Neither advocates a purely 'narrative theology'.

68. I.e., the 'experiential-expressive' model is not an adequate description of most 'mediating' or 'correlational' theologies. For Lindbeck's analysis, see *The Nature of Doctrine: Religion and Theology in a Postliberal Age*, and my "Lindbeck's New Program for Theology: A Reflection." The philosophical issue here is the relationship between 'experience' and 'language' after the 'linguistic turn'. The theological issue is more helpfully formulated as the argument on whether 'criteria of intelligibility' for theology are needed on *ad hoc* or systematic grounds. On the latter, see William Werpehowski, "Ad Hoc Apologetics," *Journal of Religion* 66 (1986): 282–301, and David Tracy, "The Uneasy Alliance Reconceived."

69. See *The Analogical Imagination*, 193–231.

70. It is noteworthy that many political theologies (e.g., Metz and Schillebeeckx) and liberation theologies (e.g., Gutiérrez) prefer the name 'mystical-political' to highlight the political and liberationist dimensions of the task. The journal *Concilium* has often published valuable articles on this theme. One should not remove the 'political' dimension by naming the theological readings 'prophetic'. However, one does thereby highlight the biblical-theological roots of all 'prophetic' readings—including, of course, political theologies, feminist theologies, African American theologies and liberation theologies.

71. This prophetic reading could also include the 'Jesus as prophet' portrait in the historically reconstructed 'Q sayings': see Richard A. Edwards, *A Theology of Q: Eschatology, Prophecy, and Wisdom* (Philadelphia: Fortress, 1976); the 'kerygmas' are analyzed in Willi Marxsen, *The New Testament as the Church's Book*. It is, perhaps, worth noting here that historical-critical

work (like Edwards and Marxsen) remains important even for those theologians who take the common narrative and common confession approach. This is obviously true, for me at least, in terms of criteria of intelligibility or credibility (whether *ad hoc* or systematic: some obvious apologetic questions: Did Jesus exist? Was he fraudulent or self-deceived? What can we know historically of his typical words and actions?) This is also true in terms of criteria of appropriateness (What unity exists amidst the great diversity of New Testament christologies? How do the earlier kerygmata cohere (or, in principle, fail to cohere) with the Jesus-Christ kerygma of the passion narratives? What theological difference, if any, would radical noncoherence make? By what theological criteria? Even 'canonical' approaches to theology can, in sum, be challenged (in terms of both credibility *and* appropriateness) by historical-critical results. How and why is exactly the question of the nature of theological criteria of Christian appropriateness for reading the Scriptures theologically.

72. On the 'apocalyptic' (and theocentric) dimensions of Paul, see J. Christian Beker, *Paul the Apostle: The Triumph of God in Life and Thought* (Philadelphia: Fortress, 1980).

73. See John Collins, *Apocalyptic as Genre* (Missoula: Semeia-Scholars Press, 1978); for Käsemann, see, "The Beginnings of Christian Theology" and "On the Subject of Primitive Christian Apocalyptic" in *Essays on New Testament Themes*.

74. As feminist critics have insisted, it is revealing of the patriarchal realities also concealed in our scriptural texts that the 'feminine' *Sophia* was replaced by the 'masculine' *Logos* in the tradition.

75. Louis Dupré's many studies of the mystical traditions have yielded the model of the four principal models of Christian mysticism I employ here: the Image mystics; the Trinitarian mystics; the love mystics; and the apophatic mystics. The relationship of these readings to John is my own, although clearly implicit in Dupré's magisterial philosophical (rather than strictly theological) studies of the Christian mystical traditions. There is, in my judgment, no more important retrieval of theological resources in our day than the recovery of the mystics by Dupré and his many colleagues (e.g., Ewert Cousins and Bernard McGinn). Here, too, is one of the signal theological contributions of Hans Urs von Balthasar. Inter alia, see Louis Dupré, *The Deeper Life: An Introduction to Christian Mysticism* (New York: Crossroad, 1981); idem, *The Other Dimension: A Search for the Meaning of Religious Attitudes* (Garden City, N.Y.: Doubleday, 1972).

76. Gershom Scholem, *Major Trends in Jewish Mysticism* (New York: Schocken, 1961); Moshe Idel, *Kabbalah: New Perspectives* (New Haven, Conn.: Yale University Press, 1988).

77. Eliade is, of course, not a theologian but a historian of religions. It is hardly fanciful, however, to note the influence of his own Orthodox tradition on his interpretations of Christianity.

78. The dialectic in each case: 1) when prophecy fails, apocalyptic takes over; 2) when mystical readings emerge, archaic motifs reemerge.

79. David Kelsey, "Biblical Narrative and Theological Anthropology," in Green, ed., *Scriptural Authority and Narrative Interpretation*, 121–43.

80. For a strong contemporary theological defense of the neo-Platonic tradition in Christian theology, see John Macquarrie, *In Search of Deity* (New York: Crossroad, 1987).

81. Elaine Pagels, *Adam, Eve and the Serpent* (New York: Random House, 1988).

82. Julia Kristeva, *Tales of Love* (New York: Columbia University Press, 1987), esp. 139–89, 297–318.

ABSORBING THE WORLD: CHRISTIANITY AND THE UNIVERSE OF TRUTHS

Bruce D. Marshall

"Intratextual theology," writes George Lindbeck in *The Nature of Doctrine*, "redescribes reality within the scriptural framework rather than translating scripture into extrascriptural categories. It is the text, so to speak, which absorbs the world, rather than the world the text."[1] My aim here is to investigate this metaphor to see whether it might be the heart of an adequate and plausible response to the question about whether Christian beliefs are true. In so doing it will be necessary to consider a series of objections which take Lindbeck's metaphor to be a flight from, rather than a response to, the question of truth. But first it is necessary to clarify the question and to see how the claim—and imperative—to "absorb the world into the scriptural text" might function as an answer to it.

I

Current theological discussions, especially those which draw on contemporary philosophical debates about truth, suggest that even at the most basic level the truth status of Christian discourse is not a single issue but several related ones. To put these issues in the form of questions: 1) How should the implicit or explicit ascription of truth to utterances, sentences, or beliefs (especially those which Christians are distinctively prone to hold true, but not only those) be interpreted? Or one could ask what it means to say that utter-ances, sentences, or beliefs are true, what truth is, or how "true" should be defined (allowing that "true" may have quite different senses in different contexts and also allowing for views which deal with this question by arguing that "true" should not or need not be defined). 2) By what criteria should the truth (and falsity) of these same utterances, sentences, and beliefs properly be assessed (allowing that these criteria may often function without being ad-verted to explicitly)? 3) Whatever criteria one identifies in answer to 2, why rely on these criteria rather than on others? Questions 2 and 3 together may be said to constitute the question of how we test and support our claims to truth. These two questions can also be taken jointly to pose the problem of the justification of Christian belief. Literally, "justified" beliefs are those we have some right to hold. As I am using the term, communities and individuals may sometimes differ about what beliefs they and others are justified in holding, insofar as they differ about the criteria which ought to be invoked in support of those beliefs, that is, about what precisely gives (or does not give) people in various contexts the right to hold this or that belief. To use the notion of justification in this way, it should be noted, is not necessarily to say that beliefs which are taken to be false must be regarded as unjustified. That depends on the account of truth and justification one develops in answer to the questions just outlined.

A reasonably adequate theological account of the claim to truth embedded in much Christian discourse would have to deal with all three questions and indicate how the answers proposed to each hang together in a coherent way. My aim here is more modest: I will focus on the third question, about how the criteria of truth which one takes to be theologically primary can themselves be warranted or justified. It is specifically to this question, I will argue, that the metaphor of "absorbing the world" suggests an answer.

II

The Nature of Doctrine includes a compact and schematic ac-count of religious and theological truth which suggests answers to all three of the questions I have posed. It will be useful to make some observations regarding Lindbeck's answers to the first and second questions, and their interconnection, although here I will have to be very brief.[2] With regard to the first question, the claim to truth embedded in first-order Christian speech and practice can be interpreted or defined "in epistemologically realistic fashion as involving a correspondence of the mind to divine reality," or more broadly, simply as "correspondence to reality."[3] Lindbeck does not develop in detail an account of how this correspondence should be understood, except to say that when it comes to talk about God and God's acts, the distinctive character of the referent of such speech requires that the correspondence of mind and reality to which the speech lays claim, while real, is significantly limited; he employs Aquinas's distinction between the *res significata* and the *modus significandi* of terms to characterize this limitation.[4] Thus, although Lindbeck does not develop a "correspondence theory of truth" in any significant sense, he does seem to say that the way Christians use sentences central to the faith (the example he employs is "Jesus Christ is Lord") requires that a notion of correspondence, or some functional equivalent, be employed to interpret first-order Christian practice.

To give a definition or characterization of truth, whether in Lindbeck's modestly realist fashion or in some other way, does not by itself help one even to begin to decide which sentences are true in the sense of the definition and which are not. For that some criteria are needed, and Lindbeck proposes two distinct kinds (specifically for religious truth, although the account could be extended), both of which must be met in order for uttered sentences to be true: categorial adequacy and intrasystematic coherence.[5] The "categories" of a religion are syntactic as well as lexical; they include not only the characteristic vocabulary of a religion but also normative patterns for deploying that vocabulary in story, teaching, exhortation, invocation, and so forth (patterns which Lindbeck often calls the "grammar" of a religion). In many religions, including "all the world's major faiths," the categorial scheme of the religion (that is, its lexicon and grammar) are "paradigmatically encoded" in a canon of normative texts.[6] Categorial adequacy is a test for truth—more precisely, a precondition for it—insofar as activities bound up with holding sentences true can only be successful if we have categories appropriate to whatever we are trying (for example) to refer to or describe. In many contexts this test for truth goes unnoticed, since we assume that anyone we can talk to has, for the purposes at hand, basically the same stock of mostly reliable categories that we do. But categorial adequacy is a significant test for truth in religious discourse, insofar as different religions propose particular and distinctive categorial patterns (such as particular realistic narratives) as indispensable for true speech about what the religion takes to be "most important" or "ultimately real." Those who lack the relevant categories, to the degree that they lack them, will not be able to make true (or false) statements about what a given religion holds to be in fact the most important thing in the universe.

When it comes to a criterion of truth for individual utterances, however, categorial adequacy must be complemented by intrasystematic coherence. A given utterance will ordinarily be judged to be true by adherents of a religion to the degree that it coheres with the wider web of belief and practice which constitutes the religion, especially with the paradigmatic patterns of belief and practice "encoded" in the religion's scriptures. Categorial adequacy alone, however, is not sufficient to guarantee that a given sentence when uttered will cohere in this way, even when that sentence is lexically and grammatically identical with a portion of the religion's sacred text. This is because the way a sentence is used is decisive for its meaning (in that use), or, more specifically, because the meaning (or interpretation) of a sentence actively held true is fixed by the specific circumstances in which it is held true.[7] These circumstances are often practical as well as linguistic, so that, as Lindbeck puts the point, "utterances are intrasystematically true when they cohere with the total relevant context, which, in the case of a religion when viewed in cultural-linguistic terms, is not only other utterances but also the correlative forms of life."[8] Ascertaining this intrasystematic coherence (or lack of it) in specific cases may be relatively straightforward or quite complex, but in any case it requires extensive familiarity with the religion as a cultural-linguistic system—with its characteristic and normative patterns of action, affection, and belief.

Although he himself does not put it this way, I think Lindbeck's way of handling the question about the criteria of truth can be fairly summarized by saying that he ascribes primacy to the plain sense of Scripture in the order of justification. By the "plain sense" I mean, borrowing Kathryn Tanner's definition, "what a participant in the community automatically or naturally takes a text to be saying on its face insofar as he or she has been socialized in a community's conventions for reading the text as Scripture."[9] It is chiefly by appeal to the plain sense of Scripture that the Christian community tests and reforms its own current web of belief and practice. And, since its identification of the plain sense of Scripture is itself part of the community's current web of belief and practice, the very notion of a normative plain sense funds a significant distinction between text and interpretation. The community's ongoing engagement with the text in which its categories are "paradigmatically encoded" may require revisions of the way the community identifies the plain sense of that text.[10] The importance of this latter point will become more apparent later on.

What the community tests by appeal to the plain sense is not only its own current faithfulness to its textually encoded identity, but the *truth* of its own discourse, and by extension of any discourse it may encounter. This is what it means to say that the plain sense of Scripture has justificatory primacy. More precisely, it means that the coherence of sentences (interpreted in their practical as well as linguistic context) with the plain sense is at least a necessary, and in some cases a sufficient, criterion of their truth. This test will tend to be not simply necessary, but sufficient, to the degree that the discourse in question is directly tied to the characteristic "categories" of the community; the more a given discourse addresses matters central to a Christian vision of the world (that is, one shaped by the plain sense of Scripture), the more coherence with the plain sense of the text will tend to be the decisive test of its truth.

Ascribing primacy to the plain sense of Scripture in the order of justification implies, more broadly, that beliefs and practices "internal" to Christianity are the primary criteria of truth. As I will use the term, a belief or practice is "internal" when the Christian community, in a given historical context, regards that belief or practice as (maximally) necessary or (minimally) beneficial in order for it to be faithful to its own identity. This will include chiefly, if not exclusively, what the community must say and do in order to identify and apply the plain sense of Scripture and in order to follow the communally normative rules which in certain respects help it identify and apply the plain sense (that is, its "doctrines" in Lindbeck's sense of the term). All other belief and practice can be called "external," or "alien" in William Christian's formal sense.[11] As we shall see, the distinction between "internal" and "external" beliefs is in practice often a merely provisional one. The Christian community will naturally strive to "internalize" initially alien discourse, so that although the latter may not become necessary to its identity ("internal" in the strictest sense), it nonetheless has a legitimate and traceable location within the community's comprehensive vision of the world (and so is at least beneficial for the community to hold true).

We can now see what form our third question about truth ("why these criteria?") will take when the first two are answered along lines like those Lindbeck proposes: Why ascribe justificatory primacy to internal Christian criteria of truth, specifically to the plain sense of Scripture? It is especially to this question that Lindbeck's arresting and controversial metaphor—"it is the text which absorbs the world"— suggests a response.

To speak of the biblical text "absorbing the world" can be taken as suggesting an account of both the interpretation and the assessment of truth claims encountered by the Christian community which are initially external or alien to its own belief and practice. Interpretatively, the project of "absorbing the world" can by characterized as a process of "redescription" in which the Christian community and its individual members attempt to make sense of novel or unfamiliar truth claims and worldviews in terms provided by the community's own primary idiom, that is, by its ruled reading and use of the biblical text. Viewing this process of redescription as the primary (although not exclusive) direction of the interpretative activity of the community can be contrasted with viewing as primary a process of "translation," in which the community attempts to make sense of its own truth claims in terms provided by one or more external worldviews or idioms. As Lindbeck puts the point, "Intratextual theology redescribes reality within the scriptural framework rather than translating Scripture into extrascriptual categories."[12]

But interpretation is closely bound up with assessment, testing for meaning with testing for truth. Specifically, the interpretative process of "absorbing the world" employs something along the lines of the "principle of charity" which, so Donald Davidson argues, we must invoke if we are to account for how we are able to understand sentences spoken in an initially unfamiliar natural language. Confronted by human beings making sounds which we take to be sentences in a language, but which we do not understand, we come to understand sentences in that language by being "charitable" about their truth. That is, we come to give right interpretations of sentences in an unfamiliar language by taking as many sentences as we can to be true, in the specific circumstances in which they are uttered. This, Davidson argues, is the only plausible way in which interpretation yielding satisfactory results can be taken to work: if we find ourselves attributing massive falsity to speakers and sentences in an unfamiliar natural language, we have no choice but to suppose that our interpretation, not the interpreted speakers and sentences, is in the main mistaken.[13]

Something like this "principle of charity" about truth in the process of interpretation is operative in the theological project of absorbing the world into the scriptural text.[14] Charity about truth shapes the interpretation of whatever discourse the Christian community encounters; the goal of interpretation is to find a way of understanding that discourse which allows it to be held true, that is, to find a place for it within the world or "domain of meaning" opened up by the scriptural text.[15] At the same time, there is an important dissimilarity between the theological "principle of charity" and that invoked by Davidson in the philosophy of language. The interpreter of sentences in an unfamiliar natural language, so Davidson argues, has no reliable linguistic clue to the best interpretation of those sentences except the sentences in her own language which she holds true; the best available interpretation will therefore be that which maximizes the ascription of truth to interpreted sentences by the interpreter's own standards. But maximizing agreement for the sake of interpretation does not at all preclude significant disagreement about which sentences are true and by what standards; the interpreter may understand the speaker by assuming agreement on a host of platitudes, and so discover that she and the speaker disagree about those beliefs which are for her most central. Thus the best interpretation of initially alien discourse by the Christian community will not necessarily be the one which maximizes the truth of that discourse by the community's own standards. This can be seen most clearly when (as is usually the case) Christians are striving to interpret unfamiliar sentences or worldviews in their own natural language. The shared natural language as a whole will itself provide clues to the interpretation of unfamiliar sentences, which may support a conclusion that the interpretation which would maximize agreement (the one the theological "principle of charity" urges us to seek) is not the one which is most plausible. Generally stated, therefore, the theological project of "absorbing the world" is the ongoing effort by the Christian community and individual members to construe novel, unfamiliar, or "alien" sentences in a way which *both* (a) constitutes the best available interpretation of those sentences and (b) allows them to be held true.

As I have already indicated, the primary test for whether sentences, novel or otherwise, can be held true on the sort of "intratextual" account being proposed here is whether they cohere with a wide network of Christian belief and practice which is generated and corrected by the community's ruled use of the biblical text, that is, its discernment of the plain sense of Scripture. This is not to say, of course, that the internal (especially scriptural and creedal) criteria of truth which are decisive for the project of absorbing the world are the only criteria relevant for the interpretation and assessment of the discourse the community encounters, nor that they are necessarily the most proximate ones; very often they will be neither. Nor is it to say that "coherence" with the textually governed web of Christian belief and practice is a uniform relation applicable in the same way to all encountered discourse. The type and degree of appropriate coherence will vary widely depending on the specific character of the discourse in question and the specific aspects of Christian belief and practice with which it is primarily engaged. Often the minimal relation of consistency will be appropriate and adequate; sometimes a stronger kind of coherence will be required: mutual fitness, explanatory force, or implication, for example.

The Christian internalization of initially external discourse and even whole worldviews, especially when it is highly successful, may involve giving such discourse and worldviews in important respects a different sense than they originally had, precisely in order to hold them true as much as possible. Thus the Platonism of Augustine (and even more of Anselm) is, although recognizable as Platonism, significantly different from that of Plotinus (let alone Plato) on account of the transformations wrought by absorbing it into the biblical text.

And, Augustine suggests, it is better Platonism just on account of being absorbed in this way. Similarly Aquinas, deeply engaged in and scrupulous about the text of Aristotle, creates a transformed, much expanded, and (so he modestly but clearly suggests) superior Aristotelianism by his massive effort to interpret (or "redescribe") Aristotle so that he can hold as much of Aristotle as possible true within a distinctively Christian and scriptural universe of discourse.

To be sure, "alien" sentences and worldviews and their associated practices will sometimes resist the interpretative overtures the Christian community or theology wants to make toward them. Sometimes the best available interpretation, applying the principle of charity, may still require that a certain discourse or even whole worldview be rejected; there may be no plausible interpretation on which that discourse is even minimally coherent with the scripturally normed web of Christian belief and practice. In this case, the discourse in question is "absorbed" into the biblical world by being denied any legitimate place within it, that is, by being held false. So, to mention an important modern example, Barth argued that the oath of allegience to Hitler, and thereby the Nazi worldview represented by that particular practice, was simply incompatible with the criteria of truth which must guide the Christian community and must therefore be rejected (and, as this case vividly shows, the community and theologians can fail disastrously to honor their own criteria of truth).

So, whether the results of the ongoing enterprise of absorbing the world are in any given case positive, negative, or as yet undecided, that project is constituted by two complementary (indeed, mutually implicative) imperatives: 1) as far as is practically possible, interpret all discourse in light of the community's scripturally encoded criteria of truth, with the goal of holding the discourse true by those criteria; 2) as far as is practically possible, consider all discourse, and therefore all possible truth, to make a claim upon the community's scripturally normed project of interpretation and assessment. To the degree that these imperatives are being followed, the text is absorbing the world, or, in another phrase of Lindbeck, Scripture is "not simply a source of precepts and truths, but the interpretive framework for all reality."[16]

To return to the original question: What justifies the claim that the internal criteria of truth which guide the Christian interpretative project of absorbing the world are the decisive test for the truth of the community's own discourse, and at least a necessary test for the truth of any discourse the community may encounter? On the view I am exploring here, the Christian community tests the truth of unfamiliar or alien discourse, from individual utterances to worldviews, by seeing whether that discourse can be interpreted so that it coheres with the community's own distinctive web of belief and practice. By contrast, a primary test *of* the truth of that web of belief and practice itself, and especially of the plausibility of using coherence with it as the decisive test for truth, is what Lindbeck calls its "assimilative power." "The reasonableness of a religion," he writes, "is largely a function of its assimilative powers, of its ability to provide an intelligible interpretation in its own terms of the varied situations and realities adherents encounter."[17] The scripturally shaped web of Christian belief will be warranted as the primary criterion of truth by its capacity, evinced in repeated successes, to internalize or assimilate initially alien discourse, that is, to give persuasive interpretations in its own terms of such discourse which allow that discourse to be held true, or which give compelling reasons in light of its own criteria to account for rejecting that discourse as false. Conversely, repeated failure to assimilate alien discourse or to give compelling reasons for rejecting it will argue that we are not warranted in ascribing justificatory primacy to the plain sense of Scripture.

This notion of "assimilative power" meets two conditions which ought to be satisfied in responding to the question, "Why these criteria of truth?" First, using the notion of assimilative power avoids begging the question. A non-question-begging test for criteria of truth operative within a comprehensive worldview will be one which is not rooted in beliefs whose epistemic status and justificatory primacy are as questionable for nonadherents as those of the worldview in question. It would beg the question about whether central Christian beliefs can be accorded primacy in the order of justification simply to measure them against some alternative set of beliefs (say those of another religious tradition or a philosophical worldview); the question, "Why these critieria of truth?" arises as readily for nonadherents of the alternative beliefs as it does for nonadherents of Christianity. As a test for criteria of truth, "assimilative power" avoids begging the question because it proposes no materially specific standards of judgment, Christian or otherwise, nor any specific requirements for the way these standards should function. Thus "assimilative power" is not itself a *criterion* of truth for what it tests; the idea serves instead as a kind of value which is to be upheld in the application of materially specific criteria of truth, or a rule for the application of such criteria.

Second, "assimilative power" as a test for criteria of truth is both acceptable to Christians and accessible to people outside the community. Christians can readily acknowledge the force of this test, since the scripturally shaped network of Christian belief itself involves a deep-laid imperative to "absorb the world into the text" (a point to which I will return in more detail). To be committed to the truth and justificatory primacy of this web of belief will therefore involve the expectation that the text will display significant assimilative power over the long run. Non-Christians might themselves have a number of reasons for being committed to the notion of assimilative power as a significant test for criteria of truth. They might, for example, be persuaded by arguments of the sort often advanced in favor of holist epistemologies (like those of Quine and others influenced by him) to the effect that the true view will be that which maximizes not only internal coherence but also explanatory power; it will be the one which most consistently takes the largest amount of relevant data into account. Or they might be adherents of a religious tradition which, for its own reasons, is committed to a notion of assimilative power. This is not to say that a desire to maximize the assimilative power of one's beliefs is either an implicit or empirical universal; there may be not only individuals but whole cultural-linguistic systems which lack any commitment to this value. The crucial point for present purposes is rather that one need not share the web of Christian belief, and its criteria of truth, in order to regard its assimilative power (or lack of same) as a significant test of its truth. Nor need one share the web of belief in order to apply the test. The crucial requirement is rather that one be acquainted with both the religion and the discourse it encounters in adequate detail.

Applied to encounters between Christianity and unfamiliar or apparently opposed truth claims and criteria, "assimilative power" is thus a particularly important test for the primacy of the Christian community's own criteria of truth. It represents a value which the community wants to maintain, and indeed to maximize, in its application of those criteria and at the same time a value to which it acknowledges it may be held as it does so, even by those who do not share the criteria themselves.

"Assimilative power" is, to be sure, an exceedingly formal answer to the question, "Why these criteria of truth?" In practice, such as in a theological argument which attempts to display concretely the assimilative power of the scriptural world in some disputed respect, it will need to be filled out in at least two ways. First, claims about the success of the biblical text in absorbing the world necessarily involve judgments about how to read and apply the text which the notion of "assimilative power" does not by itself provide. I am assuming for present purposes that it is right to read the Bible as a coherent narrative with a christological focus and that christological narrative readings rightly have a flexible interpretative primacy over the many other ways the text might rightly be read; other attempts to identify the plain sense must be consistent with this kind of reading. The "scriptural world" will therefore have assimilative power, I am assuming, primarily to the degree that familiar and unfamiliar discourse can plausibly be interpreted and assessed in relation to that christological narrative. Lindbeck provides a nice summary of what I have in mind when he talks about reading the Bible "as a canonically and narrationally unified and internally glossed (that is, self-referential and self-interpreting) whole centered on Jesus Christ, and telling the story of the dealings of the Triune God with his people and his world in ways which are typologically . . . applicable to the present."[18]

Moreover, on account of its formality, "assimilative power" is by itself an inadequate and incomplete answer to the question of why the criteria of truth operative in Christian discourse should be taken as primary. A more adequate and complete answer would have to make explicit reasons actually at work in Christian discourse for relying on the criteria Christians use in the interpretation and assessment of truth claims. There could be many such reasons. The point could be developed, for example, in trinitarian terms. It might be argued that the particular human being Jesus of Nazareth is, supremely in his passion and resurrection, the perfect image or self-expression of the one whom he called "the Father," whose being, mind, and will are the source and measure of all truth. If Jesus is in this way, to use the medieval expression, the *veritas Patris*, "the truth of the Father," then Christians are justified in treating coherence with the narrative which depicts him as a particular person as the primary test of truth; whatever can be counted true in the world whose center is the subject of that narrative can be counted consonant with the source and measure of all truth—or so the germ of an argument might go.[19] The structural feature of Christian discourse highlighted by an argument of this kind could function as an internal warrant for sticking with its own criteria of truth in its encounters with unfamiliar discourse, including that which seems to involve the rejection of its truth claims.

These observations suggest a significant limitation to the notion of assimilative power as a test for the viability of criteria of truth. As I have observed, the idea of assimilative power proposes no materially specific standards of judgment when used as a test for criteria of truth; it is more like a flexible formal value which (so many different communities may hold) should be maximized in the application of specific criteria of truth. So, in attempting to assimilate initially alien discourse, the Christian community will try to square that discourse with its own web of belief and practice, and will do so by testing such discourse according to its own justificatory practices; other religions or cultural-linguistic systems will likely do something similar. The beliefs and criteria of truth operative in different religions and worldviews are not only likely to differ from one another, but at important points to be incompatible (for example, in their particular and diverse claims to unsurpassability and comprehensiveness). This means that cases are likely to arise in which one community will interpret and assess (and thus assimilate) truth claims and states of affairs to its own satisfaction, which another (especially a rival) community will not only interpret and assess differently, but will regard as unassimilated and perhaps willfully ignored by its rival. As a result, what a community (and, *mutatis mutandis*, an individual) is likely to count as success or failure of assimilative power will depend in large measure on the beliefs it holds and the justificatory practices which it regards as primary.

This does not at all entail that a religion or other comprehensive worldview will always succeed by its own standards in assimilating alien truth claims; it may find itself unable plausibly to interpret in its own terms and square with its own criteria of assessment claims for which it nonetheless acknowledges compelling reasons to hold them true.[20] Lindbeck reckons explicitly with the possibility of failure as well as success. Referring to religions as comprehensive outlooks on all life and reality, he argues that "confirmation or disconfirmation occurs through an accumulation of successes or failures in making practically and cognitively coherent sense of relevant data, and the process does not conclude, in the case of religions, until the disappearance of the last communities of believers or, if the faith survives, until the end of history."[21] Nor do the limitations of this test for criteria of truth imply that a sympathetic and informed outsider cannot be a responsible judge of the assimilative power of a religion or worldview. The point is rather that "assimilative power" is always the assimilative power *of* a specific web of belief and practice and its associated criteria of truth. Assimilative power must in the nature of the case be measured with reference to a specific criterion not provided by the notion itself; there is no general standard of assimilative power. Consequently, although one can apply the test of assimilative power to many different religions and worldviews, one cannot use this value to decide between alternative religions and their respective criteria of truth in the way in which one can, within a religion, apply its criteria to decide between competing truth claims.[22] The logic of the two issues (of what I have labeled the second and the third questions) is quite different, as are the results: clarity and decisiveness of judgment are regularly achieved in the application of religion-specific justificatory practices and criteria to competing truth claims, but there are manifold religions and worldviews which can reasonably claim significant assimilative power. The assimilative power of a religion or other cultural-linguistic system will display itself only gradually over a long period of time and perhaps with ambiguous results. Failure of assimilative power may often be more obvious than success, so the capacity to absorb the world may function more effectively as a negative than a positive test.

III

I have suggested that the assimilative power of the textually shaped network of Christian belief and practice, its success or failure at absorbing the world into itself in an ongoing project of interpretation and judgment, is a limited but important test of its standards of truth. Success will tend to justify the Christian community in taking coherence with that network of belief and practice as the primary (that is, at least necessary and in some cases sufficient) criterion of truth, and failure will suggest that it is not justified in doing so. The importance of this test lies in its relative accessibility to those outside the community. Unlike more internal warrants (for example, the trinitarian ones to which I alluded earlier) for taking the scripturally shaped web of belief as the primary criterion of truth, assimilative power is a test whose (albeit modest) force can be accepted by people who do not share the web of belief, much less use it as a criterion of truth. So, although assimilative power is not by itself a complete warrant for Christian criteria of truth, it is an adequate warrant to be offered to those outside the Christian community, and seems to be the type of justification best suited for that purpose. At the same time it is not a test which is simply imposed on the Christian community from without, but one which the community itself recognizes; the content and logic of scripturally shaped discourse require an ongoing effort to absorb the world into the text.

My present purpose is not to argue that the biblical world does in fact have the kind of assimilative power which I have outlined; that would not be possible in a single essay, but only on a much larger scale. It is important, though, to reply to an obvious objection to the claim that "assimilative power," if it obtains, provides at least a minimally adequate answer (in connection with more purely internal warrants) to our third question about the truth of Christian belief (namely, "Why these criteria?"). For many theologians, a flexible formal value like "assimilative power," because of its intrinsic limitations, cannot be an adequate test for Christian criteria of truth. Indeed many will suspect that the "testing" going on here is more apparent than real; the whole process has the whiff of fideism about it. The suspicion, to put the charge of fideism in broad terms, is that the project of absorbing the world into the biblical text, precisely because it takes the scripturally shaped web of Christian belief as primary in interpretation and assessment, cannot possibly take external truth claims (especially apparently conflicting ones) with sufficient seriousness. Therefore *success* at that project cannot possibly be an adequate warrant for taking the scriptural web of belief as epistemically primary. This general line of objection could be pursued in several different ways. I will consider three.

1) The project of "absorbing the world" by interpreting and assessing alien truth claims in terms of internally Christian criteria, and maintaining that the project is justified when it succeeds by its own standards, seems to be willful theological isolationism of the worst sort. It seems to imply a decision to rest content solely with the internal discourse of the Christian community and a correlative refusal to engage, much less take seriously, external and potentially threatening truth claims. Jeffrey Stout nicely summarizes (although he does not himself make) the charge of isolationism: the attempt to absorb the world into the biblical text seems to be "an irresponsible willingness to abandon public discourse and critical thought altogether—a kind of fideism whose natural social expression is sectarianism."[23]

This isolationist version of the charge of fideism misses the basic point of the metaphor of "absorbing the world." The point of theological undertakings funded by this metaphor is precisely not, as the objection suggests, to replace the world with the scriptural text, or to treat the text as a means of escape from the world, but to interpret the world (all of it) through the text. Since we know the world by holding sentences true, the imperative to absorb the world into the text does not exclude, but rather requires, an open-ended engagement with whatever truth claims are being made in the times and places in which the Christian community exists. This engagement is open-ended in at least two ways: it is always a necessary task, and it is always an incomplete task.

Whatever the exigencies of a particular historical situation, the imperative to absorb the world, the necessity of the task, is woven into the fabric of Christian belief itself. In Paul's words, Christians are called to "take every thought captive to obey Christ" (2 Cor. 10:5), to reinterpret and reassess what they think they know by trying to find a place for it in the world opened up by the biblical text, the world of the triune God who makes all things new by drawing them into the interior space of his own life through Jesus' passion and resurrection, where nothing has the place we would otherwise have thought.[24] It goes without saying that this includes, indeed applies first of all, to what Christians think they know about God and what God is doing in the world. It could be argued further that this ongoing effort of reinterpretation and reassessment is a practical necessity in order to live within the world of the biblical text at all. Even the most practiced Christians are neophyte and imperfect dwellers in that strange new world (as Barth called it), who are just beginning "to learn its rhythms, to follow the twists and turns of the deep-laid plot, to tremble at the warnings it has in store, and to celebrate the victories it relates."[25] It is in part in the process of testing and redescribing what they think they know in terms of the scriptural narrative that Christians come to appreciate more fully the complexity and subtlety of its "deep-laid plot," which must happen in order for adequately complex and subtle redescriptions to be given and tests to be made. And it is only in this process that the implicit comprehensiveness of the biblical world, especially the claim that its central narratives have unlimited assimilative power, can begin to be grasped and attempts can be made to measure its success.

With the imperative to absorb the world also comes a recognition that the task will always be incomplete. This is not only because of the finite resources of the people who undertake it. In new historical and cultural situations, the Christian community will continually encounter new truth claims, practices, and worldviews, which must be interpreted and assessed with the aim of drawing them into the biblical world. As Lindbeck observes, "the worlds in which we live change. They need to be inscribed anew into the world of the text. It is only by constant re-explication, re-meditation and re-application that this can be done."[26] One could argue, furthermore, that this side of the eschaton our *comprehension* of "the deep-laid plot," of the creative and redemptive dealings of the triune God with the world in Israel and Jesus Christ, is itself too inchoate and feeble to enable us wholly to fulfill, even in limited and specific areas, the imperative to understand all things in light of that plot. Incompleteness, ambiguity, and intractability are bound to be present in even our most successful efforts—but that does not weaken the imperative.

So the theological project of absorbing the world into the biblical text does not constitute or imply a Christian isolationism which shuns the external and alien. It embodies an imperative to do quite the opposite: to internalize everything.

2) This suggests that the real problem is not isolationism but imperialism. The difficulty with the sort of "postliberal" account I have offered of the justification of Christian belief is not that it ignores non-Christian truth claims, but rather that it consistently gives primacy

to Christian standards in assessing those claims. Coherence with the scripturally and doctrinally normed web of Christian belief might be a partial test Christians would rightly want to employ in assessing truth claims, but, so the argument might go, primacy or at least parity must be granted to some external standards of truth; it is fideistic to subordinate all other standards of truth to Christian ones. This seems most obvious in regard to external truth claims with clearly established criteria of their own (for example, historical or scientific ones), but it can apply readily to internally Christian claims as well: if Christians want the right to take their own truth claims seriously, they ought to try to vindicate them by external standards, which non-Christians can also accept.[27] If this objection sticks, then it clearly follows that success at assimilating the universe of truth claims into the Christian web of belief (success at holding them true by its own standards) would not count as an adequate justification for treating coherence with that web of belief as the primary criterion of truth; it seems that some stronger, less ambiguous, more clearly external justification would be required.

We need to consider, though, what sort of external criteria might be invoked by contrast with which taking Christian criteria as primary would seem imperialistic. Clearly these will not be criteria which are themselves internal to some other comprehensive cultural-linguistic system or worldview, religious or otherwise, such that the justification of Christian beliefs would avoid fideism by taking criteria native to that other system as primary. As I have already suggested, this would beg the question. Presumably it is no more (or less) imperialistic to interpret and assess truth claims external to Christianity primarily by Christian standards than it is to treat, for example, the standards of Therevada Buddhism or democratic capitalism as primary.

Nor does it seem useful to strive for the highest level of criteriological generality, so that primacy would be accorded to those standards of truth which are most widely shared by Christianity and other similarly comprehensive cultural-linguistic systems. Aside from the considerable difficulty of identifying and characterizing these putative standards in ways which are not either wholly vacuous (and therefore criteriologically useless) or already slanted toward one system or another (and therefore beg the issue), attempting to satisfy a craving for generality on this score seems an unpromising way to

achieve the aim of taking external truth claims with sufficient seriousness. Such an attempt wants to propose in effect a measure for truth
which is either external to all religions and other cultural-linguistic
systems, or (putatively) internal to them all, and so seems fated to
take none of them with real seriousness. In the nature of the case,
attempts to find and apply the most general and widely shared criteria
will tend to devalue truth claims and criteria which are distinctive to
any particular tradition and thereby to work in all traditions not only
against their own distinctiveness, but against the aim of promoting
serious engagement with truth claims which are truly alien to and
different from one's own.

One could, however, propose a rather different kind of external
standard by which Christian beliefs might be tested. One could be a
foundationalist and argue that the endeavor to absorb the world into
the biblical text is fideistic because it fails to provide an adequate
basis for central Christian beliefs, and thus for using coherence with
those beliefs as a criterion of truth. This would involve trying to show
that there are some beliefs which are basic or primitive, such that the
primary justification for all other beliefs is some suitable linkage with
those which are basic. What justifies the basic or foundational beliefs,
however, is not other beliefs, but the world itself. So Descartes argues
that other beliefs are justified insofar as they can be derived from
clear and distinct ideas, and Locke holds that beliefs are justified to
the extent that they can be traced to simple ideas of sensation; the
"ideas" in each case are, it is claimed, directly and perspicuously tied
to the world. It is this putative justificatory link to the world which
makes some beliefs ineluctable and incorrigible, and so warrants our
taking them as the justificatory foundation for the rest of our beliefs.
Foundational beliefs thus impose themselves on all rational people;
indeed recognizing the incorrigible truth of these beliefs and therewith
their status as primitive is typically the *sine qua non* of rationality in
foundationalist epistemologies. For our present purposes, the appeal of
foundationalism lies mainly in the promise of a relatively unambiguous
adjudication of competing truth claims on a basis which all parties to
the discussion (including, of course, Christian theologians) can accept
as binding, indeed must accept on pain of forfeiting their claim to be
engaged in rational discourse.

Foundationalism, though, has fallen on hard times in recent philosophical debates about truth and justification. There are many different reasons for this. One reason widely shared by philosophers of otherwise different conviction is a family of arguments to the effect that foundationalist talk about the world justifying our beliefs is incoherent. Neither the way the world is nor the causal relations that may obtain between the world and our beliefs can count as a *reason* (that is, a justification) for holding a belief; only other beliefs can do that. As Davidson puts the point regarding the empiricist foundationalism which has dominated much Anglo-American philosophy, such an outlook depends on the notion of the knower "confronting certain of his beliefs with the deliverances of the senses one by one, or perhaps confronting the totality of his beliefs with the tribunal of experience. No such confrontation makes sense, for of course we can't get outside our skins to find out what is causing the internal happenings of which we are aware."[28] For this and other reasons foundationalism is also being increasingly repudiated in contemporary theology, not only by postliberals, for whom it is clearly incongenial, but among theologians with strong revisionist or liberal commitments as well. This means, however, that the charge of epistemic imperialism against the theological project of absorbing the world into the biblical text has not so far been sustained. It has turned out to be difficult to characterize plausibly the sort of external and shared criteria by contrast with which according justificatory primacy to Christian belief was supposed to appear imperialistic.

3) The charge of imperialism could, however, be made in a different way. Perhaps the problem with the theological attempt to absorb the world is not its refusal to be bound by shared criteria (foundational or otherwise) in its interpretation and assessment of novel truth claims, but rather its insistence that there need to be or even can be fixed, stable criteria which guide the project. If we insist on repairing to established internal criteria in conversation with those who make alien truth claims, so the argument might go, we will inevitably fail to take those claims with sufficient seriousness. Pressed by alien claims which seem not to fit with our established web of Christian belief, we will be inclined simply to reject those claims and so to bring the conversation to a premature close. The theologian who appeals to the value of assimilative power as a justification for

the primacy of Christian criteria of truth is in effect an imperialist who suddenly becomes an isolationist whenever battle seems likely to break out. This still seems like fideism, even though of a kind more difficult to pin down than the more straightforward varieties I have already talked about. In order to avoid fideism, this line of criticism suggests, it is necessary to grant that all of our established beliefs, and with them all of our criteria of truth, are at hazard whenever we enter into conversation with those who hold beliefs different from our own.[29]

In the strong sense just outlined this criticism of the theological project of absorbing the world into the text seems untenable. It proposes a standard for rational (that is, non-fideistic) conversation which seems impossible to meet, in theology or in any other type of discourse. It seems logically (and therefore psychologically) impossible to doubt all of our beliefs at once, or even to be prepared to doubt them all. The most familiar arguments against this possibility are those proposed by Wittgenstein to the effect that doubt is logically possible only against a background of beliefs held true, since rational doubt (or preparedness to doubt) requires reasons for doubting (or being prepared to), and giving reasons requires appeal to beliefs held true (that is, not doubted).[30] This kind of argument obviously suggests that questionable or doubted beliefs can only be justified by reference to those which are not doubted, an observation which has served to warrant foundationalist claims that there must be some beliefs which are self-evident or self-justifying; otherwise there will be no adequate way to terminate justificatory arguments. But if foundationalism is untenable, as this third objection assumes, then it becomes all the more important to recognize that rational conversation and argument do not require, but rather preclude, holding all of our beliefs (including our criteria of truth) open to doubt at the same time. As Michael Williams argues, "if we reject intrinsically credible foundations, we shall take the impossibility of there being an infinite regress of justification to show that we cannot go about justifying, or doubting, everything we believe at once, though the possibility of coming to doubt *anything* we believe will of course be left open."[31]

The concluding clause of Williams's remark suggests a weaker but more plausible form of the objection that the project of absorbing the world leads to a fideisticly premature closure of conversation with those who hold alien beliefs. We do not have to be prepared *per impossible* to give up everything we believe in order to avoid a fideistic attitude toward our beliefs, but perhaps we should be prepared to give up any particular belief if confronted with good reasons for doing so.

As I have already suggested, different all-embracing cultural-linguistic systems (such as religions) will differ with regard to the beliefs which, in various contexts of conversation and inquiry, they hold as the background or basis against which beliefs to be doubted and potentially given up are to be measured and so may differ at any given point on what counts as a good reason for giving up or retaining a particular belief. In the nonfoundationalist context assumed by the present objection, there will be no neutral or necessarily shared standards by which such differences could be adjudicated, that is, by reference to which refusal to give up any particular belief could be judged fideistic. Nevertheless, Christians surely ought to be prepared for the possibility that encounters with alien belief systems may give them good reasons to give up or revise at least some of their beliefs, even if there is no external standard for deciding when this should happen or which beliefs should be changed. This is just what justificatory appeals to the assimilative power of the scripturally and doctrinally shaped web of Christian belief seem to deny. If coherence with that web of belief is decisive, not only for determining what sentences should be held true, but even for determining what counts as a good reason for holding a sentence true, it seems impossible for alien belief systems to give Christians any good reasons for changing some of their beliefs and thus impossible for Christians to approach alien belief systems with sufficient openness. In order to dispel this last whiff of fideism, we need to show how it is possible to ascribe consistent justificatory primacy to the plain sense of Scripture while allowing that the established beliefs of the Christian community can be changed by encounters with alien belief systems.

IV

Here a reasonably detailed example will help, preferably one which is materially noncontroversial. Let us look at Thomas Aquinas's attempt to absorb elements of Aristotle's physics, metaphysics, and cosmology into the text of Genesis 1. Thomas's theological aim is to give an account of the beginning of the world (what he calls the *prin-cipium mundi*) which both is coherent with the plain sense of Scripture (primarily but not exclusively the text of Genesis) and incorporates what is for him the best current external knowledge pertinent to the issue, namely Aristotle's hylomorphic theory and his account of the four basic "elements," earth, water, air, and fire. The usefulness of this example lies partly in its utterly noncontroversial character—it has been hundreds of years since anyone worried about whether Aristotelian science could be reconciled with the plain sense of Scripture, so we are free to concentrate on the formal issues which are our present concern. Thomas and his contempories, however, worried a great deal about this question (so also many theologians in our day are worried about whether and how current science and Scripture are compatible) and devoted considerable energy and ingenuity to exhibiting the assimilative power of Christianity at just this point. And in the process Thomas made some illuminating procedural comments about the way theologians should try to absorb alien truth claims into the biblical world.

The text of Genesis 1:2, "The earth was empty and void" ("Terra erat inanis et vacua," in the Latin of Aquinas's Vulgate) poses for Thomas a complex problem of interpretation and assessment. The problem centers on how to understand "inanis et vacua," and leads Thomas to compose the two very lengthy articles of *De Potentia* 4, under the general heading, "Concerning the creation of unformed matter."[32] In the context of Genesis 1, with its succession of "days" in which the contours of creation become gradually more definite and rich in detail, it seems as though "inanis et vacua" should be taken to mean that the first thing God created was unformed matter, and that the existence of this unformed matter preceeded in time the creation of particular substances with definite forms. But if *materia informis* is taken in the strict sense, as that which is "without all form, existing in potency to all forms," then "inanis et vacua" cannot possibly be interpreted in this way.[33] There are, Aquinas argues, basically two reasons for this. First, false sentences cannot be identified as the plain sense of Scripture: "What is false can never be the literal sense of sacred Scripture."[34] Second, we have persuasive arguments, which originate precisely in alien belief systems, against the assertion that matter can exist in reality without any form and therefore against the assertion that matter can exist prior in time to receiving any form. Aquinas summarizes the general point in a slightly different connection when he observes, "This interpretation (*expositio*) seems deficient, since it asserts that Scripture should be understood to mean certain things the contraries of which are shown by sufficiently evident reasons."[35]

In this case, the alien arguments which Aquinas finds persuasive have a mainly Aristotelian cast. So he argues, for example, that whatever we find in reality (*in rerum natura*) "exists in act, but matter does not exist in act except through a form, which is its act; hence matter without form is not found in reality."[36] So if "inanis et vacua" in Genesis 1:2 is interpreted as "without all form," then the text cannot be taken to say that the creation of matter is temporally prior to the imposition of form upon it; unformed matter is prior "only in the order of nature, insofar as that out of which something is made is naturally prior to that which is made."[37] Thomas finds this view in Augustine, and he is in fact prepared to accept the whole of Augustine's interpretation of Genesis 1, in which the distinction of days is not understood temporally at all: "Augustine proposes that the work of the six days was done all at once (*simul*)."[38]

One could, however, interpret "Terra erat inanis et vacua" differently. "Empty and void" might not be taken for matter conceived as lacking all form, but rather as "unformed" insofar as it "does not yet have the ultimate completeness and beauty of its nature."[39] If at its first creation matter is "unformed" in this more limited sense, then there are no compelling arguments against saying that unformed matter exists before (in time) the particulars of various kinds which come to fill the creation: God first creates the (Aristotelian) elements and then brings creation to its full "completeness and beauty" by gradually bestowing upon these elements higher and more complex forms. And if "inanis et vacua" is read along these lines, then the "days" of creation can be taken as a genuine temporal sequence. This, as Aquinas notes, is the reading preferred by the Cappadocians and their followers. Though quite different, both of these readings have important advantages. Augustine's "is more profound and better upholds Scripture against the mockery of unbelievers," while the majority view is "more obvious and more in agreement with the words of the text in their surface meaning" (*quantum ad superficiem*).[40] But "the way the words go allows both senses," and since there are currently no persuasive external reasons for rejecting either as false, both are theologically permissible.[41] Attempts to force a choice between the two interpretations are needlessly narrow and reduce the richness of the text's plain sense; such attempts should therefore be avoided. "One should not want to force Scripture to have a single sense in such a way that other senses which have truth in them and can be adapted to Scripture by agreeing with the way the words go (*salva circumstantia litterae*) are completely excluded."[42]

The moral of this story for understanding the relation between Christian beliefs and alien truth claims is twofold. (a) Encounters with external truth claims can lead Christians, and under some circumstances whole Christian communities, to change their established beliefs, including internal ones. When supported by persuasive arguments, alien truth claims can lead Christians to change the way they identify and specify the plain sense of Scripture and therefore what beliefs cohere with the plain sense. Encounters with alien truth claims can thus lead Christians to change their vision of the scriptural world in which they strive to live and think.[43] The changes which can be brought about by dialogue with alien ways of understanding the world are consequently not at all superficial but affect the ways Christians specify and articulate in a particular historical and intellectual context those beliefs which are essential to their own identity. As I suggested earlier, this is logically bound to take place in a partial and piecemeal fashion, against a background of stable belief, particularly stable identification of the plain sense of much of Scripture. An external belief which the Christian community could only hold true by engaging in a massive or wholesale repudiation of its current identification of the plain sense of Scripture (for example, repudiation of a christological narrative reading) would reasonably be taken by the community as a good candidate for falsity. At the same time, Christians cannot regard their identification of the plain sense as entirely fixed, nor their identification of those beliefs which are coherent with the plain sense. It is always possible that external (or internal, although that is not the present concern) arguments may arise which lead the community to reconsider its identification of the plain sense. Aquinas thought both of the cosmologies he discusses were coherent with the plain sense of Scripture and supported by the best available relevant knowledge, and so were justifiable for Christians to hold; we would regard neither of them as justifiable for Christians to hold, since each is excluded by the best current cosmology (on the whole; each may be plausible in some limited formal respects, such as the evolutionary cast of the Cappadocian view). Following Aquinas's rule that nothing should be identified as the plain sense of Scripture which is obviously false, these cosmologies cannot now be considered as the plain sense of Scripture. If the plain sense calls for the construction of a cosmology (whether and to what degree it does is of course debatable), one which Christians will regard as justifiable to hold true will be both coherent with the plain sense and supported by the best available knowledge; in this case coherence with the plain sense is a necessary but not sufficient criterion for the truth of belief.

(b) While dialogue with external truth claims may lead Christians to change the way they identify the plain sense of Scripture, this does not entail that justificatory primacy must be ascribed to these external beliefs, or to the criteria of truth they bring with them. On the view I have been developing, justificatory primacy is ascribed to the plain sense of Scripture. If the plain sense could be defined adequately as that interpretation which one has the best external reasons for holding true (or as any interpretation which one has good external reasons for holding true), then of course primacy in the order of justification would shift from the plain sense to external beliefs and criteria. But part of the notion of the plain sense, to use Thomas's language, is interpretation which agrees with the way the words go (interpretation *salva circumstantia litterae*).[44] To say that the plain sense is primary in the order of justification is to say that one does not take Scripture to be false, although what we identify as its plain sense may at any given point be false. And this implies, as Aquinas puts it, that we should not identify as the sense of Scripture anything which is obviously false. When the plain sense is thought of in this way, it is possible to retain the primacy of the plain sense in the order of justification, while still allowing that external arguments may lead to a change in the way the plain sense is construed. This is because, while it is always possible for external arguments to foster a reconsideration of the plain sense, no interpretation can count as an identification of the plain sense, no matter how well supported by external argument, which fails to agree with the way the words go—not simply in this or that passage, but in the scriptural canon as a whole.[45] Thus beliefs cannot be justified, or function as a criterion for the justification of other beliefs, which do not agree with the way the words go, that is, which cannot count as or cohere with the plain sense.

It may happen, of course, that the only interpretations which agree with the way the words go (or those which best do so) will also seem obviously false by the measure of our best current external beliefs, or perhaps less drastically will seem to lack any support in our best current external beliefs. In such situations, to ascribe justificatory primacy to the plain sense of Scripture means to continue to hold true those sentences which agree with the way the words go, that is, which can be identified as, or as coherent with, the plain sense of the text. Correlatively, it means not to hold true sentences which are inconsistent with the plain sense in place of those which are. So, when confronted with evident conflict between ranges of internal and external beliefs both of which we would like to hold true, there are basically two courses of action consistent with the justificatory primacy of the plain sense—that is, with the requirement that beliefs held true be consistent with the way the words go: i) we can revise our identification of the plain sense in light of external beliefs; ii) we can revise our estimate of our external beliefs in light of the requirements of the plain sense.[46]

Both of these courses of action are in fact strategies for absorbing the world into the biblical text, for constructing a vision of all life and reality which is decisively shaped by the plain sense of Scripture. But neither involves a failure to take external truth claims seriously. This is obvious in the first course of action, but is true of the second as well. To revise our estimate of our (initially) external beliefs, or to revise the beliefs themselves, is not necessarily to reject them—indeed this is to be avoided as far as possible. The aim rather is to show how assumptions and arguments which seem to generate beliefs incompatible with anything which could plausibly be interpreted as the plain sense of the text need not do so and thus can be internalized rather than rejected. To continue with our example from medieval cosmology: it seemed to many theologians in the mid-thirteenth century that Aristotle's physics required those who accepted its basic assumptions and arguments to assert the eternity of the world. Since all were agreed that this could not plausibly be taken as consistent with the plain sense of Scripture, a number of theologians (most notably Bonaventure) argued forcefully that this was so much the worse for Aristotle's physics; despite its attractiveness on other grounds, some of its central assumptions must be rejected because of the inconsistency they generate with Scripture. Aquinas, while agreeing about the requirements of the plain sense in the matter, argued that Aristotle could be quite plausibly interpreted in such a way that the eternity of the world, while possible, is not necessary (indeed, he denys that Aristotle should be read as though he were really attempting to demonstrate the eternity of the world).[47] He further argued that the appearance of contradiction between Scripture and Aristotle on this point could be traced in part to the erroneous assumption by some of his contemporaries that the beginning of the world in time should be accessible on the basis of a sound natural philosophy. Not so, Aquinas maintained; (the best available) physics by itself cannot decide the issue, and certainty about the creation of the world in time is accessible only to faith, tutored by Scripture. In this way, Aquinas tried to show that the bulk of Aristotle's physics, that is, the best available natural science, did not conflict with the plain sense of Scripture and so could flourish in a Christian vision of reality—could be absorbed, in other words, into the biblical world.[48]

Thus the rule articulated by Aquinas, that Scripture is not false and therefore in seeking the plain sense one must not ascribe patent falsity to Scripture, is not a device for insulating Scripture and the wider web of Christian belief from external criticism. On the contrary: precisely in order to minimize the likelihood that their identifications of the plain sense ascribe falsity to Scripture, Christians ought to be prepared, wherever possible (that is, insofar as the words allow), to revise and expand what they take to be the plain sense in light of whatever well-supported alien claims are pertinent. In doing so they will uphold what I have called the principle of charity, which stipulates that alien claims ought to be interpreted in a way which, without ceasing to be a plausible interpretation, maximizes the range of such claims which can be held true according to standards internal to the Christian web of belief, primarily coherence with the plain sense of Scripture. We can now see that this principle of charity about truth extends to the identification of the plain sense itself: Christians should seek the plain sense in ways which maximize the number of well-supported beliefs they can hold true without prejudice to the way the words go. Thomas formulates a nice summary of the principle of charity and its link to the identification and justificatory primacy of the plain sense: "Every truth which can be adapted (*aptari*) to divine Scripture, while agreeing with the way the words go, is the sense of Scripture."[49]

If Christians find that they must consistently reject beliefs they have good reasons for holding true because they cannot successfully revise their identification of the plain sense in order to "adapt" plausible external beliefs to the biblical text, then this would show that Christianity, and particularly the biblical text, lacks assimilative power. The objection I have been considering is that a theological position is fideistic which does not grant both that established Christian beliefs are in some significant sense revisable and that failure of revisability when warranted in encounters with alien belief systems counts against the truth of Christianity and particularly against the primacy of its criteria of justification. If this is what constitutes fideism, then to argue that a formal value like assimilative power is an adequate test for Christian criteria of truth (and thereby for the larger web of Christian belief) does not exemplify fideism, but excludes it by definition.

To be sure, assimilative power is a test which can be applied only over a long period of time and with inherently ambiguous results. But within those limits it is a genuine, nonfideistic test, one which Christianity, or any comprehensive cultural-linguistic system, could conceivably fail. We might long for a more decisive, less ambiguous test. But it is not clear that a stronger test for a comprehensive belief system like Christianity is available. Formal values like assimilative power seem the best way of answering the question posed to any comprehensive belief system, "why these criteria of truth?" As George Lindbeck writes, appeal to assimilative power "certainly does not enable individuals to decide between major alternatives on the basis of reason alone, but it does help provide warrants for taking reasonableness in religion seriously, and it helps explain why the intellectual labors of theologians, though vacuous without corresponding practice, do sometimes make significant contributions to the health of religious traditions."[50]

NOTES

I am very grateful to Kathryn Tanner and J. A. DiNoia, O.P. for their comments on an earlier draft of this paper.

1. George A. Lindbeck, *The Nature of Doctrine* (hereafter *ND*), (Philadelphia: Westminster, 1984), 118.

2. I have discussed in more detail Lindbeck's treatment of these issues and argued that it has deep affinities with Thomas Aquinas's account of truth, in "Aquinas as Postliberal Theologian," *The Thomist* 53 (1989), 353–402.

3. *ND*, 66, 64.

4. *ND*, 66–67.

5. As he has subsequently acknowledged, Lindbeck confuses the issue in *The Nature of Doctrine* by speaking of "categorial truth" and "intrasystematic truth," rather than characterizing adequate categories and intrasystematic coherence as pertinent to the justification, as distinguished from the truth, of beliefs. See his "Response to Bruce Marshall," *The Thomist* 53 (1989): 403–4.

6. See *ND*, 116.

7. It should be noted that a sentence can be actively held true not only by uttering it but in many other ways (such as, to name a theologically significant case, by hearing it).

8. *ND*, 64.

9. Kathryn E. Tanner, "Theology and the Plain Sense," in *Scriptural Authority and Narrative Interpretation*, ed. Garrett Green (Philadelphia: Fortress, 1987), 63.

10. Tanner stresses the self-revisionary force Christian practice builds into the notion of the plain sense: "The distinction between 'what the text itself says' and further 'interpretive' or 'applied' senses comes to infiltrate the very discussion of the plain sense, to produce a more radical differentiation of text and interpretation. The text and its plain sense are now distinguished from, and privileged with respect to, the specifications of that sense by the community" ("Theology and the Plain Sense," 72).

11. "A claim that what is proposed in some assertion is true, or that some course of action is right, is an alien claim, with respect to some community, if and only if what is proposed in the claim is not an authentic doctrine of that community," where an "authentic doctrine" of a community is what that community holds it is "bound to teach" (William A. Christian, Sr., *Doctrines of Religious Communities: A Philosophical Study* [New Haven, Conn.: Yale University Press, 1987], 145, 74).

12. *ND*, 118. On the need to allow for situation-specific efforts at "translation" or "ad hoc apologetics," *within* an overall project of "redescription," see *ND*, 131–32: "A postliberal theology need not exclude an ad

hoc apologetics, but only [an apologetics] which is systematically prior and controlling in the fashion of post-Cartesian natural theology and of later liberalism."

13. This line of argument is central to Davidson's philosophy of language, where it is developed in considerable technical detail, and also generates a distinctive argument against skepticism. See his "A Coherence Theory of Truth and Knowledge," in *Truth and Interpretation: Perspectives on the Philosophy of Donald Davidson*, ed. Ernest LePore, (Oxford: Basil Blackwell, 1986), especially 316–19; "The Method of Truth in Metaphysics," in *Inquiries into Truth and Interpretation* (Oxford: Oxford University Press, 1984), 199–201.

14. Christians will, of course, have their own distinctive reasons for insisting on a principle of charity about truth in interpreting the utterances of other people, just as there are internal Christian imperatives for the very project of absorbing the world shaped by this principle; some of these are briefly discussed below in section III, under point 1.

15. The phrase "domain of meaning" is Lindbeck's; see *ND*, 116, 117.

16. George Lindbeck, "Scripture, Consensus, and Community," in *Biblical Interpretation in Crisis*, ed. Richard John Neuhaus (Grand Rapids, Mich: Eerdmans, 1989), 77.

17. *ND*, 131.

18. "Scripture, Consensus, and Community," 75.

19. In the first volume of his theological aesthetics, von Balthasar suggests (although he does not there develop) an argument along these lines. "The relationship between the Father and the Son—*that* is the truth. . . . It is only through faith in Christ's divinity that one can gain access to this sphere of truth within the Godhead, in which one learns to see and understand the very essence of truth" (Hans Urs von Balthasar, *The Glory of the Lord: A Theological Aesthetics*, vol. 1: *Seeing the Form*, trans. by Erasmo Leiva-Merikakis [Edinburgh: T & T Clark, 1982], 135; see also 615f.).

20. Alasdair MacIntyre discusses one way this can happen in *Whose Justice? Which Rationality?* (Notre Dame, Ind.: University of Notre Dame Press, 1988): A tradition of inquiry may undergo an "epistemological crisis," in which "it ceases to make progress" in coping with its current "agenda of unsolved problems and unresolved issues" (p. 361). Such crises are sometimes resolved by a tradition on its own terms, but sometimes they are not; "all attempts to develop the imaginative and inventive resources which the adherents of the tradition can provide may founder," precisely "by its own standards" (p. 364). As a result, "that particular tradition's claims to truth can at some point in this process no longer be sustained" (p. 364). Indeed, a particular tradition may find that it has suffered "defeat in respect of truth"

at the hands of an "alien tradition," when the latter provides the resources (which it lacked) for solving its epistomological crisis (p. 365).

21. *ND*, 131.

22. I take this line of thought to be congruent with the force of Lindbeck's observation that "the issue is not whether there are universal norms of reasonableness, but whether these can be formulated in some neutral, framework-independent language" (*ND*, 130).

23. Jeffrey Stout, *Ethics After Babel* (Boston: Beacon Press, 1988), 186. Stout himself declines judgment in this book on the viability of Lindbeck's "postliberal" theological project and others like it; see 301, s.v. "Post-modern theology."

24. This way of putting the matter is suggested by von Balthasar, *The Glory of the Lord*, vol. 1: 618. Lindbeck has stressed the internal or intra-textual imperatives for absorbing the world into the text; see "Barth and Textuality," *Theology Today* 43 (1986): 368–69.

25. The quoted phrases are those of William Christian, *Doctrines of Religious Communities*, 95 (cited in Lindbeck, "Barth and Textuality," 362).

26. Lindbeck, "Barth and Textuality," 375.

27. Christians will of course regularly share with non-Christians criteria for the assessment of specific truth claims. The question is not whether internal criteria are the only ones Christians ought to use, but whether primacy can be given to those internal standards among the wide variety of criteria that will inevitably come into use.

28. Davidson, "A Coherence Theory of Truth and Knowledge," 312.

29. For a presentation of "conversation" as the primary interpretative model, see David Tracy, *Plurality and Ambiguity* (San Francisco: Harper & Row, 1987).

30. See Ludwig Wittgenstein, *On Certainty*, ed. G. E. M. Anscombe and G. H. von Wright (Oxford: Basil Blackwell, 1969).

31. Michael Williams, "Coherence, Justification, and Truth," *Review of Metaphysics* 34 (1980): 253.

32. *Quaestiones Disputatae de Potentia* (hereafter *De Pot.*), in *S. Thomae Aquinatis Quaestiones Disputatae*, vol. 2, ed. P. Bazzi et al. (Turin, 1965). All translations from Latin are my own.

33. Quotation from *De Pot.* 4, 1, r.

34. *Summa Theologiae* (hereafter *ST*) I, 1, 10, ad 3 (*S. Thomae Aquinatis Summa Theologiae*, 4 vols., ed. P. Caramello [Turin, 1948–52]). Cf. *De Pot.* 4, 1, r: "One should not say that what is plainly false ought to be understood in the words of Scripture, for divine Scripture given by the Holy Spirit cannot be false, nor can faith, which is taught by it." How close what I am calling

the "plain sense" is to what Aquinas calls the "literal sense" need not be decided here. I will use the terms interchangeably.

35. *De Pot.* 4, 1, ad 5.

36. *De Pot.* 4, 1, r.

37. Ibid.

38. *ST* I, 74, 2, r. It should be stressed that Aquinas does not regard Augustine's atemporal reading of Genesis 1 as allegory (i.e., as one of the "spiritual senses"), but rather as a proposal about the plain sense of the text: "the way the *words* go allows this meaning" ("sensum circumstantia litterae patitur," *De Pot.* 4, 1, r; cf. 4, 2, r.). More generally, the literal sense for Aquinas embraces the use and interpretation of words both "in their proper sense" (*secundum proprietatem locutionis*; this includes but is not limited to interpreting language as historical description; see *ST* I, 1, 10, ad 2) and "in the figurative or metaphorical sense" (*secundum similitudinem seu metaphoram*); *In* 4 *Gal.* 7, #253 (*S. Thomae Aquinatis Super Epistolas Pauli Lectura*, vol. 1, ed. R. Cai, O.P. [Turin, 1953]). This implies that while Aquinas himself reads Genesis 1 as the outline of a scientific account of the beginning of the universe, to be filled in by the best current cosomology, one could read it quite differently without, on Aquinas's own principles, departing from the realm of the literal or plain sense.

39. *De Pot.* 4, 1, r.

40. *De Pot.* 4, 2, r.

41. See ibid.: "utrumque sensum circumstantia litterae patitur."

42. *De Pot.* 4, 1, r.

43. Of course, the community's continuing encounter with and reflection upon the text itself and upon the riches and logic of its internal beliefs can also do this, although that has not been my concern here.

44. See Tanner (above, note 10): "The text and its plain sense are now distinguished from, and privileged with respect to, the specifications of that sense by the community." The "way the words go" limits the revision of the plain sense in a way directly parallel to that in which the need for interpretations to be plausible limits the redescription of alien claims by the Christian community (i.e., the application of "the principle of charity"): in neither case can the best interpretation of a given discourse (Scripture or alien claims) simply be identified with an interpretation which allows one to hold that discourse true on external grounds (external to Christian belief or the alien claims, respectively).

45. The function of "the way the words go" in shaping decisions about when and how specifications of the plain sense can be revised is complex and can only be outlined here. As I have already suggested, the willingness of the Christian commuity to revise its identification of the plain sense at any given

point is, quite reasonably, tied to the relative importance or insignificance of that specification of the plain sense in the community's overall web of belief and practice. It may happen, for example, that pressures to revise the plain sense which impinge on the wider web of Christian belief only in peripheral and limited ways may be accommodated in passing and without explicit attention, or simply ignored. Pressures to revise more central beliefs will naturally be treated more carefully, eliciting greater attention to the precise specification of the plain sense. In attending to such pressures, the community will seek to ensure that its specifications of the plain sense, including its judgments about what is peripheral and what is central, are supported by the way the words go in the canon as a whole.

46. There is a clear analogy at this point with scientific procedures. Sometimes anomolous observations lead us to revise our established theories, and sometimes our established theories lead us to question the reliability or pertinence of our observations.

47. See ST I, 46, 1, r; ad 5.

48. For discussions in Aquinas of these issues, much debated in his day, see De Pot. 3, 17; ST I, 46, 1–2; De Aeternitate Mundi (D. Thomae Aquinatis Opuscula Philosophica, ed. R. Spiazzi [Turin, 1954]).

49. De Pot. 4, 1, r.

50. ND, 131.

PART TWO:

Theology in Dialogue

AQUINAS AND SCOTUS: CONTRARY PATTERNS FOR PHILOSOPHICAL THEOLOGY

DAVID B. BURRELL, C.S.C.

It is notorious that theological controversies have philosophical roots, so teachers intent on explicating the controversy will often help students trace the philosophical influences which could lead to opposing theological positions. Yet the "influence" is hardly one-way, since theologians of particular doctrinal persuasions will often be drawn to those philosophical approaches which they find consonant with their beliefs. The relation between convictions and conceptualizations is one of mutual interaction, according to the time-honored phrase of *fides quaerens intellectum*, making the task of philosophical theologian especially demanding. One must be attentive to historical articulations of faith as well as adept at conceptual clarity, since theological inquiry occurs in that space of communal self-understanding where faith seeks an appropriate conceptual articulation while the philosophical notions employed are stretched to accommodate a transcendental reach. Yet anyone who hopes to explicate a theological controversy simply by tracing it to its philosophical roots or by laying bare its conceptual frame has overlooked the dialectical situation which actually obtains.

So philosophical theologians must eschew such one-way pictures, which offer an *ersatz* clarity, while continuing to work toward displaying the conceptual or structural dimensions of theological developments and controversies. Yet where controversy is concerned, their work may not succeed in resolving the conflict so much as in clarifying the opposing philosophical approaches that may well have exacerbated matters. And at that point one may feel oneself faced with a choice between "fundamental intuitions of reality." Indeed, some philosophers even seem content to speak that way, however un-philosophical it sounds to leave root intellectual questions the prey of "choice" and "intuition." As we have insisted, however, a philosophi-cal theologian cannot rest there, but will be constrained to recast the language of choice into the texture of a faith-commitment and try to show how one of the philosophical approaches is more amenable than the other to providing a grammar for the lived language of faith. This exercise is inherently dialectical, working as it does with two sets of criteria, yet it is incumbent on a philosophical theologian to carry it through.

My essay attempts the task of clarification and will leave the comparative task at the level of suggestion, allowing the reader to complete it. My excuse is space, but the reason is that I am not yet sure how to do it. Perhaps, however, criticism of my analysis will sug-gest ways of carrying out the comparative stage as well, since the entire process of conceptual clarification in matters theological is dialecti-cal throughout. I have chosen Aquinas and Scotus as representative figures. This is especially appropriate to my appreciation for both the work and person of George Lindbeck—for I have learned equally from both—since he did his doctoral work on Scotus and has focused much of his scholarly life on Aquinas. The valuations are my own, of course, as to some extent my rendering of Aquinas and Scotus will also be, though I shall try to profit from those critics who read earlier drafts of this essay to help me present my protagonists fairly.[1] In taking two historical figures as embodying two approaches which appear quite irreducible and often incompatible, however, I wish also to make a further point about method in philosophical theology: Appropriating the struggles of the giants in our respective traditions offers the most salutary way of developing the set of complex skills required to do philosophical theology.

The theological controversy at issue is the thorny one for Jews, Christians, and Muslims: the relation between divine and human free-dom. The One who freely creates the universe holds absolute sway over it, as Job's divine protagonist reminds him in the end. Yet when

that same One values only the free responses of those creatures created in God's own image, we can find ourselves hard put to articulate
that encounter in a way which adequately respects both free partners.
To be sure, the biblical background of covenant (alluded to in the
Qur'an as well) offers some pregnant leads, and the narrative portions
of the Scriptures provide paradigms for the interaction which may
well surpass any attempt at conceptual articulation, yet the challenge
continually confronts us.[2] I shall not enter into the particulars of the
so-called *de auxiliis* controversy in the Western church, except to say
that anyone tempted to identify the Banezian (or "Thomist") position with Aquinas will be severely misled, as Bernard Lonergan has
definitively shown.[3] Rather than provide a benchmark, that controversy offers no more than an episode in the continuing inquiry and
one especially dogged by conceptual confusions. It will be the burden
of my essay that the critical questions are determined by issues quite
a bit prior to freedom, which nonetheless affect how we think about
that feature of human (and divine) existence. By choosing Aquinas
and Scotus as protagonists, I have in fact identified the critical issue
as *existence*, and with existence, quite different views on the ways in
which language and world relate; only after which shall I consider
the operation of human intentionality concerning action which we
characterize as "freedom."[4]

1. OBJECT PROPER TO HUMAN UNDERSTANDING.

I said that the approaches would divide on *existence*—concern
for it, how to deal with it; relations of language and language user
to the world, and the operation of human intentionality—specifically
that orientation toward an end which directs our choices and shapes
what we mean by freedom (without reducing it to "free choice"). Yet
I would like to introduce the contrast epistemologically, to bring the
principal actors—Aquinas and Scotus—directly on stage. Consider
the responses each gives to the characteristically medieval question:
What is the proper object of human knowing? or the object proper
to a human knower? Briefly, for Aquinas, it is a "nature existing in
corporeal matter" (*ST* 1.84.7); while for Scotus it is the essence taken
"absolutely."[5]

1.1. Some Thomists like to put this in terms of Being (often capitalized): For Aquinas the intellect aspires to know Being. I would rather parse him (and them) by saying: For Aquinas the intellect aspires to know what is the case. Fulfilling that aspiration may well involve a great deal of speculation regarding what might be the case, or what it might have been, but such considerations are at the service of a teleology intrinsic to understanding itself: to know what is.

1.2. Beginning in this way, however, hardly seems likely to set up a contrast with Scotus. For Scotus's celebrated concern to know the individual *in its individuality* seems to offer immediate parallels with Aquinas, and to contrast strikingly with my way of characterizing the proper object of human understanding for him: the essence taken "absolutely." The apparent conflict is resolved, however, when we consider how Scotus characterizes individuality—by a property making this a *this: haecceity*.[6] So the individual is identified by an individualizing *kind* (or property), thus retaining the focus on essences taken "absolutely." Before exploring this solution, however, let us return to Aquinas's treatment.

1.11. In the formula "nature existing in corporeal matter," neither 'existing' nor 'in corporeal matter' (or 'materially') names or expresses a *feature* of things. For 'existing' eludes our grasp (as Scotus insists *haecceity* does, yet for different reasons), while 'materially' expresses a manner of being rather than something said of a subject. (Strawson, in *Individuals*, locates such things as *presuppositions*.)[7] "In corporeal matter" is something presupposed in those things of which we connaturally speak and with which we customarily interact. What we say of such things is that they exist, are "concrete" entities (as opposed to abstract objects), are spatio-temporally identifiable, and the rest. For Aquinas, since items like these are proper objects for human understanding, they are paradigms for us of what is. These are familiar Aristotelian roots.

1.21. What about Scotus? Has he such a paradigm for knowing? Or for substance? The answer, as usual, is less straightforward. Gerard Manley Hopkins celebrates his exaltation of the individual, crediting Scotus with inspiring his own poetic rendition of "inscape."[8] Gilson, on the other hand, links him with Avicenna, where a process of concept formation shaped by Neoplationist emanation schemes allows the intellect to know the natures of things by its link with the first intelligence from whom essences emanate.[9] Gilson finds this picture imbedded in illumination theories which medieval thinkers associated with Augustine without realizing their Arab origins. My response is closer to that of Gilson: for Scotus the formula gives the essence of a thing, and formulas are what we connaturally grasp. The evidence for this contention is cumulative: his concern for distinctions and definitions, plus his demand for univocity, together with a confidence that such an approach captures the things we are concerned with. As a result, there is little or no reflection on actual usage; distinctions are more constructed than found.

1.12. For Aquinas, on the other hand, distinctions are employed to serve a current purpose: to understand what is the case. A distinction made in one context may not serve at all in another.[10] Understanding is contextual and language inherently analogous, so we must scrutinize actual usage to discern how analogous terms are functioning and so be led to understand how things actually are.

2. HOW ATTAIN CLARITY ABOUT EXISTING?

2.1. One way to highlight the distinctiveness of Aquinas's paradigm (for being and for knowing)—a "nature existing in corporeal matter"—is to compare and contrast it with Aristotle, for whom substance paradigmatically is a material thing of a certain kind.[11] There is no question for Aristotle but that such a thing *exists*, for to be a material thing of a certain kind *is* to exist. Nothing more need be said, or can be said. Why must 'existing' be explicitly mentioned for Aquinas, and how can it be expressed?

Aquinas must make existing explicit because something has happened; someone named Moses has intervened: Moses the author of Genesis, and Moses the author of the *Guide for the Perplexed*. The upshot of that intervention was to realize that such things not only might have been otherwise (Aristotle), but that they might not have been at all.[12] It was a Muslim philosopher—Ibn-Sina—who gave to both Maimonides and Aquinas the conceptual tools for articulating that new situation, by dividing all that is into *necessary* being and possible being according as its existence is underived or derived.[13] As Moses Maimonides employed the distinction, everything derives from One underived; and while he had some difficulties with Ibn-Sina's presentation of that originating relationship, the distinction served well enough for him as an articulation of the earlier Moses.[14]

Identifying necessary being with underived existence and possible being with derived existence, however, led Ibn-Sina to characterize *existing* as something "coming to a thing," which thing was known, insofar as it was knowable, in its *essence*.[15] The all-important fact of something's actually existing, then, which relates each individual thing to its source in the One, sounds like it is *accidental* to the thing itself. Yet that assertion is incoherent, of course, since accidents must be accidents *of* substance—so what makes something to *be* one of those paradigmatic items cannot be extrinsic to it as accidents are.

So Aquinas (not Maimonides) proposes that we conceive *existing*, not as an ordinary feature (or property) of things, but as a formal or constitutive feature of whatever is—as Aristotle conceived matter/form.[16] One does not notice a thing's matter or form, but rather presupposes that "mode of composition" in constructing the sentences we do construct to speak about it. The constructions themselves *display* the matter/form composition in their subject/predicate structure. Yet the ambiguity Aristotle left between *assertion* and *proposition* hides another correlative set of formal (or constitutive) features in which the roles played by matter/form, respectively, are assumed by essence/*esse* (existence). This new proposal of Aquinas allows him to express that each "nature *existing* in corporeal matter" has been made to do so by the creator—the One who brings into being and sustains all that is. This new constitutive feature of things, then, is the sign in things of a relation which links them to their transcendent source and so is best characterized as an *act* (ST 1.45.5).[17]

This final move is at the heart of Aquinas's account of why individual existing things are paradigmatic of what is. It offers justification, if you will, for Aristotle's founding intuition: a justification in that the "proper effect" of the creative activity of the One from whom all else is derived must itself be an act—that is, can only be conceived as an act. This is an analogous use of the term 'act', of course, since only existing things can act (*actiones sunt suppositorum*). Yet they can be said to act only because they are (as existing things) already *in act*.

The actuality of existing things, then, derives from the One whose underived (or *necessary*) existence is expressed by identifying essence with existence (*ST* 1.4.1). And since existing offers the paradigm for actuality, such a One whose nature is to-be will embody all the perfections which flow from existing. Here we have a condensed description of what Gilson and others have called Aquinas's "existentialism." It is no longer Aristotle, yet is certainly consonant with his founding insight: Individual existing things are paradigmatic for what is. It is rather an effort to articulate the new mode of contingency introduced by Moses: that the world need not be at all; and the positive effect of this articulation is to treat existing as a perfection—indeed the perfection of perfections, as that from which all others flow.

2.2. So Aquinas's manner of both articulating and celebrating existence is hardly "Greek" in inspiration. It is in fact quite unintelligible to those for whom contingency remains bounded by the classical "could have been otherwise."[18] For that view concentrates on formal structures—essences taken "absolutely"—without attempting to articulate what distinguishes the world in which we live. That approach will thus find differentiating fact from fantasy difficult to articulate, presuming that " 'histories' of possible individuals" could be available, if not to us, at least to God.[19] Indeed something like that must be available to God if God is to know which world God *chooses* to create. So "middle knowledge" scenarios are not only conceptually unproblematic in this approach; they are required if God is to act freely. (So if "middle knowledge" be incoherent on Aquinas's approach, he must have a very different view of freedom, and hence of divine freedom as well. We shall see that he does.)

Scotus will carry us a long way toward constituting this other approach. If Aquinas's thesis about the unity of the virtues is rooted ontologically in his conception of all perfections flowing from existence, Scotus's queries about that unitary thesis suggest that he was beginning to look more at features of things than at things themselves, so that things become conceived as a coalescence of features.[20] Existence functions more as the precondition for things being what they are than as the source of a thing's being and becoming. For as we have seen, what makes a thing individual is not its actual existing, but a formal feature corresponding to 'this' and called *haecceitas*.[21]

Since language mirrors reality for the medievals, as for the Greeks, it should prove useful to articulate this difference in treating existence linguistically. For Scotus, each item in the sentence 'roses are red' names a corresponding element in the world, with the copula standing for existence or being—the precondition for saying anything at all about something.[22] (Correlatively, if crudely, the item which 'this' stands for in 'this horse is frisky' would be that feature called *haecceitas*.) Aside from its being the first thing known by the intellect and showing up in the copula of every statement, however, nothing more can be said about it.

2.11. Aquinas, however, parses 'roses are red' differently, as composed of two (not three) items: a subject ('roses') which relates to the predicate ('are red') as matter to its form.[23] So at the structural level primacy is given to the predicate, which is not a name nor should it be thought of as naming a property or feature; it rather predicates that feature *of* the subject. Moreover, the proposition *roses are red* is secondary to the *assertion* "roses are red," for names succeed in referring only as we employ them in asserting a proposition—either explicitly or implicitly (as in one-word answers to questions). On such an account 'this' becomes a pure indexical, replaceable by the act of pointing, and hence cannot be a feature of possible worlds (wherein one could speak of 'some particular horse' but never of 'this horse') but only of the one in which we live.

The primacy of assertion underscores two points made earlier: (1) the primacy of individual existing things, including speakers; (2) the finality of intellect—to come to know what is the case. And it adds a third: the activity of judgment. I assert what I ascertain to be the case, by contrast to what I propose might be the case. While philosophers have a penchant for proposals, Aquinas insists that proposing be at the service of asserting. As a consequence, we are warned off speaking of true/false propositions by analogy with well or ill-formed strings of sentences. A proposition needs to be asserted to be true; even then, of course, it may be denied. Aquinas's observation that what 'true' adds to 'being' is a relation to intellect (*De Ver.* 1.1) does not favor a "correspondence" over a "coherence" view of truth, as these terms are sometimes used currently, for an attestation of the truth of *p* will require a constructive as well as a verifying role for the mind. What it does demand, however, is a distinct intellectual activity—judgment—to assert that *p* expresses the way things are.[24]

2.21. Activity, then, is the keynote of Aquinas's view of the world and of language use. To understand what something is involves an activity; so it is consonant with his thinking to propose that we understand *existing* on the model of this second activity of the mind (judgment), so that existing is conceived as an activity.[25] Moreover, activity finds expression in structures but is not itself structural. For Scotus, on the other hand, structure is primary, as what is articulatable. Some of these essential structures obtain, but that is not what interests him; what is interesting is what could or might obtain.[26]

It is doubtful whether "intuitions" can decide between these two approaches, yet if I have characterized them accurately the differences are quite basic. Grasping Aquinas's approach depends on one's appreciating how asserting a proposition differs from entertaining it, as well as the import of that difference. One could mark it but find it of little philosophical relevance. I have tried to identify this impasse by contrasting activity with structure, much as the later Wittgenstein became taken with language use. By identifying judgment as a distinct activity of the mind, which does not, however, alter the shape of a proposition entertained by asserting it, Aquinas found a way of articulating the difference which existence makes without having to locate it as a feature of things. A closer look at this analogy between judging as the premier activity of intellect and existing as what "is more intimately and profoundly interior to things than anything else" (*ST* 1.8.1) will help us locate another salient contrast between Aquinas and Scotus.

3. EXISTENCE, JUDGMENT, AND ANALOGY

3.1. In the background (for both thinkers) lies Avicenna's distinction in being between the One as necessary and the rest as possible, as well as Aristotle's views on the relation between semantics and ontology—though each of our thinkers will soon divide on their use of Aristotle. Aquinas parses subject and predicate as parts of an assertion, as matter and form are parts of an existing thing. And the manner of being is determined by the form (*esse viventibus est vivere*), as the manner of knowing is determined by the subject matter.

So both 'being' and 'true' will be (and must be) used analogously if they are to be used accurately. Propositions may be the vehicles of truth/falsity, yet the manner of verifying/falsifying them will differ according to the subject matter, so the truth affirmed or denied will be a function of the judgment rendered on the proposition proposed.

Similarly, the assertion that something exists cannot be an ordinary statement about it (since existence is not an accident), but rather expresses the judgment concerning its availability for full-blooded predication: that statements made about it may be verified/falsified in appropriate ways. This precision picks up Aristotle's founding intuition that the paradigmatic sense for 'F is true of x' is of an existing individual, and others are parasitic upon that. Aquinas formulates that intuition in terms of the finality of intellect, and identifies the crowning activity of intellect as a judgment. And since the activity of judging is always at least virtually conscious of its warrants,[27] one can distinguish different uses of 'exists' in the assertion that something exists: what Geach calls the "there is" sense—in which elephants exist but mermaids do not, and the "actuality" sense—in which elephants exist but dinosaurs do not.[28] These are not the same, since the *actuality* sense entails the *there is* sense, but not vice-versa; yet they are systematically ambiguous—that is, their relatedness will prove significant as well as their difference.

3.2. If the activity of judgment is so central to Aquinas's treatment of knowledge, especially in his attempt to articulate the relation of language to the world, what role does it play in Scotus? The short answer is none. Epistemologically there is no need for a distinct activity of judgment, neither to verify what is the case nor to capture the individual, since (in principle, at least) the individual is knowable this side of its actually existing.[29] (And Scotus acknowledges that what the tradition calls *judgment* has to do with verifying that something is indeed the case.) For, ontologically, Scotus does not conceive existing as the actuality of a thing such that it will differ with each kind of thing (as in Aristotle's *esse viventibus est vivere*), but considers existing rather to be the precondition for concrete discourse, thus distinguishing it from abstract consideration.[30] Again, as we shall see and have seen, the difference lies less in the formulae each uses than in the use to which they put them: the import of their respective articulations. These differences may be captured best by their respective attitudes toward language: Is a philosophically precise language univocal or analogous? Here we have two clearly disparate positions. For Scotus, such discourse must be univocal, as the precondition for straight talk and coherent argument. (Besides, what clear sense can we make of "analogical"? And if Henry of Ghent were one's primary interlocutor, that would be a most plausible question.)[31] For Aquinas, however, analogous usage alone reflects the related differences in reality, so he will be preoccupied to show how these eminently useful resources of language may be employed in a disciplined philosophical argument. His sense of "analogical" is "systematic ambiguity" guided by astute judgment.[32]

3.11. It is clear, then, that Aquinas presumes here the finality of the intellect: to understand the actual world; whereas Scotus focuses on "world" as a conceptual system. That is, Aquinas wants and needs to exploit the analogical resources of language because language is the human instrument of knowing, and the paradigm object of human knowing is the individual existing thing. Whatever else may be said to be *known* must be said with respect to that paradigmatic object, and our knowing it will only be completed in the activity of judgment: the activity which relates us to the actual world. (These observations help resolve a dispute among Thomists initiated by Ralph McInerny's insistence that "analogy is a linguistic doctrine"—that is, it regards the resources and uses of language. And indeed it does, but language functions in the ways it does because it allows us to come to grips with the world as it is. However one explains that fact—theologically or evolutionarily, or both—one need not oppose language to the world so much as regard them together.)

3.21. Scotus, too, presumably regards language as an instrument of human knowing, and a human instrument of knowing, yet the proper object of human knowledge differs for him. And since essence taken "absolutely" prescinds from existence, there is no need for the language fitted to such an object to function analogously. One need not refer diverse ways of being to a primary sense, since one prescinds from existing in understanding things; one need only multiply distinctions to accommodate the diverse "modes of being."

3.22. How, then, ought we conceive the relations between language and the world for Scotus? I am tempted to respond: There is no need to do so, since the formula which accompanies one's grasp of the essence taken "absolutely" will normally be presumed to have captured that essence. Or alternatively, one could be tolerant of diverse formulae, confident one has grasped the nature in question. In either case, closer attention to the use of language, or probing to settle nuances of interpretation, will be considered superfluous.[33] For all that the intellect needs to do is to "universalize the common nature, [which] it finds [in the real singular known by the senses] in immediate potency to be universalized."[34]

Since the entire preoccupation is with understanding essences in their relations to one another, there is no discernible difference between possibilities and actualities except that the world in which we live *obtains*. For "the subject must be fully constituted, i.e., be determined to individuality as a *possible* existent," to qualify as an individual, since "Scotus holds that the individual constituent is of the same order as the specific constituent." This will allow Scotus to secure "that existence is of another order, its own, and that, consequently, existence does not confer individuality."[35]

It is but a short way from here to a "middle knowledge" scenario, in which one will speak straightforwardly of God simulating "possible histories," for a virtual inattention to the difference existence makes will lead one to overlook the differences between a *precise* individual and *precisely one* of a kind.[36] Scotus will go on to insist, nevertheless, that "nothing exists but for individuals and there *are* not individuals which do not exist."[37] But the only thing left to secure that insistence is God's will, since the notion of an individual is complete before its actuality, so existing adds nothing intelligible to it.

3.12. For Aquinas, on the contrary, it is precisely existence which makes something an individual, so that it can be indicated by an indexical ('this,' 'that') and given a name.[38] Aristotle's answer to that question—matter—merely distinguished items numerically, and allowed an Aristotelian to speak adequately of individuals as *instances* of a kind.[39] By locating the individuality of living (and hence indivisible) beings in their "act of existing," however, Aquinas not only secured such individuals as paradigms for what exists, but also specified a role proper to existence: that which makes something a real individual.

Moreover, since there are many kinds of things, what it means to exist will differ with each kind (*esse viventibus est vivere*). So the role Aquinas gives to existence demands that it be analogous, varying with the kinds of individuals we encounter or otherwise become acquainted with: plants, snails, water buffalo, human beings, or angels. By contrast, one can see why Scotus appears relatively indifferent to the question of the analogy of being, for the issue is little more than an annoying residue if existence is a mere precondition which adds no intelligibility to the individual.

3.3. Typically diverse attitudes toward univocity/analogy in language reflect the differences we have already noted regarding the three issues of (1) the proper object of human understanding, (2) the role which existence does (or does not) play, (3) recognizing (or not) the distinction between a precise individual and precisely one of a kind. One's philosophical predilections for univocal or analogous discourse also indicate how these three issues are interrelated.

3.32. Where the proper object of human understanding is essences taken "absolutely," and existence is quite extrinsic even to individuality, then one is free to insist upon *univocity*. For one need not struggle to convey by one's language a sensitive and accurate rendering of the (actual) world, but is free to inquire among possible connections. "Realism" of this sort, where "true propositions" can be counted upon as the counterpart of each coherent assertion, readily metamorphoses into "coherentism"—a nice puzzle for anyone with a penchant for doing philosophy by "isms."[40]

3.31. Where the proper object of human understanding is the nature of existing things, however, and where their existing determines their individuality, one will need to have recourse to a language which contrasts as it compares, in an effort to offer an accurate description of the individual about which one wants to make true statements. The more sensitive and nuanced the description, the better chance one has to verify or falsify it. Therefore philosophical analysis cannot set itself up as a separate discipline, but needs both to employ and bring its skills to bear upon those of the working lawyer or judge, novelist or poet, or the astute historian—each of whom employs analogous expressions in a quite disciplined fashion.

3.4. It follows as a corollary that approaches akin to Scotus will see their task as developing "theories of . . . ," while those in the

family of Aquinas will exercise their philosophical acumen in sorting out, appreciating, and thereby sharpening our capacities to use
the resources latent in ordinary language—resources inherently analogous, as Ross has shown clearly and extensively.[41] These approaches
may even utilize the aforementioned "theories" in their inquiry, but
employing them as testimony among others, never dreaming that the
"definitions" they contain would offer a more "basic" understanding
of an item of reality than any other working language. Put otherwise,
analogical discourse needs no univocal *ground*. The demand for such
a "ground" simply wants to canonize the requirement imbedded in a
responsible use of our inherently analogous language: that we relate
such expressions to a paradigmatic sense each time we employ them.

3.41. This corollary returns us to the role which Aquinas re-
served for judgment. For where understanding is regarded as culminating in a judgment of the veracity of one's proposals, where a statement
is deemed to be true in the measure that it offers a faithful rendering
of what is the case, then the skills prized and exercised by philosophers will be ones designed to enhance that capacity for judgment. So
philosophical training will include dialectical exchange between historically developed positions as a way of sharpening one's capacities
for assessment by pitting them against formidable peers. Moreover,
the upshot of such a dialectical interchange could offer an appropriately indirect but nonetheless germane introduction to a keenness of
philosophical judgment.

3.42. Where judgment is not so highly valued, philosophy will
consist of carefully developing the logical consequences of quite arbitrary intuitions, as Alasdair MacIntyre depicts much of contemporary
philosophizing, and Robert Nozick conveniently exemplifies in his
Philosophical Explanations.[42] Put otherwise, when we take so little care
to discern what others have said, or better, to apprentice ourselves
to their way of inquiring to help us develop the skills of philosophical investigation, something must explain that oversight. It would be
explicable—that is, it would not amount to an oversight—were philosophy regarded as an exercise in conceptual virtuosity unconnected
with sound judgment. Then possible worlds would be as engaging
as the actual world, since nothing distinguishes actual from possible
except the "mere fact" that it happens to exist.

4. TWO APPROACHES TO HUMAN FREEDOM

How does this contrast on existence, analogy, and judgment affect our understanding of the operation of human intentionality regarding action, or freedom? It is bound to do so, since one's views on history and human possibility are intimately connected with one's understanding of how we impinge on what is. Moreover, the current polarities of libertarian and compatibilist overlook a significant middle ground, as will be clear when we see that Aquinas's position will fit in neither camp. (Those who presume the bifurcation to be exhaustive will try to put Aquinas in the "compatibilist" camp, but a recent article by Kretzmann and Stump shows how foreign the presuppositions of this distinction are to Aquinas's analysis.)[43] Finally, it is probably inevitable that a position like Aquinas's be overlooked in a liberal society where *choice* spontaneously dominates discussions of freedom, as ethicists are preoccupied with decisions and economists concerned with trade-offs. What is conspicuously missing from such parlays is a vision of the end or goal of a society, and understandably so, since such questions become procedural in a society where the reigning "theory of justice" finds it both possible and expedient to bracket any discussion of the human good.

4.2. Let us first consider Scotus's views on freedom as more in tune with the current discussion. They are firmly "libertarian," presuming freedom to imply a radical "indifference" before a set of options, so that it is always possible to do otherwise in each particular human act which we would call free. For it is *will*, for Scotus, which determines what one does; the role of intellect is to present to the will a list of possible actions from which to choose. As God's will chooses among possible alternative "histories," so our will chooses among alternative scenarios for action.[44]

In the absence of an existential (or prudential) judgment to ascertain the truth of one's understanding of and orientation toward an actual situation, the will must "decide" by a spontaneous act of self-movement. Such an autonomous movement, prepared of course by what understanding delivers to it, yet itself moving us beyond proposals to action, fairly defines *willing* for Scotus.[45] It also marks him as a "modern man," for whom freedom is auto-determination of an "indifferent" power, as in "the church of your choice."

It does not take a great deal of imagination to move a few steps further to see how Luis de Molina, presuming freedom to be autonomy (i.e., the ability to do otherwise) and wishing to elaborate a notion of divine omniscience, would have recourse to the fabrication of "middle knowledge."[46] The goal of so elaborate a construction was to sever God's foreknowledge from any casual connection with human actions. The way was eminently prepared by what we have seen of Scotus's ontology of individuals, such that one could coherently conceive of God simulating "possible histories" of "possible individuals." Moreover, the notion of freedom as indifference plus auto-determination left no room for divine subvention except as a form of intervention; no way for God to empower a free act without interfering.

So it is not one's antecedent notion of God so much as one's conception of human freedom (together with an ontology lacking the resources to mark the difference between a precise individual and precisely one of a kind) which finds "middle knowledge" to be an attractive strategy. That dominant picture of human freedom, however, will return to characterize God's free act of creating as a *choice* among possible scenarios.[47] Which only confirms the contention that one's theology is frequently a function of one's anthropology, whether consciously or unconsciously so.

4.1. But what alternatives have we? What Joseph Incandela has felicitously called "situated freedom" will allow us to show how Aquinas's views on human freedom are of a piece with his views of creation as (1) primarily an exercise of practical knowledge, (2) whose principal effect is the to-be of things, (3) itself recovered intellectually in the role which Aquinas assigns to judgment.[48] That is, the picture of a plethora of possible worlds (replete with possible individuals) over against a God whose free act of creating is conceived as choosing one of these scenarios, finds a clear alternative in a conception of God's action in creating as preeminently one of making (ST 1.45.3). The knowledge involved will then be primarily practical knowing, issuing in the *being* of creatures, some of which are so constituted as to act freely.[49] Yet their freedom is conceived not as sovereign indifference, but the principal component of an intentional orientation toward their origin.[50]

And since existence is to be thought of as an act, this specific manner of existing is seen as the source of a specific power or capacity with a correlative *telos* or perfection. And that capacity ought not be thought of as *will* alone, but as an intellectual appetite or orientation toward the end or goal inscribed in a derived existence. Just as judgment is required to bring our considerations up against the actual situation as their final measure, and so ascertain the truth of our proposals, so a practical judgment directs our actions in accordance with the way we have perceived things ought to be.

On this view, no separate step (of *willing*) is required to incline us to what we perceive to be our genuine good, though a distinct "faculty" or capacity must be presumed, since perceiving alone could not generate wanting.[51] Yet that wanting is the result of an orientation of the whole person—intellectual and sensitive as well—toward that One from which its existence comes. Aquinas does not (and need not) conceive *willing*, then, as a separate act, but subsumes it under the practical judgment of a being endowed with intellect and will—that is, with a capacity for understanding and judgment plus a spontaneous tendency toward its proper good.[52] It is the judgment which suffices to elicit and direct the natural inclination.

This analysis allows him to appropriate Aristotle's recursive analysis of means/ends, whereby we find ourselves ever choosing means in relation to ends—in principle, at least, up to that point where we come to an end which cannot itself serve as means to a yet more comprehensive goal. At that point we can no longer properly speak of *choosing*, but of consenting to (or refusing) the end which presents itself as ultimate.[53] Institutionalization, the public face of habit, spares us such a recursive analysis of our everyday actions, but certain junctures in life are called "crises" because they require the kind of judgment we call "decision."

On this analysis, then, freedom cannot be identified with choice, since freedom of choice is rooted in a constituting consent (or refusal) regarding what we judge to be our proper good—that is, in a yet deeper freedom. Nor may we conceive that judgment willfully, but rather as the practical analogue of Aristotle's remarks about his predecessors—"constrained as they were by the things themselves"—since the only goal or good which elicits consent with full spontaneity is the ultimate end (*ST* 2–1.15.3). That means, of course, that refusing such a good is tantamount to denying our nature, the complexus of orientations with which we come into being as humans. So it would not be strange were so normative a view of freedom to be alien to a liberal ethos. For if one's ultimate goal be inscribed in one's nature, then freedom is no longer indifference but contains an orientation and a capacity for growth.

Consenting freely to that orientation brings one to a greater measure of freedom, whereas freely refusing it leads one toward enslavement by lesser goods. Enslavement because one is only free to choose goods not ordered to one's final goal *via* a mistaken judgment (i.e., thinking that they are so ordered) or as a consequence of refusing one's own orientation to that good. Such an exercise of freedom will be doubly *situated*, then, in an orientation of our nature and in the light available to us in concrete historical circumstances to judge wisely.

So everything turns, for Aquinas, on practical judgment in analyzing a free act. *Will* is nowhere invoked as a separate action, though it is ever presumed as a distinct faculty or orienting power. If free acts are those by which we constitute ourselves in the character which is ours (as a "second nature"), and are claimed to be free because we assume responsibility for them, then they are at once originating and constituting, like creation itself. So it is not surprising that one's view of human freedom parallels one's view of creation. And so it is here. For Scotus, freedom is accounted "indifference" so that the will decides, while creation is pictured as God's free choice among "worlds." For Aquinas, freedom consists in the response to the orientation of our nature in a concrete practical judgment; and God's practical knowing of what it is God wills to bring forth, in response to the divine nature, is accounted creation.

The general outlines should be clear, then: For Aquinas, the orientation of the intellect to what is true is matched by the will's inclination to what is good. And since the good must be perceived as such, the mediating activity is that of judgment. In speculative knowing we ascertain what is the case; in practical knowing, what is to be made or done. What moves us, in each case, are the "facts of the matter," calling for *assent* in the case of the intellect and *consent* in the case of the will. The power to act freely, and hence to move oneself for Aquinas, then, becomes a function of a person's orientation and inclination to one's proper end (ST 2–1.15.2).

This will also allow him to conceive of God entering into our actions without interfering. For if God, who is our sovereign good in so intimate a fashion that "in desiring its own perfection everything is desiring God himself" (*ST* 1.6.1.2), were to move us to do something, the natural way for God to do so would be as the final cause of our actions. Such was the insight of Augustine, whose reflections on freedom in the eighth book of the *Confessions* established that nothing—neither God nor myself—can make me will something, unless it draws or entices me.[54] And if I cannot be pushed to will something, but only drawn to do so, not even God can cause me to do something freely, if we are thinking of an efficient cause. Yet God, as my sovereign good, could so draw my will as to bring me freely to consent to the end for which my nature craves.

So freedom is less a question of self-determination of what otherwise remains undetermined than it is one of attuning oneself to one's ultimate end. There are plenty of choices, of course, but these are to be made rationally, by taking counsel regarding the way perceived goods relate to that to which we have already consented. Ends function like principles (*ST* 2–1.14.2), guiding the inquiry in which we must engage while taking counsel (*ST* 2–1.14.1). So Aquinas's model for free action remains one of inquiry, concluding this time in a performance rather than a proposition: "just as the end functions like a principle, so whatever is done for the sake of the end functions like a conclusion" (*ST* 2–1.14.6).

Such are the main lines of Aquinas's resolution of God's unfailing providential care with human freedom. They imply that any good choice will presuppose an orientation to the end, where the orientation itself is not a choice but a consent to the orientation of one's very being. And where that end is enhanced beyond our imagining, as in the ways revealed by God to Jewish, Christian, or Muslim believers, the consent becomes a *response* of faith. Many questions remain regarding the character of that divine initiative, questions familiar to Christians under the rubrics of "predestination" or the "irresistibility of God's grace." Suffice it to say here that Aquinas's theorem of divine eternity makes the notion of *predestination* as incoherent as "foreknowledge" and that human freedom does retain for him those mysterious reaches where it can renounce its own good.[55] Bare refusal, of course, is seldom available to humans, though the angels' sin can be explained no other way (*ST* 1.63). The limiting case is, however, just that; in the course of human events we find ourselves operating within an orientation originally supplied or freely offered, and our freedom is structured by consenting to the first and responding gratefully to the second.

5. CONCLUDING REMARKS

It should be clear which approach I prefer, as well as my reasons. Yet I hope my inability to keep a poker face did not entail unfairness to the other side. For the aim of this exercise was to delineate as clearly as possible two irreducibly different ways of doing philosophical theology, by showing them to be irreducible. That is, the coherence of each reveals presuppositions incompatible with the other. How might one adjudicate between them? If each proves to be coherent philosophically, then the balance may be tipped, as I have suggested, by a better fit with doctrinal positions. As Thomas Tracy suggests, "systematic consistency may sometimes be less highly prized in theology than the ability to provide a place for enduring (even if conflicting) tendencies in religious self-expression."[56] I would add: notably liturgical expression, where the relation of creature to creator attains cultural expression, and worshippers' presence to God accentuates the actual communication between them.

My preference for Aquinas stems from the way his approach links us with Augustinian restlessness by attending to existence and to its source. And that attention assures us that one is speaking, when speaking of God, of the source of all, and not simply of some "maximal being." It is fair to say that the greatest objection to Aquinas's view turns on the conception of God's eternity. I have tried a look at that question, assisted by Kretzmann and Stump, but there is neither time nor space to deal with it here.[57] One thing must be said, however: God's eternity, for Aquinas, hardly reflects a Hellenic prejudice, but is rather rooted in divine simpleness as "subsistent existence itself." The model is not the atemporal mode of being proper to mathematicals, but the eternal source of the present actuality of existing individuals.

It is equally fair to remark that the "divine foreknowledge" and "middle knowledge" scenarios overlook a crucial distinction between a precise individual and precisely one of a kind. So that leaves us— in fairness—with two ontological and epistemological chestnuts! But what else could one expect in trying to conceive the relation between the One and all that derives from that One? The chestnuts, though, are of different order: God's eternity can be regarded as part of the mystery of divinity, indeed the place where that peculiar unknowableness linked to simpleness makes itself felt, whereas the structures demanded by "middle knowledge" ask us to revise what we mean by *individual*. The doctrinal issue most directly involved is that of creation and how to understand it. For creation remains, for Jews and Christians, the fundamental mystery revealing God to us and us to ourselves.

NOTES

1. I am indebted to Tom Flint for his comments at a joint Philosophy/Theology colloquium at Notre Dame, and to a communication from Douglas Langston (author of *God's Willing Knowledge: The Influence of Scotus' Analysis of Omniscience* [University Park: Pennsylvania State University Press, 1986]). For the theological dimensions, I am beholden to Gary Gutting's "The Catholic and the Calvinist: A Dialogue on Faith and Reason," *Faith and Philosophy* 2 (1985): 236–56.

2. For an example of attention to the conceptual fruit of narrative, see Robert Alter, *The Art of Biblical Narrative* (New York: Basic Books, 1981) and A. H. Johns, "Joseph in the Qur'an: Dramatic Dialogue, Human Emotion and Prophetic Wisdom," *Islamochristiana* (Rome) 7 (1981): 29–55.

3. Bernard J. F. Lonergan, *Grace and Freedom* (New York: Herder and Herder, 1971) offers comprehensive textual and analytic evidence of the subtlety of Aquinas's position on these matters.

4. See my *Aquinas: God and Action* (Notre Dame, Ind.: University of Notre Dame Press, 1979), esp. ch. 3.

5. References to the works of Thomas Aquinas will be abbreviated in a perspicuous way, so that *Summa Theologiae* 1, q.3, a.4, ad2, for example, will read 'ST 1.3.4.2', and, where possible, references to Scotus will adopt a similar format. In any case, the *Ordinatio*, ed. Carl Balic (Vatican City, 1954-) will be abbreviated 'Ord.' This observation can be found in Etienne Gilson, *Jean Duns Scot* (Paris: Vrin, 1952), 535 ff. Subtitle numbering of paragraphs herein is attempted to facilitate comparison throughout the text.

6. Hence "something can be considered a metaphysical individual if it can be identified in a world by virtue of its individual nature" (Simo

Knuuttila, "Being qua Being in Thomas Aquinas and John Duns Scotus," in S. Knuuttila and J. Hintikka, eds., *The Logic of Being* [Dordrecht: Reidel, 1986], 210; cf. *Ord.* II, d.3 pars 1, q.5–6, n.191). Also *Ord.* II, d.16, q.un., n.5: "Illud enim individuum, quod nunc est in actu, illud idem fuit in potentia."

7. P. F. Strawson, *Individuals* (London: Metheun, 1959), *passim*.

8. For the manner in which Scotus's epistemology influenced Hopkins, see W. H. Gardner, ed., *Poems and Prose of Gerard Manley Hopkins* (Baltimore: Penguin, 1953), xxiii-xxv.

9. Etienne Gilson, "Pourquoi S. Thomas a critiqué S. Augustin," *Archives d'histoire littéraire et doctrinale du moyen-âge* 1 (1926): 5–127.

10. Robert Sokolowski, "Making Distinctions," *Review of Metaphysics* 32 (1979): 652–61.

11. The *Metaphysics* is not that straightforward, of course (but cf. Bk.Z [104lbll]), yet this does turn out to be the best reading of his discriminating dialectic, and the one accepted by medieval and modern readers alike. For Aquinas, see *ST* 1.84.7, 85.1.

12. For a perceptive development of this contrast, see Robert Sokolowski, *The God of Faith and Reason* (Notre Dame, Ind.: University of Notre Dame Press, 1982), where he introduces "the distinction" of God from the world as a distinctively Christian achievement.

13. Ibn-Sina, *al-Shifa, al-Ilahiyyat*, ed. G. Anawati and S. Zayed (Cairo, 1960), French trans.: G. C. Anawati, *La Metaphysique du Shifa* (Paris: Vrin, 1978, 1986), 1.7. On Ibn-Sina, see Fadlou Shehadi, *Metaphysics in Islamic Philosophy* (Delmar, N.Y.: Caravan, 1982), 77–83.

14. Moses Maimonides, *The Guide of the Perplexed*, trans. Schlomo Pines (Chicago: University of Chicago Press, 1963), 1.57.

15. Ibn-Sina, *al-Shifa* 1.5 (Anawati, 108); on the notorious dictum of Ibn-Sina that "existence is an accident," see Fazlur Rahman, "Essence and Existence in Avicenna," in R. Hunt, R. Klibansky, L. Lobowsky, eds., *Mediaeval and Renaissance Studies* 4 (London, 1958): 1–16; also Fadlou Shehadi, *Metaphysics*, 71–118.

16. This is, of course, the thesis of Aquinas's *De Ente et Essentia* (*On Being and Essence*, trans. A. Maurer [Toronto: Pontifical Institute of Medieval Studies, 1982]); see my *Knowing the Unknowable God* (Notre Dame, Ind.: University of Notre Dame Press, 1986), ch. 2.

17. For Aquinas's use of this metaphor (and analogy), see my *Aquinas: God and Action* (note 4 above) ch. 3.

18. For an extended development of this point, see my "Creation, Will and Knowledge in Aquinas and Duns Scotus," *Pragmatik* (Hamburg: Felix Meiner, 1986), 247–48.

19. See Knuuttila's way of articulating this position by contrast with that of Aquinas, "Being qua Being . . ." (note 6 above), 210.

20. See the dissertation by Bonnie D. Kent: "Aristotle and the Franciscans: Gerald Odonis' Commentary on the *Nichomachean Ethics*" (Columbia University, 1984).

21. See William O'Meara, "Actual Existence and the Individual according to Duns Scotus," *Monist* 49 (1965) 659–69; and Knuuttila (note 6 above), nn. 6, 19.

22. See *In Peri Hermenias* q. 5 (Vives ed. 1, 591). For a more extensive commentary on this point, see my *Analogy and Philosophical Language* (New Haven, Conn.: Yale University Press, 1973), 108.

23. *In Peri Hermenias* L. 1, *lectio* 8 (esp.[9]).

24. Bernard J. F. Lonergan has developed the central role of judgment in Aquinas, in *Verbum: Word and Idea in Aquinas* (Notre Dame, Ind.: University of Notre Dame Press, 1968), where he presents a copious and well-ordered collection of texts.

25. This specific chain of reasoning will not be found in Aquinas; yet it is presented as a summary of Lonergan's careful analysis of Aquinas's "metaphysics of knowing" in *Verbum*, which forms the basis for Lonergan's own constructive metaphysics in *Insight* (London: Longmans, 1957). I have shown how this presents a plausible way of reading the transition from Ibn-Sina to Thomas Aquinas, in *Knowing the Unknowable God* (note 16 above).

26. Knuuttila identifies the context for this shift in his concern to show how a new theory of modality developed—see "Being qua Being . . .," 209.

27. This is Lonergan's proposal for understanding the reasonableness of judgment as "virtually unconditioned," in *Insight*, 280–81.

28. For this important distinction, see Barry Miller, "In Defense of the Predicate 'Exists'," *Mind* 84 (1975): 338–54.

29. As William O'Meara puts it (in "Actual Existence and the Individual . . ."[note 21 above]), "existence does not confer individuality"—cf. my "Creation, Will . . ." [note 18 above], 250 n. 18.

30. For this development, see Gilson's *Jean Duns Scot* (note 5 above) 454–66. Judgment will of course play a role, but its role has little or no metaphysical import, since it is not language use but language structure which tells us about reality. The formulation of Aristotle is Aquinas's, in *Aristotelis Librum de Anima* L. 1, *lectio* 14 [209].

31. Cf. Gilson's extended discussion of analogy/univocity in Scotus, especially with reference to Henry of Ghent, in *Jean Duns Scot*, 87–116.

32. That is my thesis in *Analogy and Philosophical Language* (New Haven, Conn.: Yale University Press, 1973), but also see James Ross, *Portraying Analogy* (Cambridge: Cambridge University Press, 1982).

33. I have been accused of unfairness here, so will leave it to readers to assess this criticism of a prevalent way of doing philosophy today; cf. Alasdair MacIntyre's "Postscript" to *After Virtue*, 2nd ed. (Notre Dame, Ind.: University of Notre Dame Press, 1984), 264–78.

34. Gilson, *Scot*, 535–36.

35. O'Meara, "Actual Existence . . . ," 664–65.

36. Miller, "In Defense . . . ," 340.

37. O'Meara, "Actual Existence . . . ," 665.

38. This is the upshot of the argument in *De Ente et Essentia* (note 16 above).

39. Where this becomes decisive is in God's knowledge of individuals: see Maimonides' caustic rendition of Aristotle on such matters in the *Guide* 3.17.

40. Once 'true' can be employed as '*true* in a possible world', and coherent assertions are defined by "possible worlds," then it follows that one can speak of "true propositions" without relation to actuality. It is indeed ironic that this variety of "Platonism" is called "realism," but of course that intends, after the usage of philosophers, to call our attention to the fact that statements express propositions, which are presumed to be "real." Yet one has a right to remain baffled.

41. James Ross, *Portraying Analogy* (note 32 above).

42. Alasdair MacIntyre, "Afterword" (note 33 above); Robert Nozick, *Philosophical Explanations* (Cambridge, Mass.: Harvard University Press, 1981).

43. Calvin Normore, "Divine Omniscience, Omnipotence, and Future Contingents: An Overview," in Tamar Rudavsky, ed., *Divine Omniscience and Medieval Philosophy* (Dordrecht: Reidel, 1985), 3–22; Norman Kretzmann and Eleonore Stump, "Absolute Simplicity," *Faith and Philosophy* 2 (1985): 353–82.

44. Patrick Lee has given a careful historical development of these issues in "The Relation between Intellect and Will in Free Choice according to Aquinas and Scotus," *Thomist* 49 (1985): 321–42. But see Douglas Langston's treatment of the issue in *God's Willing Knowledge* (note 1 above).

45. Walter Höres, *Der Wille als reine Vollkommenheit nach Duns Scotus* (Munich: Pustet, 1962), 269–74.

46. On Molina, see the Introduction by Alfred J. Freddoso, trans., Luis de Molina, *On Divine Foreknowledge* (Ithaca, N.Y.: Cornell University Press, 1988).

47. Gilson, *Scot*, 323.

48. Joseph Incandela, "Aquinas' Lost Legacy: God's Practical Knowledge and Situated Human Freedom" (Ph.D. diss., Princeton University, 1986).

49. Cf. James Ross, "Creation II," in Alfred J. Freddoso, ed., *Existence and Nature of God* (Notre Dame, Ind.: University of Notre Dame Press, 1983), 115–41.

50. See Frederick Crowe, S.J., "Complacency and Concern in the Thought of St. Thomas Aquinas," *Theological Studies* 20 (1959): 1–39, 198–230, 343–95.

51. Here I would disagree with Lee (note 44 above); see Incandela (note 48 above) for a close argument against such an "autonomous" view of willing in Aquinas; also Mary T. Clark, "Willing Freely according to Thomas Aquinas," in Ruth Link-Salinger et al., eds., *A Straight Path: Studies in Medieval Philosophy and Culture* (Washington, D.C.: Catholic University of America Press, 1988), 49–56.

52. See my *Aquinas* (note 4 above), ch. 12.

53. My source here is Crowe (note 50 above), though I prefer 'consent' as a translation of *complacentia*.

54. See Augustine, *Confessions*, trans. R.S. Pine-Coffin (Baltimore: Penguin, 1961), 8.8–10.

55. A close examination of Aquinas' treatment of "predestination" (ST 1.23) will show that he takes it up for completeness' sake. Nothing new is added; the principles have been developed elsewhere. So it would be inaccurate to say "there is predestination in Aquinas" just because he devotes a question to it. The general principles are given in his treatment of providence in *De Veritate* 2.12, where he remarks that "God's knowledge of future things is more properly called *pro*videntia than *prae*videntia [because] it would be impossible for God to have knowledge of future contingents were God to know them as future."

56. Thomas Tracy, *God, Action, and Embodiment* (Grand Rapids, Mich.: Eerdmans, 1984), xi.

57. Cf. my "God's Eternity," *Faith and Philosophy* 1 (1984), 389–406, which relies on and extends an earlier article by Norman Kretzmann and Eleonore Stump, "Eternity," *Journal of Philosophy* 78 (1981): 429–58.

WHEN DID THE THEOLOGIANS LOSE INTEREST IN THEOLOGY?

Nicholas Lash

INTRODUCTION

Consideration of how the word "God" *goes*, of the grammar of its usage, is of central concern to any tradition of theological investigation. And it would surely not be quite arbitrary to propose that consideration of the uses of "God" is not to be counted *Christian* unless it includes some mention of, or reference to, the figure of Jesus. In this sense, at least, a theological tradition whose doctrine of God lacked any christological component might be said to have "lost interest" in the proper subject matter of Christian theology. And yet Michael Buckley's magisterial study of the origins of modern atheism has shown that already in the early seventeenth century, thirty years before Newton's birth and within half a century of Calvin's death, patterns of theological enquiry were being laid down which "abstracted God from Christ as either definition or manifestation." In their developed forms, these patterns of enquiry took Jesus as a teacher of morals, while looking to nature and the cosmos alone to teach us about God.[1] Even to this day, ask almost any unsuspecting passerby what they take the word "God" to mean and the likelihood is that the answer (even from quite conservative Christians) will make no mention of Jesus.

Now, a state of affairs in which it is possible for people not only to indicate what they mean by "God," but also to specify the ways in which we come to know whatever we know of God, without reference to Jesus, would seem at least *prima facie* incompatible with

131

the effective operation of the three "regulative principles" which, according to George Lindbeck, were at work in the elaboration of the ancient creeds.[2] And some such state of affairs was widespread by the end of the seventeenth century. But when did the rot set in? According to Buckley, the answer is to be sought as far back as the thirteenth century, with Aquinas's momentous decision, when designing the *Summa Theologiae*, to consider what can and cannot be said concerning "divina essentia" *before* discussing those things which pertain to the distinction of persons in God (as Aquinas himself put it in the Prologue to the *Prima Pars*).

In this essay, offered in celebration of Lindbeck's work and in gratitude for his friendship, I propose, after some introductory remarks on the regulative character of Christian doctrine, to challenge Buckley's interpretation of Aquinas. My aim in so doing is constructive: freed from the spurious support of the subplot, Buckley's main argument, concerning the sea-change in both method and content which Christian theology underwent in the seventeenth and eighteenth centuries, stands out with greater force and freshness.

PATTERNS OF SPEECH

The concept of "the Christian doctrine of God" is, I suggest, best taken as referring to the declaration, by the Christian community, of identity-sustaining rules of discourse and behavior governing Christian uses of the word "God." In a nutshell: the concept of the Christian doctrine of God refers to the use of the creed as *"regula fidei."* This account of the regulative character of Christian doctrine has evident affinities with that offered by Lindbeck in *The Nature of Doctrine*. For the purposes of this paper, it is not necessary to examine in any detail the similarities and differences between our two accounts.[3] There are, however, two points that need to be made.

In the first place, without wishing to open the Pandora's box of questions concerning the ways in which metaphors of "intra-" and "extratextuality" are best construed, there is a word to be said about *reference*. If God is not a figment of our imagination, then, in our worship of God, our address to God, we may hope successfully to refer to him, to make true mention of him. Our worship, in other words, has cognitive implications: it entails the conviction that there is something that we can truly say of God. And this conviction is quite compatible with insistent nescience so far as our knowledge of "the nature" of God is concerned. On this account, one of the principal functions of doctrine, as regulative of Christian speech and action, would be to help protect correct reference by disciplining our manifold propensity toward idolatry. Idolatry is a matter of getting the reference wrong: of taking that to be God which is not God, of mistaking some fact or thing or nation or person or dream or possession or ideal for our heart's need and the mystery "that moves the sun and other stars."

In other words, I set as much store by the distinction between reference and description as Lindbeck does by that between description and regulation. But whereas I see these two distinctions as lying along different axes, much that Lindbeck has to say about cognition, about propositions, and about what he sometimes calls "ontological reference," leads me to suspect that, in his concern to secure the second distinction, he has overlooked the importance of the first.[4]

In the second place, there is the matter of what I will call the *pattern* of Christian doctrine. This is an issue barely touched on in *The Nature of Doctrine*. There, in spite of the emphasis on the comprehensively regulative character of doctrine, the emphasis is on "doctrines," in the plural, rather than on their unity and the forms of their coherence.[5]

The Christian doctrine of God is the doctrine of God's Trinity, which serves, in Walter Kasper's admirable description, as "the grammar and summation of the entire Christian mystery of salvation."[6] I have recently attempted to develop this view of the matter in some detail, arguing that the creed, as paradigmatic expression of Christian doctrine, provides a pattern of self-correction for each of the three principal modes of our propensity to freeze the form of relation with God into an object or imagined possessed description of the divine nature. The unceasing dialectically corrective movement, which the pattern requires, between the three fundamental regulations for Christian speech and action that are indicated in the three articles of the creed, is, we might say, a matter of *perichoresis*. It is only in this movement, and not apart from it, that the oneness or unity of him whom we triply worship is apprehended. It does not follow that there is nothing to be said about "godness," or what Aquinas called "divina essentia"—nothing to be said about God in abstraction from consideration of the three modes or aspects of our relationship to him. But whatever is thus said is said, precisely, in *abstraction*. To put it with perhaps misleading brevity: God is not an object whose nature we are capable of describing.[7]

Such thoughts will hold no surprises for George Lindbeck, any more than they would have done for theologians during the first one thousand six hundred years of Christian history. And if they seem, to many people today, obscure, eccentric, bordering on the unintelligible, this is perhaps because our modern imagination is still so dominated by a quite different account of what a doctrine of God might be and of the functions that it might perform, an account first formulated in the seventeenth century.

CHANGING THE SUBJECT

Michael Buckley's study is so rich in detail and elegant in design that summary of its aims and argument can hardly fail to be misleadingly banal. The enquiry proceeds on the assumption that "The emergence of modern atheism lies with Diderot and d'Holbach," to the discussion of whom nearly one third of the book is devoted. But what processes and what factors *account* for this emergence, in the precise form that it took? From the confused contradictions (as he saw them) of theology, d'Holbach, systematizing Diderot's more eclectic achievement, singled out two theologians of indisputable significance: "Dr. Samuel Clarke of England and Father Nicholas Malebranche of France. Both of these theologians are descended from figures that dominated the European philosophic and scientific world: Clarke sits at the feet of Newton and Malebranche on every page bears witness to his extraordinary conversion to Descartes." The chapter on Malebranche and Clarke, which precedes those on Diderot and d'Holbach, is, therefore, in turn preceded by a chapter on Descartes and Newton.[8]

The enquiry is not yet at an end, however, because it has not yet accounted for the most surprising characteristic of "this emergence of the denial of the Christian God," which is that "Christianity as such, more specifically the person and teaching of Jesus or the experience and history of the Christian church, did not enter the discussion."[9]

In order, therefore, to answer the question: "how did the issue of Christianity and atheism become purely philosophical?" Buckley takes the enquiry a stage further back to the early years of the seventeenth century. Then, the Louvain Jesuit Leonard Lessius and the prodigiously polymathic Parisian Franciscan Marin Mersenne "treated the atheistic question as if it were a philosophic issue, not a religious one. Both acted as if the rising movement were not a rejection of Jesus Christ as the supreme presence of God in human history, whose spirit continued that presence and made it abidingly evocative, but a philosophic stance toward life brought about by either the scandal of the state of the world, the personal dissolution of the moral virtues, or the collapse of religious unity and the horror of the religious wars." Buckley urges the importance of remembering that, in their repudiation of atheism, the major figures of the Enlightenment "counted the Church and confessional religion not as allies, but as adversaries." As Thomas Jefferson was eventually to argue, since only one-sixth of the known world is Christian, to affirm revelation in Christ as necessary for knowledge of God is to deny human beings that awareness which underlies the argument from universal consent and thus to encourage atheism and unrest.[10] The theologians agreed with the philosophers that the evidence for the reality of God, evidence the buzzword for which as early as the first decades of the seventeenth century is "design," must be obtained—independently of any religious community or tradition of discourse—from a philosophical consideration of the world.

As Buckley traces the discussions and debates from Lessius to d'Holbach by way of Newton's Cambridge, we see that original resolute dissociation of apologetics from spirituality (both of which flourished in the same place and often in the same hands, yet "never intersected except in a genius such as Blaise Pascal") constructs the elements for its own subversion. Thus, for example, in the mid-eighteenth century, "Diderot's *Pensées* exhibit in miniature the development of natural theology since the days of Lessius and Mersenne. Theology gives way to Cartesianism, which gives way to Newtonian mechanics. The great argument, the only evidence for theism, is design, and experimental physics reveals that design." All Diderot had to do was take weapons from Newton and Descartes and turn them against their forgers, "mingling the method of Newton with the issues against their forgers, "mingling the method of Newton with the issues and principles posed by Descartes."[11] There are several ways in which the story might be summarized. The theologians begin to tackle the question of God as a philosophical, and not a theological, question. But philosophical questions become, increasingly, questions in natural philosophy, which is to say: questions in science (and specifically, in mechanics). But scientific questions came increasingly, and quite properly, to receive only scientific answers. Or, as Buckley himself put it: "Theology alienated its own nature by generating a philosophy that functioned as apologetics. Philosophy eventually developed into natural philosophy, which became mechanics. And mechanics established its own nature by denying that its evidence possessed any theological significance and by negating any theological interest. . . . The origin of atheism in the intellectual culture of the West lies thus with the self-alienation of religion itself."[12]

PHILOSOPHY AND THE PHILOSOPHICAL

At the heart of that self-alienation which generated modern atheism, then, there lay the treatment of what is at issue between Christianity and atheism as a "purely philosophical" affair. But what are the parameters of the philosophical? What is it about the subject matter of a question, or about the manner in which that question is treated, which renders the question (or at least its treatment) "philosophical"?

At the period which marks the *end* of Buckley's story, such questions receive fairly clear answers. Thus, for example, with metaphysics transmuted into Newtonian mechanics, the stage is set for Kant, who was "heart and soul a Newtonian," to shift the territory of the philosophical from ontology to epistemology and ethics.[13] But what was the state of affairs at the *outset*? How are distinctions between theology and philosophy to be drawn in respect of the early seventeenth century?

I have already indicated the negative component in Buckley's answer: Lessius's treatment of the question of God was not theological, because it lacked any christological dimension and drew not at all upon the experience of Christ's followers. Positively, his reply has two main elements. "The attack mounted against the atheists is fought or mind over nature as the final explanation of things." Lessius's apologetic is philosophical in that the sources of its arguments are, in respect of both structure and vocabulary, not Christian but Stoic. Mersenne drew largely upon more recent sources, but it was equally true of him that the battle with atheism was to be fought on "common ground . . . provided by the cosmos"[14] and not in respect of anything specific to Christian life or memory.

Over and above this decision to take the question of the world's design as battleground, however, there was a further component to the "philosophical" character of seventeenth-century apologetic. There occurred, during this period, a "textbook revolution" in the theological schools. Lessius brought to Louvain an innovation which Francisco de Vitoria had introduced in Salamanca in 1526: the replacement of Peter Lombard's *Sentences* by Aquinas's *Summa Theologiae* as matter for magisterial commentary.[15]

Commenting, twenty years ago, on Herbert Butterfield's claim that the rise of modern science in the seventeenth century "outshines everything since the rise of Christianity and reduces the Renaissance and the Reformation to the ranks of mere episodes, mere internal displacements, within the system of medieval Christendom," Bernard Lonergan said of the theologians of the period that they "replaced the inquiry of the *quaestio* by the pedagogy of the thesis." Buckley registers this shift (so central to the burgeoning apologetic obsessions of the new theology) and also the transposition of Aquinas's arguments concerning "*divina essentia*" from "metaphysics, which is obscure, to the more evident data of the universe of Tycho Brahe . . . and the biological measurements of the human body." Notwithstanding these profound displacements of topic and treatment, however, Buckley takes it for granted that a fundamental continuity still obtained between Lessius and Aquinas. For both men, questions concerning the existence and attributes of God pertain to "*praeambula fidei*": they "provide a preamble to Christian convictions about god which does not include Christ."[16] That Lessius read Aquinas this way, I have no reason to doubt. But I do now want to challenge the view that thus to read Aquinas is to read him well.

AQUINAS: GODFATHER OF THE ENLIGHTENMENT?

The claim that "Lessius took from the Thomistic tradition . . . the persuasion that the existence of god was essentially a philosophical problem rather than a theological or religious one" is vague enough to be unexceptionable. And the historian exhibits admirable caution when he says that "The theologians followed the Thomistic lead, or what they understood as the Thomistic lead." Elsewhere, the cat gets out of the bag, as with the claim that "the surrender to natural philosophy of the foundations of religion" occurred, not in the seventeenth century, but "many centuries before the Enlightenment."[17] In context, this can only mean that the surrender occurred in the thirteenth century.

There are two distinct components to the well-known suspicion that Aquinas's doctrine of God is "philosophical," and hence not properly "theological," in character. The first concerns the relationship between the consideration of "divina essentia" (Prima Pars, qq. 2–26) and the discussion of God's Trinity (qq. 27–43). The second arises from the belief that "In the Summa theologiae, Christ makes a central appearance only in the third part—after the doctrines of god, providence, the nature of the human person, creation, and human finality have already been defined."[18] The implication, it seems clear, is that all these other topics have been "defined" without reference to Christ.

For all its undoubted importance, the second of these problems is far too complex to be treated here. Suffice it to say that, in order to understand the design of the Summa, it is necessary, firstly, to take serious account of what Aquinas himself has to say in his opening question about the character and subject matter of "that theology which pertains to holy teaching"[19] and, secondly, to bear in mind how deeply neoplatonic remained the scheme with which he worked. We might almost say that, for Aquinas, the "soundness" of his "educational method"[20] depended upon the extent to which the movement of his exposition reflected the rhythms of God's own act and movement: of that self-movement "outwards" from divine simplicity to the utterance of the Word and breathing of the Gift which God is, to the "overflowing" of God's goodness in the work of his creation (Prima Pars); the "return" to God along that one way of the world's healing which is Christ (Tertia Pars); and, because there lies across this movement the shadow of the mystery of sin, between the whence and whither, the "outgoing" and "return," of creaturely existence, there is the drama of conversion, of sin and virtue, of rejection or acceptance of God's grace (*Secunda Pars*).[21]

When Aquinas speaks of the effect of "holy teaching" (which is first to last *God's* teaching and only by his free grace our human participation in such pedagogy) as being to set a kind of "imprint" on our minds of God's own knowledge, he is speaking in a different figure of putting on the mind of Christ.[22] *Everything* in the *Summa* "pertains to holy teaching." I see no reason, whether of topic or treatment, to doubt that Aquinas meant what he said when he asserted that such theology differs root and branch ("*differt secundum genus*") from that theology which ranks as a part of philosophy.[23] But if this *is* true, not only of the *Summa* as a whole, but also of each of its constituent parts, then what are we to make of the apparently purely "philosophical" consideration of "*divina essentia*" in questions 2 to 26? Even if these questions are, as Buckley allows, "integrated into theology as a moment within theology," are they not nevertheless (as he also says) "philosophical in their issues and methods?"[24]

Buckley calls on no less authoritative a witness than Etienne Gilson, according to whom "The existence of God is a philosophical problem" concerning which "a theologian cannot do much more than apply to the philosopher for philosophical information."[25] When, however, we remember that Gilson was a doughty advocate of the concept of "Christian philosophy," we are alerted to the possibility that the sense, in his thought, of both "philosophy" and "theology," and hence also his account of the relationships between these two enterprises, may have been very different from that entertained by those for whom the notion of a "Christian" *philosophy* would seem quite evidently mistaken or confused.

We touch at this point on a general issue of quite fundamental importance. I earlier referred to the suspicion that Aquinas's doctrine of God is philosophical and *hence* not properly theological in character. That way of putting the matter, however, presupposes that no text or argument could be, at one and the same time, thoroughly and quite properly theological and also philosophical in character. I shall suggest in due course that this presupposition is crucial to Buckley's misreading of Aquinas. For the time being, however, I do no more than register the possibility that not all philosophical investigation is necessarily untheological or irreligious.

When undertaking the massive redistribution of material which differentiates the *Summa Theologiae* from Peter Lombard's *Sentences* (and from his own earlier *Commentary* on those *Sentences*), why did Aquinas divide "what in Peter Lombard is the 'de mysterio Trinitatis' into a *de deo uno* and a *de deo trino*,"[26] taking the former topic first? Was it because he sought, apologetically, to provide some areligious "preamble" to the consideration of Christian beliefs, or had he quite different aims in view? The third article of question 2 is quite certainly the best-known item in the *Summa*. It considers whether God exists: "*utrum Deus sit.*" Philosophers, rushing to consider the "five ways" outlined in reply, seldom pause to notice where the argument begins: namely from God's pronouncement (reported in Exodus 3:14) "*Ego sum qui sum.*" Aquinas, in other words, "starts from what God in his own person says; he begins treating God's existence from what we have been told." If, from this starting point, he then proceeds to work with what he takes to be familiar features of common human experience, he does so (in Cornelius Ernst's felicitous description of the Five Ways) "to show how one might go on speaking of God in the ordinary world."[27]

The fundamental reason, according to Aquinas, for beginning theology with the *unity* of God, rather than with God's Trinity is "because the one is by nature principle."[28] The sequence of topics in the *Prima Pars* follows "the step-by-step derivation of multiplicity from the divine unity," it moves from the "simpleness" of God's being through increasing complexity (even in God himself) to the scattered diversity of his creatures. Hence, on the specific question of the relationship between the treatment of God's being and the consideration of God's Trinity, we can say that "the *de deo trino* communicates with the *de deo uno* in virtue of the gradual development toward greater distinction in the terms of the various forms of self-relation in the divine."[29]

The structure of the *Sentences* derived (as Aquinas knew and pointed out) from the "*exitus-reditus*" rhythms of Augustinian neoplatonism. Paradoxical as it may seem, the effect of Aquinas's refashioning of that structure was to make the *Summa Theologiae* more, not less, neoplatonic than the work it superceded. The subject matter of the *Summa*, its "formal object," is God himself and all things in relation to God, their origin and end. The design of Aquinas's doctrine of God comes to him "through Dionysius and is Proclan in its philosophical origins. The step-by-step development from the unity of substance through the conceptual division of the operations to the real relation and opposition of the persons also has a late Neoplatonic logic behind it."[30]

I hope already to have provided some indication as to why the technicality and formal abstractness of Aquinas's doctrine of God is better read as being "for the sake of making God's revelation thinkable" than as providing a "preamble to Christian convictions about God," let alone as marking the "surrender to natural philosophy of the foundations of religion."[31] Nevertheless, it is still necessary to focus more exactly on the question of what the relationship between "theology" and "philosophy" in his texts might be.

According to Hankey, the neoplatonic rhythms beat not merely in the structure of the *Summa* as a whole, but in the movement of its every part. "Not only is the whole a movement from God to material creation and back through man, but this pulse of going out and return runs through the individual parts of the work."[32] Nor are the relationships between "outgoing" and "return," between God's self-gift and our appropriation of it, between God's reaching down to us and our raising of our minds and hearts to him, between (to risk the slogan-words worn most misleading through subsequent sea-changes in their use) "grace" and "nature," "revelation" and "reason," to be thought of simply as *successive*. On the contrary, we only get near the heart of the matter when we notice Aquinas's concern to hold both "beats" in some approximation to divine simultaneity, such that all our language is wholly fashioned to the pressures of God's grace while grace comes visible in wholly human speech: "Natural reason moves up to knowledge of God through creatures; conversely, knowledge of faith moves down from God to us by divine revelation; *the upward and the downward path are but one way*."[33] And even if neoplatonic thought, both within and without Christianity, furnished Aquinas with the conceptual apparatus for this view of the matter, it was a view controlled and radicalized by the conviction that that "one way" has now a name, a date, a history, a cloud of witnesses.[34]

Let us go back for a moment to that second question of the *Summa*: *"utrum Deus sit."* To many of our contemporaries, the question as to whether or not "God is" is an empirical question, a matter of fact. And according to some people, it is important to settle this question, to ascertain whether or not God exists, before moving on to the riskier business of religious belief (hence the notion of "preambles" to faith).

Aquinas, however, was not asking an empirical question, nor seeking to settle some question of fact. His enquiry was much more limited in scope and quite different in character. It was grammatical; it concerned, we might say, our handling of "existence talk" in respect of God. (It was, in other words, more like a discussion of whether numbers "exist" than like an enquiry as to whether you have any cousins.)

Now if, by "philosophical issues and methods" one means the kinds of question which invite—and best receive—grammatical rather than empirical investigation, then, in *this* sense it seems correct to say (as Gilson did) that the existence of God is treated by Aquinas as a philosophical question. But this says nothing either way concerning the kind of place, if any, which such grammatical consideration might occupy within the loving obedience of faith in quest of understanding. In other words, whether consideration of God's existence which is, in *this* sense, "philosophical" is or is not also properly theological will depend, not upon the pattern of words on the page, but upon the context and climate of their use.

We tend to consider contemplative wonder, the docility of faith, as standing in sharp contrast to the requirements of critical rationality. The priedieu, we imagine, is not the place to do philosophy. A glance at Anselm's *Proslogion*, however, should be sufficient to remind us that there have been *other* ways of handling the relationship between "faith" and "reason."[35] (Both words are set in quotation marks as a reminder, once again, that *none* of the key terms in this discussion, nor any of the relationships between them, have constant sense or connotation.)

Eventually, of course, a day was to dawn when the question of God's existence *would* become an empirical question, a matter of fact, if only for the excellent reason that, at this time, *all* philosophical questions were on their way to becoming matters of fact, matters of natural philosophy, matters of terrestrial, celestial, or transcelestial mechanics. But, for that shift, it would be less than reasonable to blame Aquinas's neoplatonism!

Michael Buckley takes Descartes and Newton, "the most influential thinkers at the dawn of modernity," as the best examples going "of what Martin Heidegger characterizes as the malaise of our world: *Seinsvergessenheit*—a forgetfulness of being, with its concomitant inability to ask the question of God at the depth which alone can give any theological sense to the content of the answer." Both Descartes and Newton, he goes on, "achieved a god commensurate with the evidence they explored . . . an explanatory factor in a larger, more complete system."[37] All that I have tried to indicate is that such "forgetfulness" may not plausibly be laid at Aquinas's door.

DATING THE GREAT REVERSAL

"What Lessius presents," in the *De providentia numinis*, "is not the person and message of Jesus, but those cosmological and historical experiences which are open to any human being." Here, in 1613, we are evidently already in the presence of what Hans Frei called the "great reversal," that shift in interpretative strategy as a result of which theological interpretation became "a matter of fitting the biblical story into another world" (namely, the world now taken to be constituted by those ranges of experience deemed open to any human being) "rather than incorporating that world into the biblical story."[37] In the self-assured world of modernity, people seek to make sense of the Scriptures, instead of hoping, with the aid of the Scriptures, to make some sense of themselves.

Although Frei mentions, in passing, the possibility that the "roots" of this modern world's theology go back to the seventeenth century, he firmly dated the great reversal somewhat later: "If historical periods may be said to have a single chronological and geographical starting-point, modern theology began in England at the turn from the seventeenth to the eighteenth century."[38] (That there is some implausibility in this account might have been suspected from the fact that the characteristic watchwords of the new theology, "theism" and "deism," were coined in *France* several decades before they were taken up in England.)

When did the theologians lose interest in theology? If we take my title as polemical paraphrase of that revolution in method and subject matter which marked, for good and ill, the "great reversal," then the answer, I suggest, is: not in early eighteenth-century England, as Frei proposed, nor in the thirteenth-century Parisian schools, as Buckley assumes (misled by modern Thomism's enduring tendency to read the thirteenth century through spectacles fashioned in the seventeenth), but in the France and Low Countries of the early seventeenth century, the world of Lessius and Mersenne. The weight of argument of Buckley's splendid study points massively to this conclusion. All that I have tried to do is to scrape one barnacle off the hull.[39]

NOTES

1. Michael J. Buckley, *At the Origins of Modern Atheism* (New Haven, Conn.: Yale University Press, 1987), 346; cf. p. 55. Leonard Lessius's *De Providentia Numinis et animi immortalitate. Libri duo adversus atheos et Politicos* was first published in 1613 (see Buckley, p. 42).

2. "Three regulative principles at least were obviously at work. First, there is the monotheistic principle: there is only one God, the God of Abraham, Isaac, Jacob, and Jesus. Second, there is the principle of historical specificity: the stories of Jesus refer to a genuine human being who was born, lived, and died in a particular time and place. Third, there is the principle of what may be infelicitously called Christological maximalism: every possible importance is to be ascribed to Jesus that is not inconsistent with the first rules" (George A. Lindbeck, *The Nature of Doctrine. Religion and Theology in a Postliberal Age* [London: SPCK, 1984], 94). For some critical comment on these principles, as stated, and especially on the third, see Lee C. Barrett, "Theology as Grammar: Regulative Principles or Paradigms and Practices?" *Modern Theology* 4 (January 1988): 167–71; Stephen Williams, "Lindbeck's Regulative Christology," *Modern Theology* 4: 183–84.

3. See Nicholas Lash, *Easter in Ordinary. Reflections on Human Experience and the Knowledge of God* (Charlottesville: University Press of Virginia, 1988). For my general reactions to *The Nature of Doctrine*, see *New Blackfriars* 66 (November 1985): 609–10. I am unpersuaded by the claim that the functions of church teaching can be *confined*, as Lindbeck proposes, to the regulative: see Avery Dulles, "Paths to Doctrinal Agreement: Ten Theses," *Theological Studies* 47 (1986): 32–47.

4. On "ontological reference," see Lindbeck, *The Nature of Doctrine*, 106. William Placher is, I think, making a point similar to mine when he suggests that, on this crucial question of reference, Lindbeck is strangely ambivalent: see William C. Placher, "Paul Ricoeur and Postliberal Theology: A Conflict of Interpretations?" *Modern Theology* 4 (October 1987): 46–47.

5. See, for example, the discussion of a "taxonomy of doctrines" (pp. 84–88).

6. Walter Kasper, *The God of Jesus Christ*, trans. Matthew J. O'Connell (London: SCM Press, 1984), 311.

7. On all this, see *Easter in Ordinary*, especially 254–85.

8. Buckley, *Origins*, 34, 32. Newton figured largely in an earlier study: see Michael J. Buckley, *Motion and Motion's God: Thematic Variations in Aristotle, Cicero, Newton, and Hegel* (Princeton, N.J.: Princeton University Press, 1971).

9. *Origins*, 33.

10. *Origins*, 33, 65–66, 38; see 40.

11. *Origins*, 345, 202, 260.

12. *Origins*, 358, 363.

13. See *Origins*, 326–28.

14. *Origins*, 48, 345.

15. *Origins*, 341, 343.

16. Herbert Butterfield, *The Origins of Modern Science, 1300–1800* (2nd ed., London: G. Bell, 1968), vii; Bernard J. F. Lonergan, "Theology in Its New Context," in Lonergan, *A Second Collection*, ed. William J. F. Ryan and Bernard J. Tyrrell (London: Darton, Longman & Todd, 1974), 57; Buckley, *Origins*, 55.

17. *Origins*, 341, 345, 283 (emphasis added).

18. *Origins*, 55.

19. Thomas Aquinas, *Summa Theologiae*, 1a, 1, 1 ad 2.

20. The reference is to the Prologue to the *Summa*, on which see Victor White, *Holy Teaching: The Idea of Theology According to St. Thomas Aquinas* (London: Blackfriars, 1958).

21. The most learned and interesting recent contribution to the discussion of both problems is W. J. Hankey, *God in Himself: Aquinas' Doctrine of God as Expounded in the Summa Theologiae* (Oxford: Oxford University Press, 1987). Hankey is concerned, above all, to demonstrate the neoplatonic background and structure of Aquinas's doctrine of God. He is sometimes overzealous in distinguishing his views from those of earlier commentators. For example: I would still recommend M.-D. Chenu's account of "the construction of the *Summa*" in his *Toward Understanding St. Thomas*, trans. A. M. Landry and D. Hughes (Chicago: Henry Regnery, 1963), 310–17. It is grossly

misleading to present Chenu's distinction between the "structure" and "history" of our return to God in Christ as a story of "*two* returns," one of nature, the other of grace (see Hankey, pp. 34, 139). There are important differences between Chenu's account and Hankey's, but they are not, I believe, as dramatic as the latter would have us suppose.

22. See *ST*, 1a, 1, 3 ad 2.

23. "Theologia quae ad sacram doctrinam pertinet differt secundum genus ab illa theologiae quae pars philosophiae ponitur" (*ST*, 1a, 1, 1 ad 2).

24. Buckley, *Origins*, 55.

25. Etienne Gilson, *Elements of Christian Philosophy*, cited from Buckley, *Origins*, 341.

26. Hankey, *God in Himself*, 23.

27. *God in Himself*, 33–37; Cornelius Ernst, "Metaphor and Ontology in *Sacra Doctrina*," in *Multiple Echo*, ed. Fergus Kerr and Timothy Radcliffe (London: Darton, Longman & Todd, 1979), 74, his emphasis.

28. For references, see *God in Himself*, 10, 37.

29. *God in Himself*, 39, 131.

30. See *ST* 1a, 1, 3 ad 2; *God in Himself*, 23.

31. *God in Himself*, 41; Buckley, *Origins*, 55, 283.

32. Hankey, *God in Himself*, 54.

33. "Quia vero naturalis ratio per creaturas in Dei cognitionem ascendit, fidei vero cognitio a Deo in nos e converso divina revelatione descendit; est autem eadem via ascensus et descensus" (Thomas Aquinas, *Summa Contra Gentiles*, bk. IV, ch. 1; cited from Hankey's discussion of this "epigrammatic formula" in *God in Himself*, 56).

34. "Over and over again Christ is called the *via*," "Christianity is able to find in Christ's union of God and man a point upon which to move the universe, which fulcrum is lacking in the Neoplatonism supplying the philosophical logic for the development" (*God in Himself*, 35, 31).

35. I have in mind the smoothness of transition between daunting logical brain twisters such as "Something-than-which-a-greater-cannot-be-thought exists so truly then, that it cannot be even thought not to exist" and (the very next words) the language of prayerful address: "And You, Lord our God, are this being . . ." (*Proslogion*, chapter 3, translation from M. J. Charlesworth's edition [Oxford, Clarendon Press, 1965], 119).

36. Buckley, *Origins*, 348–49.

37. *Origins*, 54; Hans W. Frei, *The Eclipse of Biblical Narrative: A Study in Eighteenth and Nineteenth Century Hermeneutics* (New Haven, Conn.: Yale University Press, 1974), 130.

38. *Eclipse*, 51; see 325.

39. Since drafting this paper, I have had an opportunity to discuss it with Michael Buckley who is alarmed to find me ascribing to him a particular view, concerning how Aquinas is best read, on which he had in fact intended to keep his options open.

"NARRATIVE" IN CHRISTIAN
AND MODERN READING

Hans W. Frei

I. GENERAL BACKGROUND

The association of narrative with religion generally and Christianity in particular has always been close, although the self-conscious use of the concept "narrative" is a modern invention in Christian theology. Systematic reference to the "sacred story" or "sacred history" or "salvation history" of the Bible did not arise until the seventeenth century.

Most if not all religions contain creation, loss, quest, and restoration myths, tales which symbolize reality and allow the readers or listeners access to the common identifying patterns making up that symbolized world and to the communal ways of inhabiting it. It is generally assumed that such tales are originally oral in character, with no particular author, and that they are perpetuated by a tradition of authoritative narrators or singers. These tellers adapt the content and pattern of a common story in their own, individual ways, usually under certain "formulaic" constraints imposed both by linguistic conventions and by the absence of all ironic distance between narrator, story, and audience. Tellers and listeners are part of the same symbolic and enacted world, so that the conditions for self-referencing authorial or listening perspectives are lacking.[1]

Not all oral epics can become candidates for the status of "sacred stories" within "sacred texts," especially if one accepts the speculative theory that the distinction between "profane" and "sacred" is both universal and primitive, so that "folktales" come to be distinguished

149

from "myths," which are of the same narrative order but include sacred themes.[2] However, the easy and natural fusion of historical tradition, myth, and social custom in such ancient tales makes for the natural inclusion of some of them in sacred texts, once the transition from oral to literate culture takes place.

However one speculates, in this or other ways, about the origins and universality of sacred stories—and speculation it remains—most literate cultures have them and include them in their sacred texts. Contact and conflict among religions within the same demographic area or cultural family typically results in a parasitic takeover, in altered form, of elements of one such text by a later, or even a contemporaneous, religious group as a part of its own Scripture. So it was between Hinduism and Buddhism, between Hebrew and Christian Scripture, between Hebrew and Christian Scripture and the Qu'ran. Sacred stories are obvious targets for such scriptural transformation. The adherents of Jesus did not obliterate the story of John the Baptist, assigning him instead the role of forerunner and witness in the story of Jesus.

II. NARRATIVE AND THE PRIMACY OF "LITERAL" READING IN THE CHRISTIAN TRADITION

The most striking example of this kind of takeover in the history of Near Eastern and Western culture is the inclusion of Jewish in Christian Scripture by means of "typology" or "figuration," so that not only "Old Testament" narrative (*haggadah*) but its legal texts (*halakhah*) and prophetic as well as wisdom literature are taken to point beyond themselves to their "fulfillment" in the "New Testament." The Jewish texts are taken as "types" of the story of Jesus, which is their common "antitype," an appropriating procedure that begins in the New Testament, notably in the letters of Paul, the letter to the Hebrews and the synoptic Gospels, and then becomes the common property of the Christian tradition of scriptural interpretation until modern times.

Two features in this process are especially striking. First, in contrast to Hebrew Scripture and the rabbinic tradition, in which cultic and moral regulations tend to be at once associated with and yet relatively autonomous from the narrative biblical text, Christian tradition tends to derive the meaning of such regulations—e.g., the sacraments, the place of the "law" in Christian life, the disposition of love—directly from (or refer them directly to) its sacred story, the life, teachings, death, and resurrection of Jesus the Messiah. This narrative thus has a unifying force and a prescriptive character in both the New Testament and the Christian community that neither narrative generally nor any specific narrative has in Jewish Scripture and the Jewish community.

Second, largely by reason of this centrality of the story of Jesus, the Christian interpretive tradition in the West gradually assigned clear primacy to the literal sense in the reading of Scripture, not to be contradicted by other legitimate senses—tropological, allegorical, and anagogical. In the ancient church, some of the parables of Jesus, e.g., that of the Good Samaritan (Luke 10:25–37), were interpreted allegorically as referring latently or spiritually to Jesus himself, but this could only be done because the story of Jesus itself was taken to have a literal or plain meaning: He really *was* the Messiah, just as he was depicted by means of his story. Thus, by and large, except for the school of Origen, allegorical interpretation tended to be in the service of literal interpretation rather than the reverse, although before the Reformation and outside the Antiochene school allegory remained a legitimate kind of reading. Typological or figural interpretation, applied not only to the Old Testament but to the meaning of extrabiblical life and events, including one's own, stood in an unstable equilibrium between allegorical and literal interpretation but was usually taken to be closer to the latter. An event, real in its own right, and a meaning complex, meaningful in its own right, are nonetheless understood to be incomplete and thus "figures" of the event and/or meaning that fulfills them, namely, the story of Jesus or the universal story of which it was the centerpiece.

Since the Reformation, first allegorical and then (from the Enlightenment on) typological interpretation have fallen on hard times in Christian theology, although both are enjoying a revival in very recent, purely secular, *literary* readings of biblical narrative texts.[3] The tradition of literal reading was at once continued and transformed through the procedure of historical-critical analysis and the cognate, but antithetical, outlook of fundamentalist biblical literalism. The meaning and significance of the literal sense were now judged to lie in the distinction and positive correspondence between the depiction of the narrative text and its true "referent," i.e., what had actually, historically, and in that sense literally, transpired. When the two matched, the text literally read made literal sense precisely because it was isomorphic with its actual referent; when they did not, the *literal-actual* referent was substituted as the *true* meaning of the text for the *literal-written* form, and the latter turned instead into a detective's clue to the discovery of that referent. In either case, the meaning of the text was bestowed on it by its true referent, which, being true, was taken literally. It was this way for biblical fundamentalists, who saw nothing but identity or correspondence between written text and actual referent, as well as for historical critics, who usually saw a core or residue of such correspondence amidst much that served merely as detective's clue or source to the "actual" meaning and who saw these things no matter what instruments they employed on the narrative texts—source, form, redaction criticism, religio-historical analysis or a combination. What was sought for as historical-critical meaning was the "*actual*" purposes of the final unifying editor of a gospel, the "*actual*" words of Jesus, the "*actual*" identity in content among genetically related or parallel religious patterns, etc., etc. In view of its transforming continuation of the literal tradition, historical criticism, far from being seen as a secular or religiously neutral development that was free of the ecclesiastical tradition, may actually come to be viewed by genuinely secular literary commentators as a kind of loose-jointed extension of the ecclesiastical tradition of interpretation into an Enlightenment and post-Enlightenment conceptual mode.[4]

III. POST-CRITICAL READINGS AND THE NEW TESTAMENT NARRATIVE

Biblical narrative has reemerged as an engrossing topic while the preoccupation with historical explanation as a necessary even if not sufficient criterion for the "meaning" of these narratives has faded. Biblical texts became thought of once again as texts rather than sources or clues that mean by referring beyond themselves. This development was already underway in the exegesis of Karl Barth and a few of his theological contemporaries. It has gathered momentum since then, but usually in a nontheological context, and it has caught historical critics unprepared. It was not information or explanatory hypotheses but the basic conceptual form that needed to be changed if one was to be engaged in a new and different enterprise. It was as though a previous and common conceptual frame had suddenly disappeared—a frame that had served as the common context for relating the two distinct enterprises, historical explanation and religious interpretation of the narrative texts, to each other, usually to the exclusion of other kinds of reading. Within that context one argued whether historical explanation and the judgment either affirming or denying the religious meaningfulness of the Christian sacred narrative are logically similar, logically completely distinct, or logically distinct but with an area of overlap or resemblance between them. Now this whole apparatus suddenly ceased to function (or one suddenly discovered that it had never functioned in the first place). It was the breakup of a consensus that "meaning" is an umbrella term, a single, universal category which serves as a clearinghouse within which historical explanation was traditionally taken to be the one necessary if insufficient condition for orienting oneself toward the religious meaning. Historical critics generally simply did not have the conceptual tools to orient themselves toward or within this breakup. It has widened even more the antecedent gap between historical critics and Christian theologians, but it has also tended to isolate historical criticism from other reading of biblical narratives, especially secular literary reading. In the wake of this lack of consensus over the very notion of meaning or interpretation, some writers who were previously historical critics have simply decided to conjure religious or, perhaps more accurately, homiletical rabbits directly out of theoretical hats such as structuralism or poststructuralism. But the most obvious victim of this breakup is the collapse of the transformed tradition of "literal" reading described earlier, in which "literal-actual" had come to be the comprehensive "meaning" frame for "literal," dominating "literal-written" and thus saving the reader from the threat that the narrative "means" what is written, even when the written sense does not correspond to an "actual" state of affairs. In the wake of the collapse of this comprehensive frame, the possibility arises that there is no formal "surplus" in the concept or category "meaning" to allow systematic coordination between two context-specific or substantive-meaning-specific readings of the same narrative, e.g., historical and literary.

The collapse of the common hermeneutical or conceptual frame for historical-critical and literal reading may speed up the abandonment of both, a view clearly pressed by some literary readers.[5] Alternatively, those who *persist* in the literal tradition may now want to search for analogues to it elsewhere than in traditional historical-critical reading, including some other kinds of literary readings which tend to be sympathetic to the literal tradition. However, the Babel of contemporary literary theory is such that it is too early to tell whether literary inquiry into the New Testament narratives will prove a bane, blessing, or neither to the literal tradition. It is possible that the latter may have to find hermeneutical aid and analogues elsewhere, for example, among those who try to understand the language of the New Testament by correlating its varieties, including its various belief statements, with the social matrices in which they functioned but *without* strong causal explanation for that correlation and thus without recourse to a theory of referential meaning for that language as symbol system.[6]

In the meantime professional, academic readers seem unable to avoid inventing theories for describing what it is to read a text, even if such theories (especially those that hold that "meaning" is an umbrella category of basic, indispensable, and apodictic status) by now often have poor credentials. Their multiplication has tended to make complex matters more so, sometimes only at the (second-order) level of the theories themselves, sometimes in the actual reading of texts, when theory, as often happens in contemporary academic discussion, claims entry rights into (first-order) exegesis, and the line between "literary" and "interpretive" activity becomes deliberately blurred.

In a *Christian* context, direct moral and devotional use of the gospel narratives is both distinctive and natural (see below, section IV), and reflection about it is not only rightly second-order and minimal but instructs us to leave well enough alone; but as soon as religious use also includes belief statements based on these narratives, theories of the more imperious sort begin once again, rightly or wrongly, to clamor for recognition. Are the narratives being used literally or in some other way when the sacred text in which they are included is described as "The Word of God"? When the creed says that Jesus was crucified, dead and buried, that he descended into hell and rose again from the dead on the third day? When it is said that creedal statements function only liturgically and devotionally?

Whether or not such questions necessarily force a return to the particular categorial scheme in which "meaning" includes (1) semantic "sense" and (2) its true "reference," and (3) a stateable relation between them (usually the hegemony of the latter), that is largely what has happened. A discussion in these theoretical terms has not only materialized but has been reinforced by a parallel debate among secular literary theorists, who have usually argued the status of narratives by means of that same scheme, however they have individually decided the matter. Reading narratives as texts rather than as sources for something else to which they refer, at least some theorists have nonetheless read them in a way that is logically parallel (though certainly not materially identical) to the way in which historical critics have traditionally read the gospels. And others have not only criticized them severely for this reading but have regarded it as their central error. Yet it is also an open question whether these latter folk have actually succeeded in avoiding the same pattern.

It is a matter of broad agreement among literary critics and theorists that a narrative text is its own world, whether it "refers" in some way or not, and that it should therefore be *read* as a text. And even if it should be taken to refer, it may do so in a variety of ways, though always by way of its semantic structure or form. The "heresy of paraphrase" for which the linguistic configuration is adventitious to the narrative (or poem) is universally rejected. A (nonexhaustive) list of types of contemporary theories of narrative reading, including biblical narrative, includes the following:

A. Those for whom narratives "mean" or make sense without appeal to "referring" as a category:

1. There are those who think that central biblical narratives, especially the synoptic gospels, resemble a frequently recurring narrative type, most fully embodied in the classic modern novel, i.e., a "realistic" or mimetic kind of text. As texts, especially in the portrayal of the complex interaction of character and plot, they "mean" by their history-likeness, whether or not they reproduce, either in part or in each of their details, something that actually occurred. In other words, whether or not they refer to actual historical events by means of their history-likeness is a matter that is strictly distinguishable from

the sense they make as narrative texts, even if by combined force of style and substance they seem to be characterized by an urgent or imperious claim to truth, and exclusive truth at that. Such truth claims, then, are part of their *sense* and not a matter of their sense turning into reference.[7]

2. There are those who think that narrative texts have constant, universalizable structural features (often but not necessarily always in the form of binary opposition). These features have everything to do with semiotic codes and nothing with the "meaning" or "message" that might be enacted through a text's chronologically, cumulatively narrated, and thus cumulatively realized themes or aims. Understanding such texts also has nothing to do with appeal to the "self" constituted by a universal quality called "understanding," which, as the reader's relation to the narrative, is supposedly a formal prerequisite for discerning the pattern of the narrative (or, for that matter, any other discourse). This phenomenological "subject-object" or "understanding-meaning" correlation as the formal condition of the possibility of reading narrative texts is simply pronounced irrelevant in structuralist theory. The narrative quality of understood experience and the diachronically realized thematic character of narrative are consigned to the same grave. By contrast, folktales, for example, are to be classified according to their repeatable and "deep" structural and not their particular and sequential "surface" features, to say nothing of their affinity to a structure of interpretive consciousness. Application of structural analysis to the plot, for instance, yields a number of such constant features, for example, initial situation, absentation, interdiction addressed to the hero, violation of interdiction, reconnaissance by villain, hero branded, villain defeated, initial misfortune liquidated, and so forth. And that, in essence, is the sort of pattern that constitutes a narrative, though of course some are more complex than others.[8]

3. Most drastic, perhaps most consistent, in arguing that texts do not "refer" are the poststructuralists for whom such views as the mimetic (above, A.1.) and phenomenological (below B.2.) are actually inexorably referential despite themselves, because they depend willy-nilly on an "onto-theology" in which the "signifier" (in this case the narrative itself as semantic configuration) cannot "mean" without a "signified," which is the notion of an absent and therefore of

necessity mediatingly, i.e., verbally re-presented "truth" or ideal possibility which both transcends and enables the verbal configuration. Structuralist reading, on the other hand, fails because it assumes a hidden center—in the text yet external to it (referential?)—which authorizes the orderly, systematic (in effect, the structured) character of the structure. Phenomenological and structuralist readings are illusory for different though related reasons; both impose order on the text, and the order is bound to be taken from elsewhere, whether from an illusory center to the text itself, or from the equally illusory notion of a "signified," a meaning and truth mediately present to understanding.

To cure the disease of onto-theological illusion, it is not enough to reorient verbal or phonetic discourse, which is not only by now but in principle incurably infected with it. "Logos" as the mediating principle in the Western tradition has always meant elevating oral discourse at the expense of the sensory or the letter; speech is the original medium of the illusion of "spirit" which supposedly gives life, whereas the letter supposedly kills. In contrast, one has to set forth the independence of the written text from spoken communication. For that purpose, one has to assert the actual priority of writing over speech. Texts, unlike speech, are not subject to the illusion of "reference"; and they "trace" in an indefinite series or a "durable institution" of inscribed signifiers, within which "meaning" is the "difference" of each signifier from all the others.[9]

B. For those literary theorists who think of narratives as referring, they do not do so as sources, and therefore they refer neither to specific historical occurrences, nor to historical-cultural conditions, nor yet to specific narrative themes that could serve as edifying lessons.

1. For some, narratives are specific reiterations of a number of constant, deep-seated archetypes or structures which together constitute a "self-contained literary universe" or system.[10] Despite the verbal similarity, this is not structuralism, and at least part of the difference is the different logical location of the "structure." In the case of archetypal theory, it is not a function of the text's semiotic arrangement, nor merely of its encoded pattern, but of the writer's access to that archetypal universe which is prior to him or her. That access is not only conscious but pre- or unconscious, so that in writing he does more, he is in touch with the universe that his writing

is about. The text is the medium in which that universe is exhibited. Writing is reference-by-participation, and presumably reading is not wholly different from it. Even though an explicit theory of the self as unconscious participant, related aboriginally to a mythical, archetypal ground, is eschewed by this outlook,[11] it is surely implied by it, and so is a lingering question of the relation between writer and text.[12]

2. For another perspective, usually identified as "phenomenological," an account of a historical sequence contains the same conceptual or logical elements as a fictional narrative: character and plot, "explanation" as part of the narrative rather than independent hypothesis, coherence of temporal sequence and thematic unity, relation of narrative to authorial perspective. In both history and fiction the plot's importance is inseparable from sequence and theme (or "configuration"), in contrast to the structuralists' consignment of plot to achronic deep structures, and sequence and theme to surface manifestation. To this family resemblance (if not more) between the narrative "sense" of historical and fictional sequence, there corresponds a "unity of reference" which is in fact the condition of the possibility of their resemblance in the first place. The "referent" of the text (its "about what" in contrast to its "what" or "sense") is the experience of unity or configuration through temporal sequence. "The references of empirical narrative and fictional narrative," says Paul Ricoeur, "*cross upon* what is provisionally called historicity or the historical condition of man . . . historicity is the form of life correlative to the language-game of narrating."[13] "In this experience of being historical, the subject-object relation is, as it were, undermined. We belong to history before telling stories or writing history. The game of telling is included in the reality told."[14] *De te fabula narratur*—not only morally but ontologically.

"Meaning" is then, after all, a universal category, grounded in an ontological certainty, namely, the experience of understanding that has present within it ("The subject-object relation is, as it were undermined") a true reality to which it is kin. Narrative is only one instance of the intelligible order inhering in every kind of discourse: the semiotic structure (the sign system) is subordinate to the semantic sense (the syntactical unit of the sentence, in which the functions of identification and predication, or subject and predicate, interweave); and, finally, reference "relates language [ideal or semantic sense] to the world. It is another name for discourse's claim to be true."[15] We have here a formal thematic hierarchy, the certainty and unity of which are supplied from the top of the pyramid down, as it were: The self, experiencing the real world with the intimacy of certainty, thereafter expresses that more elemental bond in language.[16] The world so experienced is not dumb or silent before the possessive onslaught of interpretive egotism. Rather, it does its own expressing: the text is its instrument. "If the reference of the text is the project of a world, then it is not the reader who primarily projects himself. The reader rather is enlarged in his capacity of self-projection by receiving a new mode of being from the text itself." The text thus has a disclosing power which is quite "distinct from any kind of ostensive reference," i.e., from any specific or objective "actuality."[17] Narrative, whose reference is the mode of being in the world called historicity, is one such type of text of disclosive power, and a privileged one at that. Biblical narrative is one instance of the general class, a special instance of a hermeneutical generality.[18]

Truth, meaning, presence, experience, selfhood, discourse as the original form of language, meaning as the mediating or making present of absent ontological truth, etc., etc.: It is as though this hermeneutical scheme of meaning-as-referential-understanding, and the deconstructionist denial of all referentiality (above, A.3) were exactly fitted out for mutual combat. And so they were; and there is no reason why Hamlet and Laertes may not wound each other mortally on their bloodless dueling ground. As long as each—the one in the assertion, the other in the denial, of certainty through reference to a reality enhancing the privileged position of the interpreting self—is taken as a kind of universal and foundational theory for reading any and all kinds of texts, including narratives, the outcome may be a fatal draw.[19]

C. Finally, there are those, chiefly followers of Wittgenstein, who rule out participation in the argument over meaning-and-reference. They do not take "meaning" to be a single term in relation to any text, nor do they take it to be one pole of a indissoluble correlation called "meaning-and-understanding." Just as they do not think of "understanding" as a universalizable inner process or event, so they do not think of "meaning" as its ideal objective counterpart, at once universal and unique, e.g., "disclosure of a mode of being in the world."

Neither phenomenologists on the one hand, nor sympathetic to the structuralists' and deconstructionists' elimination of the concept "person" from textual reading, they believe that "understanding" a text is more nearly an ability to use it appropriately in specific contexts (and the appropriate skill of judgment about whether or not to activate that capacity) than to know the rules for proper "interpretation." To construe the text properly is part of learning the requisite conceptual skills. To understand concepts is to have the ability both to explicate and to apply them, without necessarily resorting to a theory that would indicate how to couple the two.[20] In the case of the Bible, this finally cannot be done without learning how to use the Bible, including its narratives, within the church and as its canon, i.e., as authoritative "in the coincidence of letter and spirit."[21]

IV. "NARRATIVITY" AND THEOLOGY

No Christian reflection on the biblical narratives, no matter how technical, is apt to ignore the connections between those narratives and the focus of Christian identity they helped shape over the centuries. The variety of theoretical views at which we have looked has one persuasion in common: in the interaction of text and reader, the specificity of the narrative text, its literal sense if you will, is not to be ignored, no matter in what way the reader may find (s)he adjusts to it. There may well be an affinity, structural, moral, aesthetic, between reader and text. On the other hand there may not be. The conditions for a proper reading of biblical narratives may be quite accessible, even if one fails to discover such a general type of affinity, especially a structural affinity. One result of such ambiguity as to whether or not there is such an affinity is that some of the theories concerning the narrative texts of the Bible may prove quite inept with regard to the formation of Christian identity. They may give us a very different kind of reading. Still, in either event it will be a "reading."

The difference between a textually focused inquiry, working with the specificity of the narratives, and a more generally focused one, for which the biblical narratives are an illustration or illumination of "narrativity" as an elemental aspect of being human and of human experience, is not absolute. But it is important. The "hermeneutical" (or anti- or non-hermeneutical) instruments we have looked at have been shaped toward the text, even in the case of phenomenological theory. Consequently, if they make a contribution toward the definition of the shape(s) of Christian identity, it will be derivative, i.e., "text-bound."

There is, however, something else called "narrative theology." I take it that this exercise proceeds from a conviction and analysis of human nature in general and/or religion in general. It is almost invariably—covertly or overtly—a theory that texts are variable, written instances that really express a fixed, universal, and interiorized personal condition of consciousness. It is to this specimen-in-motion that the above-mentioned term "narrativity" is applied. Whether it is our personal history or autobiography, or a more general, perhaps archetypal story, the "recital" of it constitutes (a) the condition for the meaningfulness of biblical narrative, and (b) the description of the coincidence between divine influence (Spirit?) and human/Christian identity. The latter, (b), is the new shape of that liberal/neo-orthodox doctrine of revelation which used to be portrayed on the model of I-thou encounter. The coincidence of the recital of one's own story with the recital of a "disclosive" or "reinterpretive" moment in the paradigmatic story—usually that of Jesus on the cross—is the equivalent of revelation-as-event. Whatever the merits of this enterprise, it is quite different from an inquiry into the conditions for reading the narrative texts of the Bible as *texts*—and from any theology that would find the latter a "foundational" task.

NOTES

1. See Robert E. Scholes and Robert Kellogg, *The Nature of Narrative* (New York, 1966), 50ff.

2. See Mircea Eliade, *Patterns in Comparative Religion* (Cleveland, 1958), ch. 1, *inter multa, multa alia*. On the distinction between "folktale" and "myth," see Northrop Frye, *The Great Code* (New York: Harcourt Brace Jovanovich, 1982), 31ff.

3. For a striking, not untypical example see Jean Starobinski, "An Essay in Literary Analysis—Mark 5:1–20," *The Ecumenical Review* 23 (1971): 377–97.

4. See Frank Kermode, *The Genesis of Secrecy* (Cambridge, Mass: Harvard University Press, 1979), viii.

5. See, e.g., Frank Kermode, *The Genesis of Secrecy*; also Kermode, "On Being an Enemy of Humanity," *Raritan* 2, no. 2, (Fall 1982): 99f. Kermode's work, it should be added, is important because he uses historical-critical biblical scholarship skillfully for the purpose of displacing it, and with it the whole of the literal tradition in interpretation, from its hitherto central hermeneutical position.

6. See Wayne A. Meeks, *The First Urban Christians* (New Haven, Conn.: Yale University Press, 1983), ch. 6.

7. Cf. Erich Auerbach, *Mimesis: The Representation of Reality in Western Literature* (Princeton, N.J.: Princeton University Press, 1953); H. W. Frei, *The Eclipse of Biblical Narrative* (New Haven, Conn.: Yale University Press, 1974).

8. Cf. Vladimir Propp, *Morphology of the Folktale* (Austin: University of Texas Press, 1968); Roland Barthes, "Introduction to the Structural Analysis of Narratives," *Image-Music-Text* (New York: Hill & Wang, 1977), 79–124.

9. See Jacques Derrida, *Of Grammatology* (Baltimore: Johns Hopkins University Press, 1976); *Writing and Difference* (Chicago: University of Chicago Press, 1978).

10. Northrop Frye, *The Anatomy of Criticism* (Princeton: Princeton University Press, 1957), 118.

11. Cf. Northrop Frye, *The Great Code*, 48, where he calls C. G. Jung's use of archetype "idiosyncratic."

12. For this perspective, see Northrop Frye, *The Anatomy of Criticism*; *The Great Code*.

13. Paul Ricoeur, "The Narrative Function," *Hermeneutics and the Human Sciences* (New York: Cambridge University Press, 1981), 289.

14. Ibid., 294.

15. Paul Ricoeur, *Interpretation Theory: Discourse and the Surplus of Meaning* (Fort Worth: Texas Christian University Press, 1976), 20.

16. Ibid., 21.

17. Ibid., 94.

18. Cf. on all this Paul Ricoeur, "The Narrative Function," *Hermeneutics and the Human Sciences*, 274–96; *Interpretation Theory: Discourse and the Surplus of Meaning*; also *The Rule of Metaphor*, Appendix (Toronto: University of Toronto Press, 1977); *Essays on Biblical Interpretation* (Philadelphia: Fortress, 1980).

19. For some pertinent remarks about the topic of the founded certainty or the certain foundation of meaning, in connection with Husserl and Derrida, see John R. Searle, "The World Turned Upside Down," *The New York Review of Books* 30, no. 16 (October 27, 1983) especially 77–78.

20. See Charles Wood, *The Formation of Christian Understanding* (Philadelphia, 1981), 58, 64ff.

21. Ibid., 109. For this perspective, besides Wood, see David H. Kelsey, *The Uses of Scripture in Recent Theology* (Philadelphia: Fortress, 1975).

IDENTITY AND DIFFERENCE:
THE ECUMENICAL PROBLEM

Michael Root

Robert Benchley once entitled a book *Twenty Thousand Leagues under the Sea, or David Copperfield*. George Lindbeck's *The Nature of Doctrine: Religion and Theology in a Postliberal Age* is a less extreme case of the title and subtitle of a book apparently looking in different directions.[1] The title promises a book about doctrine, the normative teaching of the church. The subtitle focuses on the contextual problem of theology in the late twentieth century. The book is, of course, both: it is an analysis of the nature of normative teaching in the church and a proposal for a particular understanding of the task and method of theology in the face of the demise of a liberal hegemony. The extensive reactions to Lindbeck's book have tended to focus on the subject matter of the subtitle. The analysis of the nature of doctrine, the fruit of Lindbeck's sacrificial dedication to the goal of ecumenical reconciliation, is often treated as an adjunct to the discussion of a postliberal theology.[2] Yet Lindbeck states that the context within which he has thought out his more explicitly theological proposal has been the doctrinal discussion within ecumenical dialogues (p. 7).

In this essay I want to develop further the ecumenical usefulness of Lindbeck's analysis. I will do this, not through a direct discussion of the book, but by applying some of Lindbeck's ideas to a contemporary ecumenical problem. If imitation is the sincerest form of flattery, then I hope Professor Lindbeck will consider this appropriation of his analysis for the ecumenical cause the sincerest form of respect.

IDENTITY AND DIFFERENCE
AS ECUMENICAL PROBLEMS

On the first page of *The Nature of Doctrine*, Lindbeck identifies an ecumenical frustration that lies behind his writing: "We are often unable, for example, to specify the criteria we implicitly employ when we say that some changes are faithful to a doctrinal tradition and others unfaithful, or some doctrinal differences are church-dividing and others not" (p. 7). Lindbeck's complaint is echoed by representatives of the Christian World Communions in a 1979 review of ecumenical dialogues. Among questions requiring further clarification, it included, "How can it be decided whether different expressions of faith are truly expressions of the same faith?"[3]

In both cases, the problem concerns criteria of identity: On what basis do we say that a change has altered the identity of the faith given once for all time? On what basis do we say that the difference between ourselves and some other group is such that we are nevertheless still witnessing to the same gospel and worshipping the same Lord? By "identity" I mean nothing more than identifiability across space and time as "the same thing," in some contextually specified sense of "same."[4] My desk has an identity; today I am working at the same desk at which I was working yesterday. The two desks are numerically identical. But identity statements can be used more broadly. One might say of two different cocker spaniels that they are both cocker spaniels. There is an identity that encompasses them both. Though not numerically identical, there is a context in which I can say they are the same: they are the same breed.

Correlated with the concept of identity as applied to my desk and to cocker spaniels is the concept of difference. If I discover that the desk in my office is not the same desk as was there yesterday, I would say, "This is a different desk." Similarly, after talking of my cocker spaniels, I would say of a dachshund: "That is a different breed of dog." In each case, I would be dealing with a difference that was incompatible with the relevant identity. Not all differences are incompatible with identity. My desk today may have a scratch in it not present yesterday. But if I discover that the scratch came from a fight in my office between a night watchman and a burglar, then this difference in no way affects my judgment that I still have the same desk. Similarly, two cocker spaniels will be different in various ways which do not destroy their identity as cocker spaniels.

Issues of identity are an important concern of both theology and ecumenics. More particularly, both are concerned with the Christian identity of a particular statement, action, or community. An explicitly Christian theology seeks to articulate the Christian faith. In the process, it must have some criteria for differentiating the Christian faith from other faiths, some means for identifying the "Christian."[5] Ecumenical discussions are more explicitly concerned with the identity of the church. Virtually all churches confess that there is only one church, constituted by the one mission given by the risen Christ to the Apostles. Christian communities simultaneously existing in New York, Harare, and Fiji are all one church. The church of Paul, of Aquinas, of Bonhoeffer, and to which Christ will return is the same church. There is thus an identity that binds the church together.

From very early on, however, the unity of this one church has been disturbed by disputes in which some participants judge that the identity of the church *as church* is at stake.[6] Some in the dispute judge that if a particular course of action is followed (ordain outside of episcopal succession, preach that grace makes us merit eternal life, baptize infants), the church will lose something essential to its identity. If such a dispute is not settled, and if some communities carry out the disputed action, then a division occurs. Communities concluding that this action destroys something essential to the church's identity are to some degree divided from those which carry out this action. They cannot understand the two sides of the difference as both fully encompassed in a single ecclesial identity. A disagreement over what at least one side of a dispute considers constitutive of the identity of the church then becomes what has been called a church-dividing difference.[7]

The ecumenical movement in the twentieth century has been driven by the sense that many differences judged to be church-dividing in the past need be so no longer. If the churches have one Lord, if they confess one faith, and if they celebrate one baptism, then they are one church in the theologically most important sense. This ecclesial identity should be the decisive factor in the relations among the churches.

The explosion of ecumenical dialogues following the Second Vatican Council seemed to confirm this sense of identity. Again and again, representatives of differing traditions found an identity in the faith confessed, even if the one faith is confessed in differing ways. As a result, they claimed that church-dividing differences no longer separated the involved communities.[8] But what is the nature of a church-dividing difference and how are we to either discover or decide whether a particular difference is or is not church-dividing? These are the questions that will occupy this essay.

CHURCH-DIVIDING DIFFERENCES

When does a difference within the life of the church so threaten its identity as church that separation is preferable to compromise? This question is not new. It was implicit, for example, in Reformation debates about what is necessary for the unity of the church. One answer is given in the Augsburg Confession: "For it is sufficient for the true unity of the Christian church that the Gospel be preached in conformity with a pure understanding of it and that the sacraments be administered in accordance with the divine Word."[9] Conversely, a church-dividing difference must concern whether some preaching is in accord with a pure understanding of the gospel or whether some sacramental practice is in accord with the divine word. This definition thus provides some criteria for deciding whether a difference is church-dividing. For example, if a difference is over "ceremonies instituted by men," then it is not church dividing.[10] Church-dividing differences all concern differences over the preaching of the gospel and the administration of the sacraments. But what criteria are to be applied to distinguish issues that concern the gospel from issues that do not?

The adiaphora controversy that broke out immediately following Luther's death concerns just this question: how does one recognize in a specific situation an adiaphoron, i.e., a matter that does not involve the church's relation to the gospel and so not a matter over which the church potentially should be divided.[11] In addition, even when the gospel is clearly the subject of dispute, are all differences church-dividing? Is the *slightest* deviation from what one understands to be the right understanding of the gospel to be understood as "not being in accord" with the gospel? What criteria distinguish church-dividing differences over the proclamation of the gospel or the administration of the sacraments from non-church-dividing ones?

A similar set of questions can arise about Roman Catholic definitions of heresy. All heresy involves a "falling away from the unity of the church's faith."[12] But how is heresy to be recognized? Roman Catholic canon law states that heresy involves the "denial of some truth which must be believed with divine and catholic faith."[13] Unless one is dealing with the explicit rejection of an explicitly defined dogma, how does one recognize such a denial of such a truth?[14]

Surprisingly, the question of the criteria for recognizing church-dividing differences has received little attention in ecumenical dialogues.[15] For the most part ecumenical dialogues have not set out to establish that some differences are church-dividing but rather to deny that a particular difference need divide the churches. In the process, dialogues have tended to focus on particular theological problems, e.g., the Lord's Supper or ordained ministry, rather than on the more theoretical question of the nature and criteria of church-dividing differences. As Lindbeck notes, various criteria have been implicit in the concrete discussion of church-dividing differences in ecumenical documents, but they are not made explicit nor extensively reflected on.[16]

This statement can be verified by looking at one of the best ecumenical dialogue documents, the Common Statement on Justification by Faith produced by the Lutheran-Roman Catholic dialogue in the U.S.[17] A variety of analyses are carried out and criteria applied. Most significantly, it concludes, "In view of the convergences to which we now turn, theological disagreements about structures of thought in relation to the proclamation of the gospel, though serious, need not be church-dividing" (§154). The remaining differences in theological outlook are to be judged non-church-dividing because they are embedded in a wider or deeper set of convergences. These convergences seem to be a criterion for judging the remaining differences non-church-dividing and are summarized in a "fundamental affirmation": "Our entire hope of justification and salvation rests on Christ Jesus and on the gospel whereby the good news of God's merciful action in Christ is made known; we do not place our ultimate trust in anything other than God's promise and saving work in Christ" (§157, also §4). The joint affirmation of this statement is taken as a sign of an identity in faith: "But where the affirmation is accepted, Lutherans and Catholics can recognize each other as sharing a commitment to the same gospel of redemptive love received in faith" (§159). This agreement is described as "a fundamental consensus on the gospel" (§164). The international Roman Catholic/Lutheran Joint Commission more explicitly indicates that a (the?) criterion for judging whether a particular difference is church-dividing is the existence of a wider agreement on the nature of the gospel: "At the same time it [dialogue] should both clarify and make certain that remaining differences are based on a fundamental consensus in understanding the apostolic faith and *therefore* [*somit*] are legitimate."[18]

We have here a criterion of church-dividing differences developed within the dialogues. Differences are not church-dividing if there also exists a more basic agreement on the gospel. Without further elaboration, however, this criterion will not help us much. How do we distinguish a consensus which can serve as such a criterion from other sorts of consensus? The metaphors involved in terms such as "basic" and "fundamental" are useless unless we can state what makes a particular consensus more basic or fundamental than some related difference. To respond that a consensus sufficient for the unity of the church is a consensus on the important or fundamental aspects of the gospel only replaces one problem with another. When can we say, "We now have *sufficient* agreement on the *appropriate* topics"? To what does one appeal in justifying a judgment that a consensus has been reached that is sufficient for the unity of the church? Unfortunately, this question has been addressed no more directly than the question of how to recognize a church-dividing difference.[19]

We should not be surprised that a certain sort of consensus can serve as an indicator that differences are not church-dividing. "Church-dividing difference" and "consensus sufficient for unity" are mutually defining concepts. A church-dividing difference is one that is incompatible with a consensus sufficient for unity, and a consensus sufficient for unity is one that excludes all church-dividing differences. Such reciprocal definition of terms means that a criterion that will help us identify one will also help us identify the other. Nevertheless, we still do not have such a criterion.

Before trying to specify such a criterion, we need to ask whether such a criterion is actually needed. Are the questions raised above only the expression of a longing for "method," for some ecumenical algorithm that can settle questions of identity and difference definitively and coercively? One must be wary of such longings. The identification of criteria will not obviate the need for judgment nor exclude disagreements over their application. Nevertheless, contemporary ecumenical discussion suffers from the lack of the sort of explicit criteria sought here. We have noted Lindbeck's comment on the need for more explicit criteria within the dialogues themselves.[20] The need is even greater in the public debates that surround the reception of the dialogues by the churches. Harding Meyer states:

> This lack of a clear idea of the meaning of consensus in the context of ecumenical effort becomes painfully evident at the very latest when we come to the question of receiving the agreements reached. . . . That is why we are repeatedly confronted in the present reception process with such questions as the following: Are the dialogue results proposed for reception really "consensus" in the true meaning of the term? Or are they not just immature forms of consensus still awaiting the transition to "genuine" consensus? Are we not dealing here with no more than "convergences" falling short of "full" consensus? Are we not still in the realm of provisional and even superficial agreements which leave still unfathomed and yet unsolved the real depths of confessional differences and church division?[21]

Ecumenical agreement on previously church-dividing issues can be challenged in at least two ways. On the one hand, the agreement itself can be criticized as merely verbal or achieved at the cost of denying certain important communal beliefs. On the other hand, the claimed agreement can be accepted, but the assertion that the remaining differences are not church-dividing can be challenged. It is this latter objection which Meyer describes. To what does one appeal in a debate over such a challenge? Without some answer to this question, the debate is unfocused and can easily stray from substantive matters.

DOCTRINES AS RULES

Can we state more exactly what a church-dividing difference (or a consensus sufficient for unity) is? Many, though perhaps not all, church-dividing differences are over matters of what is usually called doctrine.[22] Thus, the doctrine of Christ's two natures was involved in the separation of the Oriental Orthodox churches from Eastern Orthodox and Catholic churches. The doctrine of justification through faith alone was important for divisions in the Western church. The doctrine of the Lord's Supper separated Lutheran and Reformed. Just as church-dividing differences have usually been in relation to doctrine, so most ecumenical dialogues have centered on doctrinal matters. But what is a doctrine? Here we will turn to Lindbeck for help.[23]

Lindbeck proposes a cultural-linguistic theory of religion and a rule theory of doctrine. His cultural-linguistic understanding of religion is not presented as a new achievement but as the common view of religion in the social sciences, suggested in particular by the anthropologist Clifford Geertz and the sociologist Peter Berger. For such a cultural-linguistic understanding, religions are "comprehensive interpretive schemes, usually embodied in myths or narratives and heavily ritualized, which structure human experience and understanding of self and world" (p. 32). A religion is more like an encompassing culture or language within which or in terms of which one acts, thinks, and feels, than it is like any group of propositions within, or experiences in terms of, that culture or language: "A comprehensive scheme or story used to structure all dimensions of existence is not primarily a set of propositions to be believed, but is rather the medium in which one moves, a set of skills that one employs in living one's life" (p. 35). Lindbeck's colleague William Christian similarly states that what a religion proposes is a "pattern of life." This pattern is composed of, among other things, "beliefs, valuations, and courses of action. . . . By way of precepts, backed by accounts of how the world is, by way of examples, pointing to individuals whose lives have manifested and defined the pattern concretely, and by way of direct induction of its members into certain practices and habituation in those practices, a community aims at shaping the lives of its members. It instills habits of appreciation, of overt behavior, and of thought, which hang together as a more or less coherent pattern of life."[24]

"Doctrine" is then defined by its function within this total pattern. Doctrines for Lindbeck are not what a religion teaches about

God or the world (what William Christian calls primary doctrines). They are not a part of the first-order discourse of a religion. Doctrines as doctrines are a form of second-order discourse, talk about talk (or at least about significant action). Doctrines are not directly about God, humanity, etc., but about the church's talk about God, humanity, etc. For example, the texts from Nicaea and Chalcedon as doctrine are not directly descriptive of Jesus. Rather they describe the sort of language that Christians should use in describing Jesus, e.g., that all attributes necessarily implied by the predicate "human" must be ascribed to Jesus. What Lindbeck calls simply "doctrine," William Christian calls "governing doctrines," i.e., "what the community has to say to itself about its [primary] doctrines."[25] In this respect, doctrines are similar to grammatical rules or the rules of a game. Grammatical rules are not about the world;[26] they are about talk, which can be about the world. The rules of a game are not the playing of the game; they regulate how the game should be played. Doctrines *as doctrines* are about how Christian life, thought, and talk should be carried out. Lindbeck thus states, "The function of church doctrines that becomes most prominent in this perspective is their use, not as expressive symbols or as truth claims, but as communally authoritative rules of discourse, attitude, and action" (p. 18).

Lindbeck's proposal strikes many as odd. When one looks at the christological definition of Chalcedon, it looks like a statement about the two natures of Christ, i.e., it looks like talk about Christ, not talk about talk about Christ. In fact, almost all the texts we would be inclined to call "doctrinal statements" seem, at first glance, to be examples of first-order Christian discourse. Lindbeck denies neither this appearance nor its truth. The christological definition of Chalcedon *is* an example of first-order language about Christ. But *as such* it is not a doctrine. It is a doctrine when it plays a certain function in the life of the church, ruling certain christological language in, ruling other christological language out. Rather than saying the definition of Chalcedon is a doctrine, it would be more correct to say that it becomes a doctrine when used in certain ways.

Most doctrinal texts or statements are, like the Chalcedon definition, less rules than examples of a rule well followed. They are paradigms from which a ruled practice is to be derived (p. 81).[27]

Thus, the Nicene and Chalcedonian texts must undergo significant analysis from Lindbeck before they offer up rules phrased as rules.[28] Nevertheless, Lindbeck's analysis seeks to lay bare what has in fact been done with these texts when they have functioned as doctrine. Thus, Lindbeck's proposal to understand doctrines as rules is first descriptive. It seeks to explain the way doctrines have in fact functioned in the life of the church. In his analysis of the rules implied in the doctrinal use of the Nicene and Chalcedonian statements, he is seeking to make explicit the rules implicit in the way the paradigm has been used.[29]

Lindbeck's understanding of doctrines as rules reinforces an aspect of William Christian's analysis. What a rule governs is an action. Grammatical rules, for example, govern linguistic actions: talking, writing, thinking in a particular language. Doctrinal rules govern actions carried out in relation to a particular religion. The actions may be entirely cerebral: "When you think about Jesus, think about him in this way . . . ." Nevertheless, that to which a rule applies is a human activity. Doctrines are not disembodied propositions, nor expressions of agentless experiences. They are rules of procedure for specific actions carried out by specific communities.

For Lindbeck, then, doctrinal agreement constitutes an agreement to have one's relevant actions governed by certain rules. To accept the Chalcedonian doctrine is to agree that whatever predicates we find inseparable from the terms "God" and "humanity" we will ascribe in a certain way to the integral person Jesus Christ. We can be in agreement in relation to this doctrine even if we disagree what those predicates are. The rule does not commit us to any particular christology. Doctrinal disagreement would be a disagreement over some rule which governs the pattern of life which a religion proposes.

DOCTRINES AND IDENTITY

If doctrines are rules of the sort Lindbeck describes, then what would a church-dividing difference over doctrine be, and how would one differentiate church-dividing from non-church-dividing differences? As noted earlier, a church-dividing difference is one that threatens the identity of the church as church. If two communities understand themselves to be church without qualification, then they cannot be divided as church if the church is one. Division can only be justified by a threat to the church's identity as church. A church-dividing difference over doctrine would thus exist when some persons believe that a particular doctrine or doctrinal proposal is not simply mistaken, but threatens the church's identity.

As noted above, if doctrines are understood as rules, then they are to be most directly related to activities: verbal, liturgical, etc. A difference over doctrine then becomes church-dividing when some persons think that having the activity of the church governed by a certain rule will compromise the church's identity. A firmer grasp on the nature of such a dispute requires a detour into more general considerations of the connections between the identity of an activity and rules which relate to it.

The identity of an activity is not as clearly defined as that of a person or material object and has not received the same degree of philosophical attention. Yet in everyday talk we use identity language in connection with activities without difficulty. The participants in a chess tournament are playing the same game. Speakers of English are speaking the same language. The activity of playing chess or speaking English is spoken of as an identity; the activity is identifiable across space and time as doing the same thing.

To be identifiable across space and time, an activity must have recurring characteristics, usually found in a certain pattern. One aspect of the patterning of many complex activities are rules which guide the activity into its identifying pattern. In this way, such rules can be closely interrelated with an activity's identity. With a chessboard and a chess set, one can play either chess or checkers. We cannot play chess without following the rules of chess. If we consistently break a sufficiently large and significant set of rules, at some point one would say we are no longer playing chess. The identity of the game we are playing as "chess" requires that the rules of chess for the most part be followed.[30]

In certain situations, a particular rule can be decisive for the identity of an activity. At a track meet, the difference between walking and running is specified by certain rules. If competitors do not keep one foot in contact with the ground at all times, they have ceased to walk and have begun to run. The identity of walking as distinct from running is specified by this and other rules. To break the rules is to engage in some activity other than walking. In the context of a track meet, this identity-specifying rule is important. If I enter the 1500 meter walk, but do not follow the rules that specify walking, I will be disqualified. One could rightly say, "He wasn't really walking." In this case, the identity of walking is inseparable from the rules that distinguish it from running. One needs to note, however, that not all rules so directly specify the identity of an activity. Take, for example, the activity "speaking English." The rules of standard English do not specify a second person plural pronoun distinct from the second person singular pronoun. Both are "you." English as spoken colloquially in the American South, however, does permit a distinctive second person plural pronoun, "y'all." There thus exists a difference in grammatical rules between standard English and English as spoken colloquially in the South. Yet it would be odd to say that this difference alone means that when I am writing this article in standard English and when I am speaking colloquially with other Southerners, I am using two different languages.

These two cases illustrate two important characteristics of the identity of activities. First, the identity of an activity is specified within some context and for some purpose. We distinguish the identity of an activity to the degree that the situation demands. Outside of a track meet, we rarely specify the identity of walking in any detail; we have no need to do so. The context of the track meet creates a need to specify more exactly the identity of different activities. Second, the specification of the identity of an activity is an ongoing process. As contexts change and human creativity alters actions, questions can arise about the continuing identity of an activity. Pragmatically, some of these questions may require an answer, perhaps in the form of new identity-specifying rules. The identities of most important human activities are constantly being respecified.[31]

This interrelation of rule and identity illuminates the nature of church-dividing differences and consensus sufficient for unity. A potentially church-dividing difference is a difference over some action which some persons think would compromise the identity of the church as church. A doctrine is a rule to govern this action so that it will (negatively put) not compromise the church's identity or (positively put) specify the church's identity in this aspect of its life. If in the face of a potentially church-dividing difference an agreement on a rule to govern the activity cannot be worked out, a division or separation in the church results.

Conversely, a consensus sufficient for unity in relation to a particular doctrine would be a consensus on the rule implicit in the doctrine as (negatively put) compatible with the identity of the church or (positively put) as specifying the identity of the church in a particular aspect of its life. A consensus on doctrine is thus a consensus on the characteristics a specific action must display to be compatible with the identity of the church. There need be no consensus on other characteristics the action might display.

A comprehensive doctrinal consensus (what might appropriately be called a "fundamental consensus") would be a comprehensive agreement on the rules presently needed to specify the identity of the church as church. Such a consensus would be sufficient for full unity, communion, or fellowship between two churches, or rather, for the full unity of the one church.

This understanding of the nature of ecumenical difference and consensus needs to be protected against a possible misunderstanding. Its focus on the identity of activities must not be taken as an abandonment of a concern for truth or of the traditional conceptual concerns of doctrinal theology. It only gives them a particular focus in the context of ecumenical dialogue. In addition, activity here must be taken to include such verbal activities as preaching and teaching. Even here, doctrine will have the character of a rule directed at an activity (e.g., in speaking of the presence of Christ in the Eucharistic elements, do not compromise the continuing identity of the bread as bread and wine as wine). Lindbeck's attack on the idea of a religiously meaningful yet prelinguistic level of experience would apply also to any attempt to find an agreement at a level of action religiously meaningful yet somehow independent of its inherence in a particular cultural-linguistic whole.[32]

Does this specification of the nature of church-dividing difference and consensus sufficient for unity cast any light on ecumenical discussions? Are there advantages in thinking about difference and consensus in these terms?[33] Let me here note one aspect of ecumenical dialogues that becomes more understandable. Ecclesiology has played a central role in ecumenical discussions. Why it has and must play a central role should now be apparent. Since in an ecumenical discussion, the concern is always the relation between the immediate topic and the identity of the church as church, ecclesiology is always an accompanying theme. Ecclesiology plays a normative role in determining the ecumenical adequacy of results. Whatever the immediate topic, one is always asking, What sort of agreement in this area is needed for the unity of the one church and has such an agreement been reached? The task of ecumenical dialogue inevitably means that ecclesiology will play there a greater role than it does in many other forms of theological discussion. This prominence of ecclesiology in ecumenical discussions need not imply ecclesiastical narcissism. The judgments made in a dialogue may imply a narcissistic and self-glorifying ecclesiology, but they may also imply a mission-oriented ecclesiology. The prominence of ecclesiology may show only that the dialogue has understood its task and sought to carry it out.

The normative character of ecclesiology within ecumenical discussions also explains some of the difficulties in adjudicating ecumenical disputes. A decisive element in deciding whether a difference is church-dividing is one's judgment about the relation between the issue at hand and the identity of the church. Behind any particular judgment about the relation of an issue and the identity of the church will stand a comprehensive sense of what makes the church the church, a comprehensive sense of the church's identity. This comprehensive sense will operate as what David Kelsey calls a *discrimen*, "a configuration of criteria that are in some way organically related to one another as reciprocal coefficients."[34] It is a synthetic imaginative judgment, pulling together many elements used as discrete criteria in particular situations into a relatively unified vision of the nature of the church.

This comprehensive sense will inevitably be the sort of synthetic imaginative construal which is not beyond rational argumentation but which also is relatively immune from decisive criticism by any single argument and involves an irreducible element of imagination. Ecumenical differences rooted in different imaginative construals of what makes the church the church can thus be exceedingly difficult to settle. Conversely, ecumenical progress can be aided by the development of new construals of the identity of the church, which make possible new understanding of differences and their significance. A careful concern with ecclesiology is thus not simply an inevitable, if perhaps regrettable, aspect of ecumenical discussion but also a means of furthering the visible unity of the church.

DOCTRINES AND THE RECOGNITION
OF DIFFERENCE AND IDENTITY

I have identified what a church-dividing difference and a consensus sufficient for unity would be for a rule theory of doctrine. Nevertheless, little specific has been said yet about the criteria for recognition of a church-dividing difference or a consensus sufficient for unity. What has been said will clarify some rather obvious cases of church-dividing differences. If some persons believe that it is an aspect of the identity of the church as church that it be in communion with the episcopal successor of Peter, then the straightforward rejection of any form of that claim will be a church-dividing difference.[35] Such cases, however, are not the problem. The problem arises in cases where, in relation to a question which has been church-dividing in the past, an agreement on some but not all aspects of the question is reached. Is this agreement a consensus sufficient for unity, or are there remaining church-dividing differences? The preceding discussion makes clear that there can be no "method" in the sense of a means of calculation which will obviate the need for personal judgment. The role of an imaginative sense of the identity of the church rules out any such possibility. But can we specify more precise tests which can give some focus to our judgments?

A test follows from what has been said so far. As noted, a church-dividing difference is simply a difference incompatible with a consensus sufficient for unity. If one can ascertain whether a consensus sufficient for unity exists, then one can ascertain whether a church-dividing difference exists. We have already seen how this interrelation was used as a criterion by both the American and international Lutheran-Roman Catholic dialogues.

Above, "consensus sufficient for unity" in relation to a particular doctrine was defined as a consensus on the rule implicit in the doctrine as compatible with, or as specifying the identity of, the church in a particular aspect of its life. A consensus on the Lord's Supper, for example, is sufficient for unity if those involved can agree on how the activities related to the Supper should be ruled so that they may realize the identity of the church as church. How would we know whether we have reached such an agreement? A straightforward test would be: Can we perform *together* the actions related to the Lord's Supper regularly and in a comprehensive range of situations without violating our understandings of the identity of the church? If we can, then remaining differences do not divide us at the level of the identity of the church as church.[36]

The nature of this test needs to be elaborated. First, performing an act *together* does not imply that all involved do exactly the same thing. Rather, we can perform an act together if we all can participate in the act. Different persons may participate in different ways. Such participation will often require extensive agreement on which aspects of the act are mandatory (e.g., in every Eucharist, the Words of Institution are to be said), which are permitted but not mandatory (e.g., the consecrated Host may but need not be elevated), and which are unacceptable (e.g., a Eucharist is never to include animal sacrifice). The middle stipulation covers cases in which persons may be willing to accept as compatible with the identity of the church someone else carrying out an action that they themselves would refuse to carry out.[37] Such a detailed agreement is necessary, however, only to the degree required for a common performance of the activity. Perhaps, in some cases, whether an aspect of an act is mandatory or merely permissible can be left undecided.[38] Thus, "together" does not imply a uniformity in how the act is done or in how different persons are involved in the act. It does imply, however, an agreement on the acceptable range of diversity and differentiated involvement.

Second, "regularly and in a comprehensive range of situations" implies that the test is whether the act can be performed together in the full range of reasonably expectable situations and not just in special cases. This requirement means that we are not concerned with what can be tolerated on rare or special occasions but with what is found generally acceptable.[39]

Third, the test is not whether performing the activities together violates one's understanding of how the activities should best be done or even of whether they should be done at all. The question is whether the way they could be performed together violates one's understanding of the identity of the church. One may think the action in question is unnecessary, inappropriate, or foolish. One may contend that if one were compelled to perform it, such compulsion would violate one's understanding of the identity of the church. But if agreement can be reached on how it *can* be performed together without violating one's understanding of the identity of the church, then the differences that remain, however significant, cannot be church-dividing.

If this test can be met, then one has achieved in relation to the issue at hand a consensus sufficient for the unity of the church. If one believes, however, that remaining differences are church-dividing, one should be able to specify what action cannot be performed together without violating one's understanding of the identity of the church.

The same test can be applied to the broader question of whether there exists a comprehensive consensus sufficient for full unity, communion, or fellowship between two churches. Can they perform together regularly and in a comprehensive range of situations the activities either considers essential to the identity of the church as church without violating either's understanding of the identity of the church? If so, then the differences that remain cannot be church-dividing, for they do not in practice affect those activities which are essential to the church's identity as church and thus its unity. A consensus exists capable of bearing all remaining differences.

When an agreement that can pass this test has been reached, to insist on greater agreement as necessary for the unity of the one church is not only unnecessary, but it is undesirable. It becomes the suppression of legitimate diversity. Without some such a test, however, there is a tendency to press for maximal consensus in ecumenical agreements, consensus on all theological topics considered in some way important.[40] Anything less appears as "lowest common denominator ecumenism." In reaction, impossible goals are set for ecumenical discussion. This situation can be avoided only if one sees that a consensus sufficient for unity is not so much a particular *degree* of agreement but a particular *kind* of agreement. Agreement on the rules of chess is not a "lower" level of agreement than agreement on the best end-game strategy. It is a different kind of agreement. Agreement on the doctrinal norms that specify the identity of preaching as *Christian* preaching will not and should not specify precisely what is preached. Agreement on precisely what should be preached is a different sort of agreement. Without a clearer sense of the sort of agreement a "consensus sufficient for unity" is, any ecumenical proposal is vulnerable to the accusation that it is somehow not true or complete consensus. The primary advantage of a clearer sense of the nature of ecumenical difference and consensus and of the criteria for their recognition is the aid they can give an ecumenical discussion in knowing when to stop.[41] The criterion or test here recommended is oriented toward practice, in the widest sense of the term.[42] Such an orientation has significant implications for ecumenical discussions. First, it orients discussion toward those aspects of a controverted topic that have been important for the life of the church. For example, a divisive topic between Catholics and Protestants has been that of purgatory. An application of the recommended test would ask, what can we not do together because of our disagreement on purgatory? Obviously, we cannot speak together about the fate of many of the dead. But is the inability to speak together on this subject in itself church-dividing? An analysis of Reformation texts quickly shows that the issue was rather different. In the Smalcald Articles, for example, when the subject of purgatory is raised, Luther immediately addresses the related practice he finds incompatible with the identity of the church, namely, works performed to aid those in purgatory.[43] Participation in this activity Luther finds unacceptable; it violates the identity of the church as a community in which salvation is strictly a gift. Applying the test here recommended would direct the discussion to the more ecumenically significant point, the relation between the church in purgatory and the church on earth.

The American Lutheran/Catholic statement on justification, in fact, applies something like the test here recommended. The thematic statement quoted above from §4 and §157 shows an agreement in an area of Christian life crucial for the doctrine of justification, namely, trust in God's work in Christ for our justification rather than in any aspect of our self, even an aspect confessed to be a work of God's grace. The statement notes that we are one in the activity most central to the concerns of the doctrine of justification. Its claim to have reached an agreement on this topic sufficient for unity rests on the judgment that the remaining differences in relation to justification do not affect this unity in the activity decisive for the identity of the church.[44]

Second, such an orientation can help to explain why some topics, such as ordained ministry, tend to play a leading role in ecumenical discussions, despite their theologically peripheral character. Topics such as ministry and sacraments become important precisely when the issue is how we can carry out together the activities of the church. When that issue is raised, the subordinate questions of "who does what how" become unavoidable. As the prominence of ecclesiology in ecumenical discussions is not necessarily a sign of ecclesial narcissism, so the time given to the doctrine of ministry need not imply creeping clericalism or ministerial self-absorption.[45] It might imply simply a concern with the practical realities of ecumenical relations.

Third, and perhaps most importantly, such an orientation roots ecumenical discussion and the consensus it seeks in the lived relations among the churches. Ecumenical discussion is first an ecclesial activity. It is an aspect of the church's concern for its identity. The visible communion that is sought between the churches is not an exclusively or even primarily intellectual or conceptual unity. It is oneness in the body of Christ, in the reality of a life lived in the Spirit. This life has forms, activities, in which its identity is realized: prayer, proclamation, sacraments, discipline, reflection. It is unity in this life that is decisive for the unity of the church. The proposed test seeks simply to make clear that the norm of the adequacy of an ecumenical consensus is its adequacy for the life of the church. Our doctrinal agreement is sufficient when we can live this life together without violating our convictions on the essential identity of that life.

CONCLUSION

When ecumenical discussion is examined through the lens of Lindbeck's understanding of the nature of doctrine, the juxtaposition of title and subtitle of *The Nature of Doctrine* becomes more understandable. As noted above, the identity of any complex human activity is in a constant process of respecification. What ecumenical discussion can and should be is a forum for the continuous process of discovering and deciding what the church and its mission are in this time. It should be a paradigm for Alasdair MacIntyre's definition of a tradition: "A living tradition then is an historically extended, socially embodied argument, and an argument precisely in part about the goods which constitute that tradition."[46] Ecumenical discussion, however, is not just "in part" but virtually entirely about the goods which constitute the tradition. The mission of the church is given once and for all by the risen Christ. In its concern to preserve the continuity of that mission, ecumenism has its conservative aspect. But, as noted above, identity judgments about an activity are inevitably contextual. Our situations change, calling for new judgments and visions of what specifies the identity of the church in this context. Our minds change, construing the identity of the church in new ways. Ecumenical discussion relates reflection on the identity of the church to concrete problems in its life and forces that reflection into a more dialogical form. Title and subtitle in Lindbeck's book do not then form a Benchley-like oddity. They represent the interrelation which should form all ecumenical reflection, the interrelation of critical reflection and the lived reality of the church.

NOTES

1. (Philadelphia: Westminster Press, 1984). Page references to this book will be given in brackets within the text.

2. Gordon Kaufman explicitly regrets that Lindbeck has yoked his theological insights with ecumenism. See his review in *Theology Today* 42 (1985): 241.

3. *The Three Reports of the Forum on Bilateral Conversations*, Faith and Order Paper 107 (Geneva: World Council of Churches, 1981), 11.

4. Identity across space and across time can present different philosophical problems. (See Avrum Stroll, "Identity," in *The Encyclopedia of Philosophy*, ed. Paul Edwards.) These differences are not important for this discussion. In this essay more general philosophical analyses of identity will be used sparingly. I do not think their introduction would help clarify the issues here addressed.

5. This concern is common to quite different theological positions. See, e.g., Schubert M. Ogden, "What Is Theology?" *Journal of Religion* 52 (1972): 25, on the norm of appropriateness and Ronald F. Thiemann, *Revelation and Theology: The Gospel as Narrated Promise* (Notre Dame, Ind.: University of Notre Dame Press, 1985), 92, on the norm of Christian aptness.

6. To avoid tedious repetition, I will often refer only to "the identity of the church" when I mean "the identity of the church as church." Unless otherwise indicated, the former phrase is a shorter form of the latter.

7. This paragraph may imply for some the unduly harsh assumption that a division within the church implies that some community judges another community as deficient in that which constitutes the identity of the church. Nevertheless, only such a judgment can justify separation, if one believes that the church is truly one. In this sense, all divisions are, to a degree, *from* the church and not simply *in* the church. Nevertheless, the identity of a community as church need not be an all or nothing matter and thus one can speak of divisions in the church.

8. For examples of dialogues claiming to have overcome church-dividing differences, see below, note 16.

9. Article 7:2. In *The Book of Concord: The Confessions of the Evangelical Lutheran Church*, trans. and ed. Theodore G. Tappert, et al. (Philadelphia: Fortress Press, 1959), 32.

10. Article 7:3.

11. See Bernhard Lohse, "Dogma und Bekenntnis in der Reformation: Von Luther bis zum Konkordienbuch," in *Handbuch der Dogmen- und Theologiegeschichte*, ed. Carl Andresen (Göttingen: Vandenhoeck & Ruprecht, 1980), vol. 2, 108–13.

12. Heribert Heinemann, in *Sacramentum Mundi*, s.v., "Heresy, I. Concept."

13. Canon 751, *Code of Canon Law: Latin-English Edition* (Washington, D.C.: Canon Law Society of America, 1983), 284f.

14. Stephen Sykes goes so far as to say, "The definition of heresy is logically dependent, therefore, on that of defined doctrine." In *The Westminster Dictionary of Christian Theology*, s.v., "Heresy."

15. An important exception is a largely ignored article by Robert W. Jenson, "Lutheran Conditions for Communion in Holy Things," in *Lutheran-Episcopal Dialogue: A Progress Report* (Cincinnati: Forward Movement Press, 1973), 127–38. While his essay focuses simply on what criteria contemporary American Lutherans should apply, Jenson's suggestion resembles the one that will be offered here. The decisive criterion for both is found in what two churches can (or cannot) do together, although this practice-oriented aspect of his proposal is not developed by Jenson.

16. The claim that church-dividing differences have been overcome or discovered not to exist is made explicitly in at least the following dialogue documents, besides those discussed in the next paragraphs of the text: Anglican-Roman Catholic Joint Commission, "Salvation and the Church: ARCIC II," *Origins* 16 (1987): 616, §32; Lutheran/Roman Catholic Joint

Commission, *The Eucharist* (Geneva: Lutheran World Federation, 1980), §51, §64; *Marburg Revisited: A Reexamination of Lutheran and Reformed Traditions*, ed. Paul C. Empie and James I. McCord (Minneapolis: Augsburg, 1966), vi; Lutheran-Reformed Dialogue Series III, 1981–1983, *An Invitation to Action: A Study of Ministry, Sacraments, and Recognition*, ed. James E. Andrews and Joseph A. Burgess (Philadelphia: Fortress Press, 1984), 16f., 31. In the Leuenberg Agreement §1, the positive statement is made that agreement exists sufficient for church fellowship. See Appendix 3 to *An Invitation to Action*, 65. None of these cases makes explicit the criteria which guided or might justify their judgments that certain differences are not church-dividing. The only dialogue I have encountered which produced a statement on this question was the Anglican-Roman Catholic Consultation in the United States. In a document entitled "Doctrinal Agreement and Christian Unity: Methodological Consideration," it specified certain "operative principles in the assessment of whether such divergent formulations do indeed constitute an essential obstacle to full communion." Nevertheless, the principles listed turn out not to be criteria that might help in deciding whether a difference is church-dividing, but reasons one might give for permitting differences to exist in the church, e.g., the possibility of doctrinal pluralism or the possibility that divine truth is captured only in a paradoxical tension. See *Journal of Ecumenical Studies* 9 (1972): 445–48.

17. H. George Anderson, T. Austin Murphy, and Joseph Burgess, eds., *Justification by Faith: Lutherans and Catholics in Dialogue* 7 (Minneapolis: Augsburg, 1985), p. 74, §164. Further references to this document will be to the paragraph number and will be included in the text.

18. *Facing Unity: Models, Forms and Phases of Catholic-Lutheran Church Fellowship* (Geneva: Lutheran World Federation, 1985), §47. Emphasis added. German original, *Einheit vor uns: Modelle, Formen und Phasen katholisch/lutherischer Kirchengemeinschaft* (Paderborn: Verlag Bonifatius; Frankfurt: Verlag Otto Lembeck, 1985). This relation between fundamental consensus and church-dividing difference is even clearer in §123: "If a fundamental consensus is reached on faith, sacramental life and ordained ministry such that remaining differences between Catholics and Lutherans no longer can appear as church dividing, . . ."

19. Harding Meyer notes, "The dialogues of the last two decades were almost exclusively concerned with the achievement of consensus and seemed hardly to consider at all the question of the nature of the consensus required and sufficient for unity." "Fundamental Consensus and Church Fellowship: A Lutheran Perspective," in *In Search of Christian Unity* (Philadelphia: Fortress Press, forthcoming).

20. See also the puzzlement expressed by J. Robert Wright over just what it means for Catholics and Anglicans (himself included) to reach agreement on the essential aspects of the doctrine of justification in the ARCIC II statement on "Salvation and the Church"; in his "Fundamental Concensus: An Anglican Perspective," in *In Search of Christian Unity*.

21. Meyer, "Fundamental Consensus and Church Fellowship," in *In Search of Christian Unity*. In relation to the 1981 Final Report of the Anglican/Roman Catholic International Commission, J. Robert Wright demonstrates the difficulties that can be created in a process of reception by unclarities about the sort of consensus claimed. See "Fundamental Consensus: An Anglican Perspective."

22. Whether all church-dividing differences are at least implicitly doctrinal need not be decided here. An answer will depend to a large degree on what one means by "doctrine." In this essay I will only be discussing doctrinal (as opposed to possibly strictly disciplinary) church-dividing differences. No explicit attention will be given to the ways in which what have come to be called nontheological factors (e.g., cultural and ethnic differences) are involved in or stand behind doctrinal differences. The role and importance of such factors does not affect the argument of this essay.

23. An explicit argument in favor of Lindbeck's understanding of doctrine will not be offered. Nevertheless, if his description helps us to clarify the implicit criteria at work in ecumenical discussions, the credibility of his description is thereby strengthened.

24. William A. Christian, Sr., *Doctrines of Religious Communities: A Philosophical Study* (New Haven, Conn.: Yale University Press, 1987), 5.

25. Ibid., 2.

26. Except in the sense that language is itself a part of the world.

27. In this respect the sort of grammatical rule a doctrine would be most like is a verb paradigm, which exemplifies rather than directly states a rule.

28. In "Theology as Grammar: Regulative Principles or Paradigms and Practices?" *Modern Theology* 4 (1988): 155–72, Lee Barrett rightly notes that the rule which a doctrine embodies is inseparable from the historical practice of the application of the paradigm from which the rule derives. He thus provides a corrective to tendencies to isolate doctrinal rules from the historical reality of the life of the church, a tendency Lindbeck himself in some passages does not sufficiently guard against. I do not think Barrett's criticism requires a thorough rethinking of Lindbeck's proposal, although such a conclusion cannot be demonstrated here.

29. Or at least, the practice this paradigm guides when it is rightly applied. That there are significant examples of the misuse and misunderstanding

of the paradigm in the history of the church cannot be denied. Nevertheless, there must be a descriptively plausible standard use against which the misuse can be understood to be a misuse. Any analysis of a doctrine as a rule will thus be *first* descriptive but then also normative.

30. I have avoided saying here that following the rules *constitutes* the identity of what we are doing as chess. Rule-following is always embedded in a wider context of practices apart from which the rules themselves cannot function. See Barrett, "Theology as Grammar."

31. To respecify identity is not necessarily to change it. Rather, new characteristics are taken to specify the identity. One might hold that the new specification picks out "the same thing" as the old specification. Analogously, the redefinition of a meter as 1,650,763.73 wavelengths of the orange-red radiation of krypton 86 in a vacuum respecified the length of a meter but did not change it.

32. Heinz-Günther Stobbe and John May in a series of essays have sought to differentiate different kinds of consensus and to interrelate consensus on doctrine and consensus on action. See their "Übereinstimmung und Handlungsfähigkeit. Zur Grundlage ökumenischer Konsensbildung und Wahrheitsfindung," in *Ökumenische Theologie: Ein Arbeitsbuch*, ed. Peter Lengsfeld (Stuttgart: W. Kohlhammer, 1980), 301–37; Stobbe's "Konsensfindung als Hermeneutisches Problem," in *Theologische Konsens und Kirchenspaltung*, ed. Peter Lengsfeld and Heinz-Günther Stobbe (Stuttgart: W. Kohlhammer, 1981), 31–51; and May's "Consensus in Religion: An Essay in Fundamental Ecumenics," *Journal of Ecumenical Studies* 17 (1980): 407–31. While their program is similar in certain respects to what is being done here, they have different goals, pursue them with different methods, and encounter different problems. They do not seek to provide a practice-oriented criterion of sufficient consensus, but rather a comprehensive explanation of the interrelation of consensus about truth, meaning, and action in the life of the church. In the process they create a complex analysis of kinds of consensus that, on the one hand, I do not find helpful for the task of this essay, and, on the other hand, I find philosophically problematic. Although they do not do so consistently and explicitly, they have a tendency to make a consensus on action foundational to consensus on meaning and truth (e.g., "Übereinstimmung, 322; "Consensus," 414) without adequately noting that the converse is equally true. This tendency (and their redefinition of a consensus on truth as a consensus on meaning, "Übereinstimmung," 332) makes their program open to the accusation that they are abandoning the valid and necessary concern for truth. See the criticism by Gerhard Sauter, "Was ist Wahrheit in der Theologie? Wahrheitsfindung und Konsens der Kirche,"

in *In der Freiheit des Geistes: Theologische Studien* (Göttingen: Vandenhoeck & Ruprecht, 1988), 80, note 6.

33. Lindbeck himself (pp. 16f.) proposes his theory as a way of explaining how earlier disagreements are ecumenically overcome without either participant compromising essential beliefs.

34. David H. Kelsey, *The Uses of Scripture in Recent Theology* (Philadelphia: Fortress Press, 1975), 160, quoting Robert Johnson. The ecumenically operative *discrimen* of a sense of the identity of the church will be closely related to the *discrimen* Kelsey identifies of a sense of the mode of God's presence. See Kelsey, 164.

35. Whether the rejection of the claim itself or only the rejection of some specific exercise of the claim would be church-dividing depends on whether one judges that a common statement of this belief is an activity essential to the identity of the church.

36. The development of new ways of performing together certain actions is one means for overcoming previously church-dividing differences.

37. In such a case the action would not be incompatible with the identity of the church, but the *insistence* that it be carried out would be. One can imagine more complicated cases. One community might not insist that anyone in particular perform an act (e.g., say a particular prayer in the context of an ordination) but might still insist that *someone* present do so. No individual is compelled to perform this act, but the community is compelled to find someone to do so. Those who deny the necessary character of this act would have to decide whether such an insistence, while possibly compelling no one, still compromises a freedom they may consider essential to the church's identity.

38. Lindbeck has raised the possibility that certain questions about the necessity or permissibility of episcopal and papal structures could be left undecided. He implicitly uses a criterion much like the one suggested here: In certain situations, the difference over the "irreversibility" of such structures produces no foreseeable "operational differences" and thus becomes "practically nugatory." See his "The Church," in *Keeping the Faith: Essays to Mark the Centenary of Lux Mundi*, ed. Geoffrey Wainwright (London: SPCK, 1989), 200.

39. That churches can perform certain important actions (e.g., the Eucharist) together in certain special situations is not trivial and indicates a significant level of unity. Nevertheless, such "limited communion" is not the full unity of the one church.

40. See comments of Reinhard Slenczka, "Kirchengemeinschaft und theologischer Konsens: Eine Thesenreihe," *Kerygma und Dogma* 29 (1983): 175. The tendency to maximize the extent of a consensus needed for unity

can be seen in Wolfgang Beinert's definition of "total consensus" as "full agreement in all important points of the common subject matter. This is the ideal case of Christian unity and expresses itself as consensus in doctrine and confession." "Der ökumenische Dialog als Einübung in die Klärung theologischer Differenzen," in *Handbuch der Ökumenik*, ed. Hans Jörg Urban and Harald Wagner (Paderborn: Verlag Bonifatius, 1987), vol. 3/1, 117 (emphasis added).

41. Harding Meyer thus notes that ecumenical dialogue needs to be directed "not towards the *maximum* but the *optimum* of consensus." "Roman Catholic/Lutheran Dialogue," *One in Christ* 22 (1986): 154.

42. Such an orientation is not new. Especially in its German version, the Augsburg Confession, Article 7, gives a practice-oriented test: Can we agree on what constitutes the right preaching of the gospel and the right administration of the sacraments? Stephen Sykes has also proposed a pragmatic criterion for the identity of Christianity in *The Identity of Christianity: Theologians and the Essence of Christianity from Schleiermacher to Barth* (Philadelphia: Fortress Press, 1984), e.g., 285. While I do not reject his emphasis on worship as the activity in which the identity of the church is focused, I am not ready to accept his sometimes exclusive characterization of worship as the one place in which common action is required (p. 8).

43. Part II, Article 2:12 (Tappert, 294f).

44. This ecumenical statement, however, can be criticized for not taking its concern for the practical implications of the doctrine seriously enough. It distinguishes agreement on "the doctrine itself" from agreement on its use as a criterion (§152, §155). If one accepts an understanding of doctrines as rules, this distinction could only be a distinction between one aspect of justification as a doctrine or rule and another aspect of justification as a doctrine or rule. In such a case, agreement has not been reached on all aspects of justification *as a doctrine*. In the formation of the response to this statement by the Lutheran Church in America, I argued against the point I am now making, which was at that time pressed by Elizabeth Bettenhausen.

45. See, for example, the criticisms by Lutheran churches of the inclusion of the topic of ministry in the Lima Document, summarized in Michael Seils, *Lutheran Convergence? An Analysis of the Lutheran Responses to the Convergence Document "Baptism, Eucharist and Ministry" of the World Council of Churches Faith and Order Commission*, LWF Report 25 (Geneva: Lutheran World Federation, 1988), 96f.

46. Alasdair MacIntyre, *After Virtue: A Study in Moral Theory* (Notre Dame, Ind.: University of Notre Dame Press, 1981), 207.

EPISCOPE AND POWER
IN THE CHURCH

S. W. Sykes

> It is not our intention to find ways of reducing the bishop's power, but
> we desire and pray they may not coerce our consciences to sin.
>
> (*Confessio Augustana* XXVIII,77)

The treatment of the power of bishops in CA 28 turns on a distinction, long familiar in medieval Western theology, between the power of the gospel and that of the temporal sword. But as George Lindbeck and Avery Dulles point out in their jointly authored essay on "Bishops and the Ministry of the Gospel," the *Confessio Augustana* "simply assumes that episcopacy should be retained."[1] The question it faced was, given bishops, what should be their powers.

Modern Lutheran theology, however, after centuries of agreement that the structures of church government (or at least the titles given to church leaders) are a matter of indifference, now presents an apparently different face. Analysis of the Lutheran responses to the section on the ministry of the World Council of Churches document, *Baptism, Eucharist and Ministry*, suggests that the relationship between the universal priesthood of all believers based on baptism and *any* form of inequality of power in the church has become extremely problematic in Lutheranism.[2] The celebrated "satis est" and "nec necesse est" of CA 7 is notoriously capable of, and receives, widely differing interpretations. What I wish to offer here is an argument about the nature of the relationship between spiritual and ecclesiastical power, addressed to the fact that power is bound to be unequally distributed in the church and most likely to be misused. It is an argument which

191

assumes that sociological and theological methods of analysis ought to be distinguished but cannot be separated. The church is, as Richard Hooker declared at the end of the sixteenth century, both a society and a society supernatural.[3] But, I propose to argue, there is a dialectic between the fundamental theological character of the church and its necessary embodiment in specific and, of course, changing organizational arrangements. With the *Confessio Augustana* we may simply assume that there will be those who govern. The question is who, and how.

THE GOVERNMENT OF THE CHURCH AS A PROBLEM

In the work of a brilliant young seventeenth-century Anglican theologian, Edward Stillingfleet, there is a passage of sustained polemic against the institution of papal monarchy which runs along the following lines; Roman Catholics, he says, argue from the manifest excellence of the monarchy as a form of political institution to the manifest excellence of monarchy in church government. But the analogy is plainly defective. It must be remembered, he says, that we are speaking about the government of the church which is spread throughout the world. How possibly could decisions taken in Rome be effective in Mexico or Japan? What is plainly needed, he argues, is decisions to be taken in those places where they can be put into practice at once. If one needs any political analogy for this procedure the more appropriate model is government by aristocracy.[4]

No one reading this passage could fail to be struck by two reflections. The first is that the cogency of Stillingfleet's argument, which derives from the extreme difficulty of communicating with Rome in the seventeenth century, is undermined by the astonishing ease of modern travel and the electronic transmission of words and images. The second thought is that the notion that aristocracy is itself politically attractive would only have occurred to certain particular people, living in certain countries at certain times, one of whom would have been a political conservative and defender of the national church writing in England in 1664. A third reflection could be added to the effect that modern Anglicanism, which has somewhat modestly enhanced the role of the primates of the communion's twenty-seven autonomous provinces, has, in fact, implemented Stillingfleet's preferred model of government, justifying it in terms of "collegial interdependence" rather than on any overt political analogy.[5]

The extent of the permeation of civil or political precedents or ways of thinking into what theologians may hope to be the unique mode of expression of authority in the church is always easier to detect in societies or cultures other than our own. We may pray that "the whole body of the Church" be "governed and sanctified" by the Holy Spirit (Collect for Good Friday, 1662 BCP), but we constantly discover, sometimes to our distress, that this government does not preclude the (at least) partial fulfillment of secular role expectations. Common sense suggests that this is what we would expect. Christians are not subject to the influences simply of the church's teaching and socialization. They carry their cultures around in their heads.[6] Cultures develop and legitimate modes of authority. Some styles of behavior or ways of making decisions will necessarily seem to be justified simply on the basis of satisfactory common experience. If people are content with local arrangements for the distribution of political power they will find them, or their nearest analogues, natural and right in the church. Stillingfleet, we note, was alert enough to detect argument by analogy and to challenge its precise applicability to the church; but he was human—or at least English—enough to commend the Anglican model by reference to another political analogy.

The relationship of secular and ecclesial ideas about modes of government is, of course, part of a much wider issue of the relationship of Christ and culture, to which very considerable thought has been given since H. Richard Niebuhr's classic work of that name. In more recent years, under the heading of "inculturation" or "indigenization" (a somewhat patronizing terminology readily concealing normative assumptions), extensive consideration has been given to the processes involved in cross-cultural missionary activity. At least four stages have been distinguished. In the first, the period of primary colonial evangelistic activity, the culture of the "gospel" and that of the preachers of the gospel has not been distinguished. In the second phase, the distinction is made and the churches attempt to adopt local styles of music, dance, language, and imagery, and tentatively explore local models of authority. Then, in the third stage, ambiguities begin to emerge in the process of so-called indigenization. The complexity and dynamic quality of local culture begins to become plain, especially if the country involved is subject to urbanization and secularization. Finally, a new critique of culture is undertaken which attempts to deepen its grasp on the distinctive model of human relationships to be found in the gospel. A critique of social processes, whose nature and dynamic is now more fully understood, begins to be developed. The document from the 1988 Lambeth Conference which lays out this process adds the following comment:

> The business of freeing the Church from the "Babylonish captivity" of colonial culture is multi-faceted and long-term; and it requires more than a merely guilty or sentimental politeness to what is thought to be "indigenous" culture. It involves an imaginative sensitivity to the concrete social processes at work in specific contexts—to how nations and peoples are *actually* becoming themselves—and a serious listening to how people themselves perceive their hopes for fuller liberation from alien systems of domination.[7]

The presupposition behind the description of such a process is that it is possible to recognize an "alien system of domination" in the light of mature and profound reflection upon the gospel. It is important to see that the process, so described, is a critical one. It is not that the gospel provides us with a series of instructions on the basis of which Christians can devise a completely satisfactory non-dominative system of church government. Rather the alien character of a system—which, until a crucial point, may have seemed to be a natural and appropriate way of arranging for the government of the church—is disclosed as dominative in the light of the gospel, either by immediate intuition or by a longer process of reflection such as has been described. In other words, the gospel functions critically in a dialectical process rather than constructively by ideal realization.

It is equally important, on the other hand, to realize that there was a political or cultural imperative in the original preaching of the gospel. It was in part through political or quasi-political terminology that Christians expressed the sense of their own identity. To a certain extent the development of the episcopate stood for a new political reality in the ancient world, corresponding to the church's consciousness of being a new people, or a new race, whose *politeuma* or commonwealth was in heaven (Phil. 3:20), at once strangers and sojourners in other people's cities, but also radically at home in God's world.[8] What we have identified as a dialectical process in relation to so called "indigenization" is kept in motion by an imperative deriving from the gospel, by the knowledge that the God with whom Christians have to do is a God who establishes relationship with human beings of a particular, determinate kind. This relationship, which is spoken of in the New Testament as communion (*koinonia*), is the foundation of the relationships between persons, which it is the church's mission to embody. How Christians arrange for the government of the church, therefore, both is, and is not, a matter of indifference, but in contrasting senses. It is indifferent in the sense that no blueprint of church government is provided in the New Testament, which witnesses to the launching of the Christian movement into the dialectical process we have described. But at the same time it is not indifferent in the sense that the church has the task of communicating a unique and distinctive pattern of relation between human beings which has its ground in the being and act of God himself. The problem of this Yes and No is what must occupy us in further detail.

DOMINEERING BEHAVIOR IN THE CHURCH

I have spoken of the Christian movement being launched into a dialectical process. That, at least, is obvious on the pages of the New Testament documents, once we stop the habit of quarrying the text for legitimation of our own denominational arrangements. There is plainly an already serious problem about domineering behavior within Christian communities. In Corinth, Paul had real difficulty in establishing his authority in the church, or churches, at least those of which he had been the founder and over which he claimed rights as a father. He was accused of being weak, and he reacted with direct divine legitimation backed by a rhetorical vigor which bordered on emotional blackmail. In its recollections about Jesus the church preserved stories greatly to the discredit of at least some of his immediate disciples, who in the version recorded in Mark asked for special positions of rank in the eschatological kingdom (Mark 10:37) or who fell into jealous dispute about which was to be regarded as the greatest (Luke 22:24). The first letter of Peter makes clear that financial gain and love of power were already discernibly part of the motivation of those "elders" who had pastoral responsibility for the community (5:2–3).

With such admissions of blatant abuse of authority we hardly need further evidence from the history of the early church. But it is, perhaps, not so readily or honestly acknowledged as in the pages of the New Testament itself. One exception occurs in Book IV of Irenaeus's *Adversus Haereses*, where in instructing the church to follow only the interpretation of the Scriptures provided in the church by the presbyters who have the succession from the apostles, Irenaeus warns his readers against unauthorized schismatics or heretics who have set themselves up in opposition to the church. He is, however, obliged to acknowledge that there are also those who are believed to be presbyters by many (their succession appears not to be in doubt), but who are proud and scornful and are "puffed up with pride by the pride of holding the chief seat." From all such persons one must keep aloof and resort only to those who guard apostolic doctrine and combine the order of priesthood (*ordine presbyterii*) with sound speech and blameless conduct.[9] Thus it appears that at an early stage in the history of the church it was perceived that neither ordination in succession nor the profession of impeccable orthodoxy necessarily protected church leaders from the moral abuses attendant on the exercise of power.

The fact that the New Testament communities themselves knew that the abuse of power was a possibility signifies one important truth, namely that domineering behavior is not the prerogative of churches which have formally structured themselves on a hierarchical pattern. The term "hierarchy" is, of course, ambiguous. Taken literally it simply refers to rule or dominion in holy things; whereas sociological usage has focused on the ordering of rule in ranks or grades, one above another. But prescinding altogether from discussion of whether the communities reflected in the synoptic gospels and the first letter of Peter were or were not hierarchical in whatever sense, it is evident that those who are what sociologists may call "higher participants" in an organization have greater access to the exercise of power than "lower participants"[10] and that this exercise of power is open to abuse and from the first has been abused in the church.

In this connection it is worth making clear that churches with what are reckoned to be hierarchies of order (for example, deacons, priests, and bishops in ascending sequence) may also have somewhat

differently constructed formal or informal hierarchies of jurisdiction
(for example, as in the Church of England, a lay sovereign—who
has been for more than one notable reign a woman—lay members
of Parliament, and lay persons of considerable power or influence
in parishes).[11] Abuse of power is on principle as possible for higher
lay participants as for ordained. Churches with large bureaucracies
exhibit, moreover, the informal power networks characteristic of any
organization, the manipulation of which by clerks and secretaries,
spouses and friends, is the common coin of ecclesiastical gossips
and novelists, by no means all of whom have the stature of
Anthony Trollope.

Merely to refer to these phenomena is sufficient to evoke recognition. And yet it appears that Christians have well-developed mech-
anisms for discounting their significance. It is a curious phenomenon
that, despite the fact that domineering behavior is ascribed to higher
participants in the New Testament communities, Christian theology
has been reluctant to give a clear account of the phenomenon of
power in the church. "Power," it has to be admitted, is by no means a
clear concept, and to that extent the failure is the less culpable. But
the root of the malaise lies deeper. The concept of power itself is, as
modern research has demonstrated, a negative one.[12] Raymond Aron
has written: "The words 'power' and 'Macht', in English and German,
'pouvoir' or 'puissance' in French, continue to be surrounded by a
kind of sacred halo or, it may be preferable to say, imbued with mysterious overtones that have something terrifying about them."[13] The
association of the terms have to do, he points out, with Machiavelli,
with *Machtpolitik*, with *die Damonie der Macht*, and with Lord Acton's
dictum, "Power corrupts, absolute power corrupts absolutely." With
such connotations as these, it is sometimes asserted or implied that
the problem is not the abuse of power but the mere phenomenon
of power. There are Christian theologians today who use the term
"power" to mean domination and for whom the only appropriate
Christian option is a posture of powerlessness.[14]

When one bears in mind the sheer quantity of reflection on the
phenomenon of power in organizations, undertaken in the last two
decades, it is clear that one of the preconditions for this extraordinary
development in Christian reflection is the wholesale abandonment

of connection with contemporary sociology. But the church's difficulties in the face of a demand for explanation for the presence of
domineering behavior in its leaders are of long standing. Two principle strategies have been developed: The first was to minimize the
possibility of identifying the behavior as domineering by maximizing
the entitlement of the officeholder to the possession and exercise of
power. A straightforward theology of the charisma of office enabled
ordained persons to claim that they spoke or acted, not on their own
behalf or in their own name, but in virtue of the bestowal on them of
the Holy Spirit and in the name of Christ. The biblical basis for this
was the commissioning of the seventy in the Gospel of Luke ("He
who hears you hears me," 10:16) and St. Paul's claim to speak on the
authority of Christ ("I am entrusted with a commission," 1 Cor. 9:17).
As we have seen, in the writings of Irenaeus it could be recognized
that commissioning of ordination by no means protected the recipi-
ent from pride and moral error. But the ambiguity of the notion of
entitlement attached to the point where the claim was greatest; from
pride there could be no escape, even into the (paradoxical) claim
to humility.

The second strategy was more subtle. This was the development
of the conception of a ministry of service, specifically on the model
of the ministry of Christ, deploying the "myth" of *kenosis*. Again
a biblical basis was to hand, especially in the synoptic and Johan-
nine passages where Christ is spoken of as a servant. This strategy
has existed in two main forms. So long as kenotic christology was
held not to involve the abandonment by the divine Son of God of
his divine power and prerogatives (that is, so long as the christology of the dogmatic Tome of Leo was approved), *kenosis* would not
have the connotation of powerlessness. However, once nineteenth-
century theology developed what we now call "kenotic christology" on
the assumption of either the pouring out, *Entaüsserung* (Thomasius),
or, more radically, of the self-emptying, *Entleerung*, of the incarnate
Lord,[15] then the way was clear for the root-and-branch denial that
leadership in the church could involve power of any kind.

Now it must be said that both of these strategies, despite their
apparent biblical foundations, attract sociological suspicion. The first
lends itself classically to analysis in terms of legitimation. One of the
observable techniques of those who wish to exercise power over others

is to clothe themselves (sometimes in ritually enacted performances) with the mantle of divine approval. The developing clash between the power of the church's hierarchy and that of a theologically conceived secular imperium is the main historical example we possess for the escalation in legitimating claims. The ideology of extreme papal monarchy implied that the pope was set over the emperor, because the pope alone had the power of eternal life or death, that is, literally the last word on an emperor's destiny.[16] This power the pope had in virtue of the gift of the keys of St. Peter, a gift sufficiently ambiguous as to require acknowledgment in an unambiguous, but alas spurious, legend of the donation of Constantine. The point of divine legitimation is to exact compliance; its weakness is that, as a claim, it depends upon voluntary acknowledgment for its impact. But it was the last weapon in the armory of an institution which was regularly threatened by force of actual weapons and whose influence could be and sometimes was swept aside by vulgar might. It was a threatened institution which equipped itself with the theological assertion of infallibility and ultimate control over human destiny. Having seen the processes of legitimation at work, we have become suspicious.

Suspicion no less certainly arises over the other strategy, that of the invocation of service and powerlessness. In fact power is not escaped by identifying it with force. The claim that one has no power is one which, in certain moral contexts, has considerable weight. For example, immigrants into the State of Israel discover that their status as the "powerless" gives them influence with officialdom. Gandhi's politics of nonviolence achieved results in a moral climate which deplores the use of force on the nonresisting and unarmed. Were the theologians who endlessly celebrate servant-ministry less sociologically innocent they would know that the service conception of power is usually and especially favored by the powerful and those employed in defending and promoting their power.[17] It also arouses the suspicion that an attempt is being made to conceal power. The invocation of service on the model of Christ is, in Christian contexts at least, also a form of legitimation.

I have spoken of these strategies as arousing suspicion, and the brevity of the discussion of the grounds for suspicion may provoke irritation. The reason for irritation is obvious enough. Those who exercise power frequently (though not invariably) have overt motives for doing so. My discussion raises what are best described as psychological considerations relating to the adequacy of the account of those motives. If church leaders or officeholders say or do something decisive and affirm that they do so because they are empowered by the Holy Spirit, or because they wish to serve the church, who is anyone to say that they are rather clothing themselves in the mantle of unchallengeability? What gives us the right to be suspicious of them? The answer can only be phrased in terms of general, not particular, considerations—for example, that we know that some of those in the past who have claimed divine support or high-minded motives have actually been in error or self-deceived and have even on occasion admitted as much subsequently. Motivation, we know, is complex, and the more important the question, or the more far-reaching the claim, the greater care which needs to be taken in its evaluation. Suspicion is appropriate, not because we know in advance that in all particular cases the least creditable motives are to be preferred to those which are honorable, but because we have a duty to take care. Suspicion does not, therefore, require the abandonment of the theological strategies we have mentioned; but it is consistent with the idea of a dialectical process which we have already developed. Sociological observations on how people who are in possession of power frequently behave must be a partner in any careful analysis of the exercise of power in the church.

THE THEOLOGICAL CONTEXT OF EPISCOPE

Anglicans or Episcopalians have the unenviable reputation in ecumenical circles for introducing episcopacy into discussion like a *deus ex machina* in an ecclesiological vacuum. There are reasons for this. They like to appeal to history; they do not wish to be tied down to one theological theory of the episcopate; their long history of permitting lay involvement in church government means that they cannot fully share the theologies of the episcopate advanced in Orthodox or Catholic circles.

But Anglicans or Episcopalians have not always appreciated why they are obliged to offer a theology of the episcopate to accompany its recommendation as a form of church government; the reason for this requirement can be very simply stated. Bishops are, for Anglicans, officeholders in the church of God. There must, therefore, exist an understanding *of the church* in the context of which the episcopate belongs. Although Anglicans have recently (that is, in the last 150 years) become reluctant to admit that they have, or ought to have, a theology of the church to bring to the ecumenical discussion table, it is ecclesiology which will make sense—or nonsense—of the office of a bishop. The same considerations hold good for any broader discussion of ministries of leadership and pastoral oversight, however they may be entitled or named, and irrespective of their view of a historic chain of ordinations. *Episcope* in the church must have an ecclesiological context.

The context in which it is intelligible, I wish to argue, is that of baptism. The reason for this view must be briefly sketched. The Christian community is the community of the baptized. Baptism defines who belongs to the church. There were baptisms of various kinds before the Christian movement came into existence; there were also groups which had a kind of relationship to Jesus' preaching, but which existed apart from what baptism signified to the later church. But in general it is the case that we can speak confidently of the existence of the church at the same time as we can confidently point to the practice of initiatory baptism.

Being baptized involves participating in the church's foundational metaphor, that is, of passing from death into life by being ritually identified with Christ in his death, so as to rise again with Christ into newness of life. Being baptized means to receive the gift of the life-giving Spirit and thus to participate in the death-conquering new life which is the gift of the risen Christ to his church. To be a "member" of Christ implies that one has passed from the domain of death into that of life and has become a living limb or organ of a new reality. Baptism therefore establishes the sense of each individual person as having an irreplaceable part in an active system of persons-in-relation. This is that new personal identity which transcends the old identifying marks of humanity. Is one male or female, Jew or Gentile, in slavery or free? No, one is a new person in Christ. Nothing more fundamental can be said about anyone's life than that it has been lived as part of Christ's body. It is for this reason that *episcope* in the church must be understood first in relation to baptism.

In order to understand the relationship of baptism to ordination it is essential to distinguish between identity and role.[18] To be a "member" of Christ is a matter of identity; to be a priest is a matter of role. It is for this reason that according to the theological definition of laity, however it may have to be used conventionally in other contexts, no priest ever ceases to be a lay person. No one ever gets "beyond" baptism. The ordained do not become "super-members" of Christ; on the contrary, as St. Paul makes clear, in the body of Christ those parts which are commonly regarded as of least importance are given a special status.

The problem of how to conceive of ordination is, of course, an aspect of the doctrine of the Holy Spirit. Here the language of "gift" needs to be deployed with discrimination, because human gifts (presents, money, attention) are all capable of being quantitatively increased. But the gift of the Spirit is not quantifiable. This gift is a divine self-giving without measure, pure superabundant grace; we note, in this context, the use of the analogy of excess which is designed to subvert our awareness of the human possibility of residual meanness of giving.[19] But God deals with all his people with superfluous generosity. Thus the idea of an increase in the Holy Spirit is, so to speak, an optical illusion; it is not the case that to certain persons is given more Holy Spirit than to others: rather, that in the lives of some there ceases to be such resistance or obstacle to the effectiveness of the Holy Spirit. For such increase of grace all Christians have both the need and the right to make daily intercession.

What then is the significance of the prayer for the bestowal of the Holy Spirit on those set aside for ordination? Ordination is the recognition by an act of special solemnity that a new role is being undertaken by a particular person which has consequences for every member of the church. Solemnity at this moment is justified as in the case of the ritual observance of marriage or of the approach of death. Ordination is a life-transforming event, the outcome of deliberate decision by both people and candidate, is carefully prepared for, and involves intimate contact with most holy things, the preaching of the word and celebration of the sacraments. It would be inconceivable that the prayers of the church at this moment of personal choice should not be given solemn, ritual focus.

Secondly, prayer for the gift of the Holy Spirit is an oblique acknowledgment of the special danger attaching to this particular role in the church. We are speaking not now of the danger of contact with the holy, but rather of the more mundane temptations of pride which the public character of the office entails. Precisely because *episcope* involves exposure to the possibility of abusing power, and thus to the risk of further obstacles to the realization of the gift of the Spirit, it is wholly appropriate that the "increase" of the gift of the Holy Spirit be sought at this moment.

Finally, inasmuch as a series of tasks are solemnly assigned to the officeholder, failure in which will have the most serious repercussions for the church, the whole church joins in common prayer to the Holy Spirit that what should be true of each baptized Christian will indeed be true of these baptized Christians, namely that they will truly be Christs to their neighbors. The service of ordination is a recognition of the public character of the life of the ordained in its assigned roles in liturgy and in preaching, undeniably a greater burden and responsibility, humanly speaking, than that of the nonordained. In the prayer for the Holy Spirit there is an implicit recognition of the social anthropology of representation in religion, a phenomenon not peculiar to Christianity, nor one from whose potential, and difficulties, it is exempt. We shall discuss further the sense in which Christian theology both affirms and simultaneously subverts the representative character of Christian priesthood.

It is a corollary of the relation of *episcope* to the theology of baptism that the Christian is able to be thoroughly realistic about the continued influence of death in the lives of individual members of the church and in its institutional structures. The recovery in contemporary theology of the eschatology of the church has enabled theologians of many denominations to recall ecclesiology from a triumphalism which seriously distorted the practice of *episcope*. This recovery is the theological precondition for the admission of the idea of a dialectical process in relationship to the realities of power in the church. It is not easy for those who hold power to perceive their own abuses of it. They have to be told, and the telling is not comfortable. Nor are those who cry foul invariably in the right. The influence of death and the politics of alien domination take many forms. Democratic institutions lend themselves to various specious distortions, as I

shall argue, to which those sensitized to the more startling manifesta-
tions of authoritarianism are sometimes blind. The acknowledgment
that we live in the midst of a dialectic enables the church to hear the
call to return to baptism, a call which is issued at every Eucharist.

ROUTINIZATION AND
THE CONTRIBUTION OF SOCIOLOGY

The contribution which sociology must be allowed to make to
any consideration of the question of *episcope* and power in the church
will largely be included with a discussion of Weber's formulation of
the "routinization (*Veralltäglichung*) of charisma," one of the most successful sociological concepts ever to have been devised.[20] But before
we examine this idea, a word is overdue about the terminology of
"power" and "authority." So far I have preferred to speak of power
in the church, and to accept the possibility that such power may be
abused or used properly. There are also those who would sharply distinguish power from authority in relationship to the church. They
would do so on the grounds that the Christian faith sponsors the
radical criticism of mundane views of power and that the resource it
possesses, or with which it is endowed, is not power but authority.

The position which is being advanced in this essay is wholly
consistent with the view that the Christian church has a way of man-
aging its institutional life which is sociologically utterly distinct, in the
sense of being constructed solely from its own, spiritual resources. In
all voluntary associations united to achieve common goals there takes
place the distribution of powers such that one may distinguish higher
participants from lower participants. In such voluntary organizations
the source of the power is not force or physical constraint but whatever can be mobilized to sustain agreement. The Christian churches,
of course, have not always been voluntary organizations. There have
taken place the forcible conversion and baptism of whole populations.
Heretics have been physically persecuted and orthodoxy protected by
censorship and far-from-idle threats. Of all these methods there has
been criticism virtually since they were deployed, precisely because
they undermine something precious to Christian faith, namely the
sincere intention of the person to love God for himself. Insofar as

the word "power" has the connotation of "force," or "violence," it is appropriate for Christians to renounce it.

But is "power" to be taken as the equivalent of "force"? Modern sociology, which is fascinated by the complexity of the idea of power, has no one answer to that question. Writers on power are obliged to define in what sense they are using the term; and one of the difficulties of such definitions is that they fail to do justice to more than a part of the problem of power, as it is known in the ordinary speech conventions of modern societies. Furthermore, one of the suspicions with which one rises from the study of modern sociological literature is that religious people use the word "authority" precisely because of its less negative connotations. It functions, in other words, to conceal behind bland vocabulary resources which in other contexts would be recognized as power.

The issue, like the literature, is vast, and all one can do here is to indicate the linguistic decisions which have been taken. The word "power" I take to be a term of very broad meaning covering a spectrum of forms which generally are given other, more precise denominations.[21] Power in this sense includes violence, coercion, and force, on the one hand, but also domination, manipulation, persuasion, and influence, on the other. Power is a term indicative of resources available to human beings, the main types of which are economic, military, legal, and ideological. It makes perfectly good sense, therefore, to speak of "the power of ideas."

On this account, therefore, authority in a religion is that form of power specifically appropriate to ideological power in a voluntary institution. When we speak of the "authority of the priest," for example, this is to refer to a complex of powers needing further analysis. In part the authority consists in that person's intrinsic qualities (some of which, like humility, will be in part distinctive of Christianity, others of which will be attributes appropriate to any public leader); hence to "speak with authority" will entail the recognition of those intrinsic qualities. But there are other aspects of the authority of the priest of greater ambiguity, for example the fact that the priest's legal status in a congregation may give him or her certain monopolistic rights in religious or even civil matters (such as marriages). Moreover the priest has, or may have, a number of sanctions at his or her disposal, such as the power of excommunication—or, in a more secular vein, the power of being in the position to spread information or disinformation about members of the congregation. If it is true that authority in a religion is a composite term in need of further analysis, the fact that such analysis may lead us into uncomfortable or embarrassing areas, where plainly secular power is an element of the picture, ought by no means deter us. Indeed, if the dialectical process we have depicted is actually to work, it is essential that our gaze does not waver at the point where we may be in danger of confusing the imperatives and power of the gospel with alien, but convenient, supports. We do not escape from the realm of human resources by speaking of authority in the church. There is much to be said for the use of the term "power" in that it compels us to confront the probability that it will be abused.

Bishops and those who occupy positions of leadership and pastoral oversight in the church have, then, powers of various kinds. Why should this have come to pass? Weber's explanation was that all religions, including Christianity, which start with charismatic leaders, have to go through a process of regularizing leadership, so as to solve at least two problems: the preservation of the goals of the movement by focusing activity and the necessity of making financial provision for ensuring the movement's continuance. He listed a series of possible solutions of the problem of leadership after the original leaders' disappearance from the scene. Two of these feature in the New Testament, the choice by the charismatic leader of his successors and the election of new leaders with the agreement of the community.

In view of the prominence in modern New Testament scholarship of the thesis about so-called early Catholicism, it is important to stress that, in Weber's view at least, St. Paul was already wrestling with problems which are recognizably those of routinization. Paul himself should be regarded as "charismatic" on Weber's definition and the leadership of the Pauline churches no doubt posed severe problems of routinization.[22] But the Corinthian correspondence needs analysis in terms of routinization and institutionalization if we are to understand the nature of Paul's appeal to his commissioning by Christ himself, as well as the doubts which many apparently felt about its authenticity. Financial problems about his own maintenance are also clearly visible.

Routinization, however, has other avenues, one of which is the development of ritual. Victor Turner has described with considerable insight the process whereby the life of a charismatic leader becomes the matter of a ritual process, and discipleship of the now long departed leader is preserved in the narration of a sacred text embodying and celebrating his significance.[23] This, we should note, is why the phenomenon of Christian baptism and the social reality of the church are conterminous and why their theologies define each other. In particular, baptism constitutes a ritual which, on Turner's account, first separates the baptizand from his or her normal place in the structures of society, thrusts the baptizand out into a realm (which Turner calls the "liminal" or "threshold situation") characterized by the absence or negation of structure, finally to reaggregate the baptizand into society again, but changed and elevated by the ritual process. For Turner the threshold is a state of what he calls "*communitas*" or holy equality, characterized by the abolition or at least suspension of structural relationships. This is a greatly simplified account of Turner's highly sophisticated study of ritual processes which has already proved fruitful in more than one study of the Pauline practice and theology of baptism.[24]

I wish to comment on my own behalf on one paradoxical feature of the situation, namely the person and status of the baptizer. St. Paul is vehement in his denial that the person of the baptizer is relevant to the identity of the Christian (1 Cor. 1:13ff). He does not even remember precisely whom he has baptized; the sole important matter was the gospel faith underlying the baptism, a faith which should guarantee unanimity. The issue may, however, already have been that of baptismal pedigree from one or other leader, Apollos or Cephas. The baptizer appears to hold a privileged position in relation to the ritual by making the process happen. But at the same time, according to the liminal understanding of the ritual, all participants, the baptizer included, belong to one holy equality. Baptism, in other words, has the paradoxical capacity simultaneously to exalt the power of the baptizer and to undermine it.

This paradox deserves further exploration. The ritual affirms that there exists a world of human relationships other than the structured relationships of human societies, which erect and perpetuate divisions and hierarchies between different groups of people. This alternative world is, in Christian theology, a new humanity remade in Christ, claiming the whole world for the redeemed order. The community of the redeemed, therefore, has to manifest the new order of things. It is to stand for the reality which will be, to manifest the new being of the kingdom. But it is never possible totally to create an "alternative culture." The process of the subversion of existing societal structures is extraordinarily complex.[25] If the subversive intentions of the Christian community are to be realized, Christians themselves have to be mobilized to achieve this goal. But such acts of mobilization impose their own organizational costs. Structures have to be created in order to focus Christianity's opposition to its competitors. Hence the paradox of the position of the baptizer, who at once is recognized as an authorized representative of the community but whose actions subvert the very structure which locates his or her role.

The importance of developing ideas concerning leadership and pastoral oversight in the church in relation to baptism becomes at once apparent. The doctrine that baptism bestows upon the baptized the fullness of the gift of the Holy Spirit is the essential precondition for understanding the relationship of the ordained to the nonordained. The roles in the Christian community of ordained and nonordained may differ according to the structure of an order necessary to the mission of the church. But if we are to understand the provisionality of the structure within human societies, its openness to abuse, and the necessity for care in its justification, we shall have to take firm hold upon the doctrine of the Holy Spirit.

We shall not be surprised to discover that the same Spirit which is given to each and every Christian as a unique gift for the common good, is the very basis on which specific individuals claim either superior status in a hierarchy, or the superior rights of a spiritual elite. But the Spirit of God is the Spirit of love and the holy equality in virtue of which Christians are taught the difficult lesson of counting others better than themselves (Phil. 2:3). In the light of such a doctrine it becomes, or should become, institutionally impossible to identify the Spirit's guidance of the church with the decisions of a hierarchy or elite.

A COMMENT ON AUTHORITARIAN LIBERALISM

With this last consideration the essay begins to take on the tone of a standard piece of theological liberalism. Academic liberals in Western institutions of higher education have not, however, invariably perceived the self-interested character of attacks upon the standing of hierarchs and bureaucrats. They have failed to observe that by any appropriate criteria they too belong to the higher participants in church government, by means of the monopoly which they have established upon entry to the position of pastoral leadership in the church. It is extraordinarily difficult to persuade scholars in the church that their learning and articulateness are resources which need as careful scrutiny as the more overt powers of hierarchs. But if it be the case that, despite Kierkegaard's caustic observation of the failure of the New Testament to refer to professors of theology, intellectual skills are also gifts of the one Spirit, then the problem of how to count others better than themselves needs careful consideration by the churches' scholars.

The authoritarian liberal is an increasingly familiar phenomenon in the modern church. Liberals generally believe in increasing the participation in decision making of those who are to be affected by the decisions and are antagonistic to elites and cabals. Authoritarian liberals become exceptionally keen on such participation when *de facto* they control the processes whereby relevant information is minted and disseminated. Power is exercised not just by the arguments of the articulate, but also by their control of the agenda and their capacity to create a climate in which beliefs and desires are modified without overt attention being drawn to the process. Authoritarian liberals are generally experts at concealing the fact that they are as ready as any totalitarian of the past to manipulate the internal communications of the church to ensure that the multitudes decide in favor of what they want to have confirmed.

Liberals also profess the principles of wide toleration of opinion, but are caught at the difficulty of tolerating opinions whose implementation would destroy the conditions of toleration for which they stand. The inevitable discovery of the limits of toleration persuades them of the need for vigilance, a vigilance which soon becomes the pretext for the return of authoritarianism, suitably disguised. Authoritarian liberals are expert at manipulation; they become spokespersons for selected minorities whose campaigns entail the promulgation of their own beliefs. In this way intellectual resistance to their systems of belief can be represented as the persecution of a minority and thus intolerable opinion. A whole series of campaigns on behalf of the genuinely persecuted or disadvantaged, whether Jews, blacks, women, homosexuals, or the mentally handicapped, have been harnessed to more or less naked expressions of the will-to-power among Christian liberals in higher education who have developed, in the process, fearsomely authoritarian traits.

But in the dialectic which I have depicted in this essay there is no guarantee that what are thought to be liberal institutional arrangements are more true and faithful resolutions of the problem of *episcope* and power in the church. It has to be realized that institutionalization itself imposes costs upon the church. A failure to appreciate this truth is responsible for the readiness of modern democrats to be suspicious enough of what are said to be—with all too little justification—representative assemblies. Liberalism itself can harden into a devious form of authoritarianism and will need to be subverted from within. The dialectic is not to be prematurely halted. The duty of a theologian is not to determine how the problem of the routinization of charisma may finally be resolved, but to identify abuses; and that, I submit, is the sense of the passage from the *Confessio Augustana* with which we began.

NOTES

1. In *Confessing One Faith*, ed. G. W. Forell and J. F. McCue, (Minneapolis: Augsburg, 1982), 149.

2. Michael Seils, *Lutheran Convergence?* Lutheran World Federation Report 25 (Geneva: Lutheran World Federation, 1988), esp. chs. 5 and 7.

3. *Of the Lawes of Ecclesiasticall Polity*, Book I, xxv, 2.

4. *A Rational Account of the Grounds of Protestant Religion* (1664; new edition, Oxford, 1844), ii, 277–80.

5. *The Truth Shall Make You Free: The Lambeth Conference 1988* (London, 1988); Resolution 18, 2a, p. 216.

6. See Wayne Meeks, *The First Urban Christians* (New Haven, Conn.: Yale University Press, 1983), 157; cf. 112–13.

7. *The Truth Shall Make You Free*, para. 36, p. 90. The section on "Christ and Culture," pp. 87–92 is extensively based on the Inter-Anglican

Theological and Doctrinal Commission's Report, *For the Sake of the Kingdom* (London, 1986), esp. chs. 6–10.

8. Compare *The Niagara Report*, The Report of the Anglican-Lutheran International Continuation Committee (London: Anglican Consultative Council, and Geneva: Lutheran World Federation, 1988), para. 46, p. 27.

9. Irenaeus, *Adversus Haereses* IV, 26, 3.

10. See Amitai Etzioni, *A Comparative Analysis of Complex Organizations* (New York: Free Press, 1961), esp. 3–21.

11. See S. W. Sykes, "Power in the Church of England," in *Power in the Church* (*Concilium* 197), ed. James Provost & Knut Wolf (Edinburgh: T & T Clark, 1988), 123–28.

12. Sik Hung Ng, *The Social Psychology of Power* (London: Academic Press, 1980), 255–57.

13. "Macht, power, puissance: prose démocratique ou poésie démoniaque," *European Journal of Sociology* 5, no. 1 (1964): 27. Article translated and reprinted in S. Lukes, ed., *Power* (Oxford, 1986), 253–77.

14. See for example the work of a Dutch Augustinian prior, Father Robert Adolfs, *The Grave of God: Has the Church a Future?* ed. and trans. D. N. Smith (London: Burns and Oates, 1967), and its endorsement by D. M. MacKinnon in *The Stripping of the Altars* (London: Collins, 1969).

15. See M. Breidert, *Die kenotische Christologie des 19 Jahrhunderts* (Gütersloh, 1977).

16. Classically expressed in the eleventh century in a letter of Gregory VII: "Every Christian king when he approaches his end asks the aid of a priest as a miserable suppliant that he may escape the prison of hell. . . . To whom among them [kings or emperors] is given the power to bind and loose in Heaven and upon earth? From this it is apparent how greatly superior in power is the priestly dignity." *The Correspondence of Pope Gregory VII*, trans. E. Emerton, Records of Civilization: Sources and Studies, 14 (New York: Columbia University Press, 1932), 171.

17. See S. Lukes, ed., *Power*, 7.

18. The usual distinction which is introduced at this point in the discussion, that between ontological and functional understandings of the priesthood, is radically unclear. Often it is a disguised way of contrasting theological and sociological views of ordination, a contrast which, it must be said, has absolutely no fixed content. In the present passage both "identity" and "role" are conceived at once theologically *and* sociologically.

19. See, on the "logic of overflow," D. W. Hardy and David F. Ford, *Jubilate: Theology in Praise* (London, 1984).

20. There is continuous discussion and refinement of Weber's original presentation, up to and including Anthony Gidden's "theory of structuration"; see his *The Constitution of Society* (Cambridge, 1984), ch. 2.

21. See D. H. Wrong, *Power: Its Forms, Bases and Uses* (Oxford, 1979).

22. See Bengt Holmberg, *Paul and Power: The Structure of Authority in the Primitive Church as Reflected in the Pauline Epistles* (Philadelphia: Fortress, 1980); and Reinhard Bendix, "Umbildung des persönlichen Charismas. Eine Anwendung von Max Webers Charismabegriff auf das Frühchristentum," in W. Schluchter, ed., *Max Webers Sicht des antiken Christentums* (Frankfurt, 1985), 404–42.

23. See esp. Turner, *Dramas, Fields and Metaphors: Symbolic Action in Human Society* (Ithaca, N.Y.: Cornell University Press, 1974).

24. See esp. Meeks, *The First Urban Christians*, ch. 5.

25. See, on the complexity of the process whereby the thrust against legitimation builds up harder legitimation, David Martin's sociological study of Christian theory and practice, *The Breaking of the Image* (London, 1980), ch. 10.

A RABBINIC PRAGMATISM

PETER OCHS

George Lindbeck's *The Nature of Doctrine* is not just for Christians. The ecumenical concerns to which it speaks are "intra-Christian"[1]—as Lindbeck's understanding of "intratextuality"[2] requires. Nevertheless, the way in which it speaks to these concerns is a model for intra-Jewish understanding as well, at least for the self-understanding of a subcommunity of recent Jewish thinkers. In this study, I examine some of the ways in which Lindbeck's approach to studying Christian doctrine helps illuminate these thinkers' own approach to studying normative Jewish teachings. Lindbeck makes claims about the nature of doctrine itself, and not just about the way some scholars think about doctrine. Consequently, it might seem that the appropriate way to extend his approach would be to examine comparable claims about the nature of classical Jewish teachings, rather than about the methodologies of what may turn out to be an idiosyncratic group of Jewish scholars. Lindbeck's "postliberalism," after all, is about getting back down to business after so many centuries of the modernist hemming and hawing we call epistemology. In reply, I hope this essay will suggest that a postliberal or pragmatic study of normative teachings is itself a study of how some particular group of people studies, interprets, and lives those teachings. The business we have to get back down to is itself a historically situated method of inquiry.

As displayed in *The Nature of Doctrine*, Lindbeck's approach allows for only a certain kind of imitation. He says that his rule theory of doctrine is a particular instance of what he calls a "cultural-linguistic" approach to the study of religion. Analogously, we may consider his practice[3] of this approach, including his labeling it "cultural-linguistic," an instance of a more general interpretive tendency.[4] The tendency is defined only through such practices, of which there may be particularly felicitous instances, but no privileged or definitive instance. If Lindbeck cites Wittgenstein, Geertz, Frei, and others among the most significant sources of his approach, this means that the works of these thinkers introduce him more effectively than others to an interpretive tendency exemplified in his own practice. As the Psalmist declares, "deep calls to deep" (Ps. 42:8):[5] in this context, an allusion to that wisdom which recognizes itself in the words of what appears to be ordinary speech. Or, again, "As face answers to face in water, so does one person's heart to another" (Prov. 27:19). The practice of one interpreter influences that of another in the way it awakens recognition of a common or mediating tendency. In the idiom of scriptural interpretation, this tendency is often labeled "word" — *dibbur* and then *logos*: as in one tradition, "My word is like fire . . . ," and in another, "In the beginning was the word . . . ." In this idiom, we may say that Lindbeck's approach is to examine church doctrines as interpretations, and in that sense instantiations, of scriptural words and that his own approach is itself an interpretation of some otherwise undesignated word. This is to suggest that the cultural-linguistic approach of Wittgenstein, Geertz, et al. may interest Lindbeck because it appears to him to be at least analogous to a more ancient and authoritative hermeneutical tendency. As William James said of pragmatism, this approach would then be "a new name for some old ways of thinking."[6]

It is as such a new name that Lindbeck's approach is pertinent to the work of what I call the "aftermodern Jewish philosophers."[7] Among the group's most well-known representatives are such thinkers as Hermann Cohen (in his later work), Martin Buber, Franz Rosenzweig, Emil Fackenheim, Emanuel Levinas, to some extent Abraham Heschel and Mordecai Kaplan, and Max Kadushin—the latter little known and not previously collected with the others but in fact very important to the group's self-definition. Admittedly, this group is a group in a Pickwickian sense. For the present purposes, however, there are good reasons for classing them together. When Rosenzweig labels his new method of thinking *Sprachdenken*, or "speech-thinking," he says it is the method also of Cohen and Buber; Levinas considers Rosenzweig the stimulus for this aspect of his work; Fackenheim offers similar credits; Heschel provides a bridge between the work of these continental aftermoderns and their American, pragmatic cousins; among the latter, Kaplan sets out the pragmatic method and Kadushin reconnects it to a theory of what we might call rabbinic speech-thinking. This attention to speech-thinking corresponds to Lindbeck's cultural-linguistic approach, and these thinkers are classed together with respect to this character alone. In sum, the aftermoderns are a collection of recent Jewish thinkers who practice, in various ways and with varying degrees of refinement and self-consciousness, what I will call a single interpretive tendency. Since the tendency is displayed only through such practices, it always appears differently. To refer to "a single interpretive tendency" is to suggest that, as face answers to face, each of these interpreters could recognize his tendency in the others' practices. The hermeneutical model of this phenomenon is illustrated in a midrash in the Babylonian Talmud *Sanhedrin* 34a:

> It was taught in the School of Rabbi Yishmael: "Behold, My word is like fire,—declares the Lord—and like a hammer that shatters rock" (Jer. 23.29). Just as a hammer produces many sparks (when it strikes the rock) so too a single verse has several meanings.[8]

We speak of one Word, even though we have in hand only the sparks.

The claim of this paper is that the aftermoderns could see in Lindbeck's practice sparks of the same hammer. I examine the claim in four ways. The first, labeled "Face Answers to Face," is to identify ways in which the aftermoderns' approach to religion is analogous to Lindbeck's postliberal approach. In order to adequate one approach to the other, I describe Lindbeck's postliberalism as if it were embodied in the practices of an emergent group of "postliberal" Christian scholars. The presumption enables me to claim that we are, in fact, drawing analogies between the practices of two comparable groups, the aftermoderns and the postliberals. The focus here is on shared method. The second way, labeled "Deep Calls to Deep," is to compare the critical claims offered by aftermoderns and postliberals. The focus here is on these thinkers' perceptions of the philosophic errors they believe they are correcting. The third way, labeled "Where Deep

Calls," is to offer initial suggestions about the contexts out of which these thinkers make their claims. The last way, labeled "A Saving Presence," is to introduce the hermeneutical program the thinkers have offered: restating their claims in terms of the context out of which they are offered.

This examination is guided by a species of pragmatic analysis. In the idiom of Charles Peirce's original pragmatism, this is to reconnect a rational inquiry to the problematic situation[9] to which it responds and in terms of which it has meaning. As employed in this essay, the method is to interpret postliberal and aftermodern theses as analogous explicit responses to comparable but as yet undisclosed problems. The paper's scriptural themes emerge from a pragmatist's reading of several verses of Psalm 42:

(2) Like a hind crying for water
　　my soul cries for You, O God;
　　my soul thirsts for God, the living God;
　　O when will I come to appear before God! . . .

(6) Why so downcast, my soul,
　　why disquieted within me?
　Have hope in God;
　　I will praise Him
　　for His saving presence.

(7) O my God, my soul is downcast;
　　therefore I think of You
　　in this land of Jordan and Hermon,
　　in Mount Mizar,

(8) 　where deep calls to deep
　　in the roar of Your cataracts,
　　all Your breakers and billows have swept over me . . .

(12) Why so downcast, my soul,
　　why disquieted within me?
　Have hope in God;
　　I will yet praise Him,
　　my ever-present help, my God.

The medieval commentator Rashi[10] reads "deep calls to deep" as "trouble calls to its fellow ('to that joined to it')"; the psalmist's troubles multiplying like the surging waters, it is as if each trouble calls to its fellow to join it.[11] For our present purposes, the text symbolizes the pragmatist's understanding of what lies beneath one interpreter's recognizing him or herself in the practice of another. They share comparable discomforts. In Peirce's terms, their inquiries arise as responses to comparably perceived inadequacies in antecedent practices. To hope for God's "saving presence" is to trust that these inadequacies will eventually be repaired. For the pragmatist, this means that the inquiries stimulated by a given problem will eventually lead to its resolution.

"Rabbinic Pragmatism" is a name for the activity of applying the pragmatic method of analysis to the argumentation of the aftermodern Jewish philosophers. It is a way of reconnecting the aftermoderns' philosophic claims to their efforts to find in the classical sources of rabbinic Judaism answers to what troubles them about modern philosophy or, more generally, about the modern project of inquiry in the academy.

1. FACE ANSWERS TO FACE:
POSTLIBERALS AND AFTERMODERNS

If Lindbeck's approach to religion typified the practices of a group of postliberal Christian scholars, then aftermodern Jews might see in postliberal Christians faces which answered their own in the mirror of as yet unidentified waters (Prov. 27:19).

Lindbeck distinguishes his cultural-linguistic approach to the study of religion from the "preliberal" approach of the "cognitivists" and the "liberal" approach of the "experiential-expressivists."[12] He says the cognitivist approach is to consider religions as systems of propositions or truth-claims about an objective reality.[13] The experiential-expressivist approach is to consider them, in Lonergan's terms, as "diverse expressions or objectifications of a common core experience,"[14] which is "the dynamic state of being in love without restriction" and "without an object."[15] The cultural-linguistic approach is, to the contrary, to place emphasis

> on those respects in which religions resemble languages together with
> their correlative forms of life and are thus similar to cultures (insofar
> as these are understood semiotically as reality and value systems—that
> is, as idioms for the construction of reality and the living of life).[16]

Following Geertz, this is to consider a religion a

> system of discursive and non-discursive symbols linking motivation and action and providing an ultimate legitimation for basic patterns of thought, feeling and behavior uniquely characteristic of a given community or society and its members.[17]

It is to consider "being religious" as "achieving competence" in a code with grammatical, lexical, and semantic dimensions or as "interiorizing a skill."[18] Lindbeck adds that, "unlike other perspectives, this approach proposes no common framework such as that supplied by the propositionalists' concept of truth or the expressivists' concept of experience within which to compare religions."[19] Religion, he says,

> can at least plausibly be construed as a class name for a variegated set of cultural-linguistic systems that, at least in some cases, differentially shape and produce our most profound sentiments, attitudes, and awarenesses.[20]

The aftermoderns do not sound like Lindbeck, because their arguments tend to be methodologically one degree less reflexive. Lindbeck's description of the cultural-linguistic approach constitutes what Peirce would call a speculative rhetoric or methodeutic of religion:[21] an analysis of the methodologies available for identifying and evaluating second-order[22] hermeneutical practices. The aftermoderns, on the other hand, usually lack a methodeutic. They argue on behalf of a new norm or reasoning, or logic, without first having surveyed and evaluated the methods available for offering such argumentation. Adopting Lindbeck's approach as paradigm, however, it is possible to provide the aftermoderns a methodeutic and, in terms of it, to show how close they are to Lindbeck in both their logic and their method of defending it.

Rosenzweig's speech-thinking is representative of the aftermoderns' new norms of reasoning. He promoted his speech-thinking as a new paradigm in which "the method of speech replaces the method of thinking maintained in all earlier philosophies."[23] The norms of this new thinking are "grammatical" rather than "logical":[24] dependent on the temporal, historical, social, and personal contexts of speech. This, he asserted, is also the new thinking of Cohen and Buber, as well as of Feuerbach and others. In a fashion reminiscent of Peirce,

Rosenzweig noted that this new thinking "actually . . . employ[s] the method of sound common sense as a method of scientific thinking."[25] He did not press his empiricism further, however, to note those everyday or traditional practices in which this thinking is a commonplace. Instead, in the manner of modern, Cartesian philosophies, he constructed his model of this thinking out of the elements of what approximates a phenomenological field; the method of argumentation remains transcendental and, ironically, *a priori*. In other words, he tends to contemplate the possibility or form of speech-thinking more than he examines historically situated cases of it.

Lindbeck's methodeutic suggests another way of formulating Rosenzweig's innovation. It is that Rosenzweig perceived in the grammar of everyday practices, including the everyday practices of the traditional rabbinic Jew, certain norms of reasoning of which the logical systems of the modern philosophers provided no adequate model. These systems did not offer him adequate tools for identifying the rationality or rule-governed character of "sound commonsense" or of the hermeneutical, legal-ethical, and liturgical practices of traditional Judaism. In the absence of such tools, he attempted to construct his own by describing what he took to be the essential features of this commonsense reasoning and then adopting his description as a template for measuring all instances of this reasoning. Employing Lindbeck's terms, we might say that Rosenzweig sought to develop a cultural-linguistic method. Unaided by Wittgenstein, Geertz, and others, he was forced to forge it from out of the recalcitrant materials of cognitivist and experiential-expressivist inquiries, whose proper objects lay in certain ideal or *a priori* systems rather than in the concrete practices of concern to Rosenzweig. Thus, following Schelling, as did Peirce and James, Rosenzweig went in search for an "absolute empiricism,"[26] by which he meant an empiricism which reached behind the "static truths"[27] of the classical empiricists to those relational truths, or "truths *for* someone,"[28] of his speech-thinking. For Lindbeck, "absolute empiricism" becomes Ryle's and Geertz's method of thick description and "relational truths" are the "intrasystematic" truths of semiotic systems which, as exemplified in the scriptural world, are "able to absorb the universe," supplying "the interpretive framework within which believers seek to live their lives and understand reality."[29] Rosenzweig initiated an inquiry which, un-hampered by his idealist heritage, the "postliberals" have nurtured into a discipline.

Among the aftermoderns, Kadushin's work comes closest to ex-hibiting the methodology of an empirical study of speech-thinking. Influenced in this regard by Peirce, as well as by the social scien-tific antecedents of Geertz in the early twentieth century,[30] Kadushin attempted to develop his methodology in the field—or at least the library—rather than in the armchair. Rather than construct a para-digm of speech-thinking *a priori*, he sought to locate practices of speech-thinking in their social, or at least literary, contexts and then fashion his particular science of thick description in accordance with what he found. His name for speech-thinking was "organic think-ing," which he predicated of "the rabbinic mind" as exhibited in the hermeneutical-ethical practices of the talmudic sages. With some degree[31] of interpretive license, he took the literary documents of rabbinic exegesis or *midrash* to be accurate indices of these practices and he took these practices to be accurate indices of public com-portment. Eschewing what correspond to cognitivist and experiential-expressivist forms of analysis,[32] he then developed a cultural-linguistic method for examining the grammar of organic thinking as it is dis-played in rabbinic midrash:

> Our theory of organic thinking bears the same relation to the concrete complex of rabbinic theology as grammar does to a language, and, like grammar, can best be grasped through the actual analysis of a good sample of that literature. The analogy—it is probably much more than that—goes even further. Just as the rules of grammar always have reference to a specific language, so the implications of the theory of organic thinking have reference to a particular organic complex.[33]

Within the language of a chronologically earlier and less-developed science, Kadushin anticipated several features of Lindbeck's study. He examined normative rabbinic teachings intratextually, attending to what Lindbeck would call their intrasystematic rather than their on-tological truths. His analysis of the stable elements of these teachings corresponds to Lindbeck's rule-theoretical interpretation of Christian doctrine.[34] Like Lindbeck, finally, he suggested that the method he used to study the grammar of rabbinic normative teachings might also be employed generally as a method of studying the grammars of other normative systems, religions in particular.

Aftermoderns and postliberals appear to share a general method of inquiry: examining the grammars of religious practices—considered typical of commonsense or everyday practices in general—with tools of inquiry apparently unavailable in the repertoire of classical and modern Western philosophy.

2. DEEP CALLS TO DEEP: THE COMPLAINTS OF POSTLIBERALS AND AFTERMODERNS

To claim that aftermoderns and postliberals practice a common interpretive tendency is, for the pragmatic interpreter, to claim that they share a comparable discomfort. To discover apparently shared methods of inquiry is to take only the first step in examining this discomfort. The second step is to identify the complaints which each group may offer in response to its discomfort and which may serve as the only indices we have of it. The complaints may appear, explicitly, as criticisms of some inherited practice of inquiry, or, only implicitly, as the articulated or unarticulated correlatives of certain recommendations, which tend to appear in terms of dichotomous or doubly dichotomous distinctions. An example of the latter is Kant's critical philosophy, which he recommends in contradistinction to dogmatic philosophy, of which there are empiricist and rationalist sorts. The task of this second stage of our inquiry is to identify the recommendations of the postliberals and aftermoderns and link them with their correlative complaints.

Lindbeck's complaint is displayed by way of the dichotomous distinctions he draws between cultural-linguistic and non-cultural-linguistic analyses of religion and then between rule-theoretical and non-rule-theoretical theories of doctrine. His complaint, in short, is that non-rule-theoretical theories of doctrine fail to account for the facts of ecumenism among doctrinally divergent groups. His diagnosis is that these theories are generated by non-cultural-linguistic tendencies of analysis, of which there are two sorts, cognitivist and experiential-expressivist. His recommendation is that Christian theologians adopt cultural-linguistic approaches to religion and apply these to developing rule-theoretical accounts of doctrine. Among the leading features of his own account are these: "Church doctrines are communally authoritative teachings regarding beliefs and practices that are considered essential to the identity or welfare of the group in question."[35] These doctrines are second-order propositions, which are propositions about first-order propositions, which latter are propositions about the world itself. The doctrines are, therefore, rules about the discourse Christians use to speak about the world, delineating the grammar of Christian discourse, which is the grammar of a language spoken by the church as a normative community of interpreter-practitioners of the scriptural word. Among church doctrines, some are unconditionally necessary in the context of a given historical period or a given civilization. As general rules, doctrines always appear in context-specific formulations, of which there is no one privileged instance. As second-order claims, the rules remain stable, while their first-order formulations adjust to changing conditions of experience.[36]

Lindbeck argues that, for cognitivists, doctrines "function as informative [first order] propositions or truth claims about objective realities."[37] From this approach, it is possible to claim that a given doctrine appears differently in different contexts only when the ontological referents of various formulations remain the same. For cognitivists, then, there are privileged formulations and there is an intolerance for ontological relativism. Lindbeck argues, finally, that experiential-expressivists understand doctrines as "noninformative and nondiscursive symbols of inner feelings, attitudes or existential orientations."[38] Here, there is room to explain any sort of change whatever, since there is no limit to the polyvalence of doctrinal symbols. All symbols symbolize a single "core experience of the Ultimate" through the media of various languages and contexts. There is, however, no way of accounting for the stability of doctrinal meaning; experientialists "tend to exclude *a priori* the traditional characteristics of doctrine."[39]

In order to compare Lindbeck's complaints and recommendations with those of the aftermoderns, I find it expedient to reformulate both sets of correlatives in terms of a variant of Peirce's pragmatic semeiotic.[40] This semeiotic provides a more rudimentary formulation of the interpretive tendency displayed in both the postliberal and aftermodern arguments. For the third stage of our inquiry, it also introduces a common idiom for identifying the postliberals' and aftermoderns' shared discomfort.

Excursus on Peirce's Semeiotic

Peirce defines a sign as

> something which stands to somebody for something in some respect
> or capacity. It addresses somebody, that is, creates in the mind of that
> person an equivalent sign, or perhaps a more developed sign. That
> sign which it creates I call the *interpretant* of the first sign. The sign
> stands for something, its *object*. It stands for that object [only in some
> respect].[41]

Among many subdivisions of signs, he distinguishes these general
divisions:

> An *icon* is a sign which refers to the Object that it denotes by
> virtue of characters of its own, and which it possesses, just the same,
> whether any such Object actually exists or not. . . .
> An *index* is a sign which refers to the Object that it denotes by
> virtue of being really affected by that Object. . . . In so far as the Index
> is affected by its Object, it necessarily has some Quality in common
> with the Object, and it is in respect to these that it refers to the
> Object. . . .
> A *symbol* is a sign which refers to the Object that it denotes
> by virtue of the law . . . which operates to cause the Symbol to be
> interpreted as referring to that Object. It is thus itself a general type,
> or law. . . . Not only is it general itself, but the Object to which it
> refers is of a general nature.[42]

Necessarily imperfect examples of icons are images, diagrams, or even
a sculpture of something. Examples—imperfect again—of indices are
weather-vanes, thermometers, or interjections such as "Ugh!" Examples of symbols, which Peirce calls "genuine" signs, are words, propositions, and arguments. Peirce labels "genuine symbols" those whose
objects are themselves symbols and, thus, whose interpretants are symbols or laws, such as a law of cognition, or a process of interpretation.
For reasons noted earlier, it seems preferable in this context to sub-
stitute the term "tendencies" for "laws."

According to Peirce, a sign signifies, or determines its interpretant, in one of two ways. A sign is determinate "in respect to
any character which inheres in it or is (universally and affirmatively)

predicated of it, as well as in respect to the negative of such characters,"[43] or if its "meaning would leave 'no latitude of interpretation,'"[44] or if it "indicates an otherwise known individual." Otherwise, the sign is indeterminate—describing in some way, but not completely, "how an individual intended is to be selected."[45] Of indeterminate signs, there are two kinds: the *vague*, or indefinite, and the *general*, or hypothetical. For Peirce, the *general* "turns over to the interpreter the right to complete the determination as he pleases."[46] If the first subject of a proposition of two or more subjects is general, the proposition is called universal:[47] the general indicates the character of a merely possible individual, representing the synthesis of a multitude of subjects. The *vague*, on the other hand, "reserves for some other possible sign or experience the function of completing the determination."[48] If the first subject of a complex proposition is vague, the proposition is called particular:[49] the vague denotes some of the characters of an *existent* individual, representing the synthesis of a multitude of predicates.

According to Peirce's definitions, genuine symbols must be indeterminate. For the sake of the following discussion, I will use the term *complete symbol* to refer to the genuine symbol which signifies its object generally, that is, non-vaguely. The complete symbol withholds no information from the interpreter, offering rules for the construction of a possible universe which the interpreter may enact as he or she sees fit. For example, the propositions "all apples are red," or "all people are created equal" may be interpreted as instructions "to take any apple you will and it'll be red," or "any person you will and he or she'll be created equal." I will then use the term *incomplete symbol* to refer to a genuine symbol which signifies its object vaguely. The incomplete symbol withholds essential information from the interpreter and therefore appeals to the interpreter to wait and listen for more, which is either to depend upon the source of the symbol for further instruction or to engage in some action to elicit more information. For example, the statement "there is some aftermodern who has expressivist tendencies" may be interpreted to mean that there is more information to be had about exactly who that someone is.

It is most helpful to begin our comparison with the aftermoderns, since their theory of incomplete symbolization is methodologically more basic than the postliberals' and therefore displays more clearly its connections to the kind of fundamental work in which Peirce was engaged. Searching for methods of interpreting scriptural texts and rabbinic practices, the aftermoderns tend to single out classical and modern Western philosophers for criticism. In terms of Peirce's semiotic model, their critique may be reformulated in the following way.[50] *They complain that a class of philosophers treats a class of incomplete symbols as if they were complete symbols.* The class of philosophers includes Kant, Hegel, Descartes, and Plato, too—that is, classical and modern philosophers who make ontological claims which would have a bearing on the fundamental norms of human conduct. The class of incomplete symbols includes various tokens of these norms. There is no privileged, or noncontextual way of characterizing the norms, and they therefore appear differently in the different contexts of each of the aftermoderns' interpretations.[51] Within the interpretive context of the present study, Buber's examination of "primary words" and Kadushin's examination of "value-concepts" serve as particularly suggestive illustrations of the aftermoderns' tendencies to analyze the fundamental norms of Judaism as incomplete symbols.

Buber's examination of primary words emerged from out of a philosophic complaint of which his loving critique of Cohen is illustrative. Cohen never departed from his commitment to a philosophically disciplined science of ethics, guided by the critical and transcendental methods of the Kantian program. Nevertheless, within the terms of that program, he complained about attempts to launch a science of ethics without "a reflection upon the nature of the good as it becomes manifest in man, concretely and personally."[52] He said the biblical prophets discovered that this is a reflection upon the fact and upon the sources of human suffering, that the reflection breeds compassion, in particular compassion for the poor, and that reflection on the good comprehends its subject matter only if it is guided by such compassion. He complained that his fellow scientists of ethics are not necessarily moved by such compassion, but, guided appropriately by the Platonic ideal of scientific inquiry, are also guided, inappropriately, by the Platonic reduction of cognition to *a priori* intellection.

Buber continued Cohen's critique of *a priori* ethics, indicting once again Plato's belief "that he possesses an abstract and general, a timeless concept of truth,"[53] in favor of Isaiah's conviction of his own inadequacy. Unlike the philosopher, the prophet "always receives only one message for one situation," which is "why, after thousands of years, his words still address the changing situations in history."[54] Buber saw in Cohen "a philosopher who has been overwhelmed by faith,"[55] yet he feared that, while "renouncing the God of the philosophers in his innermost heart," Cohen did not fully confess this renunciation consciously. Cohen therefore retained a tendency to construct in a philosophy of faith "the last home for the God of the philosophers."[56] Buber identified this persistently "philosophic" tendency with Kant's contradictory attempt to acknowledge God's reality while also identifying God with an idea of reason. In the end, the notion of ideality triumphed; lacking love of God and thus personal relation with God, Kant bequeathed to Cohen a God-Idea whose "only place is within a system of thought."[57] Buber's alternative to Kant was not strictly skeptical or fideistic. It was, rather, to replace the *a priori* of abstract ideas with "the *a priori* of relation,"[58] which is to discover both that reasoning about ethics is reasoning about relations and that we reason, in the first place, *from out of* concrete relations. These relations, furthermore, are engendered by language, and the *a priori* of relation is the primacy of words. According to Buber, we reason from out of words that establish the relations in terms of which reasoning has meaning. Among these relations are elemental ones, engendered by the *primary words*, I-Thou, I-It.[59]

In Buber's analytic vocabulary, the terms for these primary words refer to contrasting ways of symbolizing the interpretive activity through which human beings endow the elements of experience with meaning. Each term refers to a symbol which establishes relationship.[60] A relationship is a kind of law or regular practice, and, in the terms of this study,[61] a symbol which establishes—or is interpreted by—a law is a genuine symbol. "I-It" refers to the class of complete symbols. These are practices of interpreting the elements of experience by way of universal propositions: of removing from the associative penumbra of experience some discrete association of some class of objects with some set of characters, that is, of objectifying experience and thereby replacing it with its object or meaning. "I-Thou" refers to the class of incomplete symbols: practices of interpreting the elements of experience by way of particular propositions, with indefinite subjects. These are ways of insisting both that experience has some particular meaning and that the meaning is as yet incompletely disclosed. "I-Thou" words are therefore *performative* as well as representational, linking experience, speaker/text, and listener/interpreter in an interpretive relationship which *bears* meaning rather than merely representing or pointing to it. Thus Buber writes that by way of the word-pair I-It, I can claim to experience something out there, but by way of the pair I-Thou, I participate in a relationship of which experience is itself an implicit element.[62]

In these terms, Buber's critique of Cohen may be restated as follows. Cohen perceived correctly that the principles of ethics must be incomplete symbols; Cohen's notion of compassion for suffering serves as an index of the irreducibly particular, relational, and performative elements of all reflections on the good. Nonetheless, following Kant, Cohen persisted in his contrary tendency to identify rationality with completeness. Fearing that incompleteness implies irrationality, he saw no alternative to replacing particular propositions about compassion with the universal propositions of a science of ethics.

Rosenzweig's "speech-thinking" provided the model of nonreductive rationality Cohen lacked. For our present purposes, this model is perfected in Kadushin's study of what he called "organic thinking," in particular, in the instance of organic thinking he observed in the hermeneutical-ethical practices of the talmudic sages.

Kadushin labeled the grammar of these practices "the rabbinic mind" and claimed that this grammar was most clearly exhibited in the homiletical literature of rabbinic midrash. This literature is comprised, for the most part, of collections of homiletical exegeses of scriptural texts, of which one example is the interpretation of Jeremiah we considered earlier:

> In the school of R. Ishmael it is taught, "[Behold my word is like fire, declares the Lord,] and like a hammer that shatters rocks" (Jer. 23:29). Just as a hammer breaks into several shivers, so too one scriptural passage issues as several meanings.

Illustrating the theme of this particular exegesis, a given collection of midrash might include several, often conflicting interpretations of particular scriptural verses. Kadushin notes, for example, that in the midrash Mekhilta,

> there are numerous consecutive opinions accounting for the crossing of the Red Sea. Following is a partial list of these opinions and their authors: Because of Jerusalem—R. Ishmael; God only fulfilled the promise He had made their fathers (the Patriarchs)—anonymous . . . ; because they observed the rite of circumcision—Simeon of Teman . . . ; because they (Israel) trusted in me—Rabbi (Judah the Prince) . . . . [63]

To uncover the grammar of rabbinic practice, Kadushin undertook the equivalent of a pragmatic analysis of these exegeses. He reinterpreted them as performative utterances which displayed the ultimate behavioral norms of rabbinic Judaism *through the occasion* of scriptural exegesis. Lacking the vocabulary of pragmatics, Kadushin struggles somewhat to identify the following stages of his analysis and to convince his readers that he was not engaged in some idiosyncratic form of eisegesis.

He labeled each discrete exegesis a "haggadic statement,"[64] by which he meant a discrete performative utterance. Without using these terms, he conceived of the haggadic statements as propositions whose predicates are collections of what he calls "value-concepts" and whose subjects are what he calls "cognitive concepts." He defined "cognitive concepts" as the referents of "terms we use in order to describe whatever we perceive through the senses," such as "death," "table" or "angel."[65] He defined "value-concepts"[66] as the referents of terms used to represent fundamental or irreducible elements in the valuational life of the rabbinic community. Examples are "God's justice," (*middat hadin*), "God's mercy" (*middat harakhamim*), "Acts of lovingkindness" (*gemilut hasadim*), and "God's spoken word" (*dibbur*). Kadushin's definitive claim was that the rabbinic mind is a constellation of such value-concepts and that the logic of rabbinic thinking is displayed in the manner in which these concepts relate to one another and in the way each one of them exhibits what he calls its "drive to concretization"—that is, the way it guides specific acts of judgment. He said that acts of midrashic interpretation, culminating in haggadic statements, are paradigmatic of such acts. In these statements, the cognitive concepts indicate the occasions with respect to which the midrash exhibits some aspect of the complex of value-concepts. In Kadushin's illustration from the *Mekhilta*, for example, the rabbinic accounts of the crossing of the Red Sea are haggadic statements which may be analyzed, performatively, as propositions in which various value-concepts are predicated of an occasion called "the crossing of the Red Sea." We would thus have such propositions as "The crossing . . . exhibits the Merit of the Fathers (*zekhut avot*)" (anonymous), or "The crossing . . . exhibits Divine Justice (*middat hadin*) in response to Observances (*mitzvot*)" (Simeon), and so on.

Kadushin's analysis of the rabbinic mind was occasioned by his critique of what he calls "philosophy's" misrepresentations of the fundamental norms of ethical and of religious practice. He drew his dichotomy between cognitive and value concepts in order to argue that philosophers err by misrepresenting value concepts as cognitive or defined concepts: in other words, by misrepresenting incomplete symbols as complete ones. Kadushin argued, for example, that Maimonides' critique of anthropomorphism misrepresents the indefinite character of the rabbis' portrayals of God: "To ascribe to the Rabbis any sort of stand on anthropomorphism is to do violence . . . to rabbinic thought."[67] In the terms of Peirce's semeiotic, this means that, as incomplete symbols, the rabbis' portrayals do not obey the law of excluded middle. In similar fashion, Kadushin criticized Whitehead's tendency to argue against his own organismic thinking by describing the "mutual relatedness" of "eternal objects." In different terms, Kadushin argued that only incomplete symbols enter into relationship, while eternal and therefore fixed or formal objects must be complete.[68]

Kadushin's analysis of the value-concept requires a slight modification before it can serve as a model of the aftermodern analysis of incomplete symbols. Kadushin has been justifiably criticized for interpreting the rabbinic literature nondiachronically and thus exaggerating the stability of the rabbinic value-concepts.[69] Another way to state the criticism is that Kadushin minimized the performative character of his own analysis: as if, contrary to his own methodology, the value-concepts represented "essences" of the rabbinic mind, rather than ways through which he, as an aftermodern interpreter, may conceptualize the performative force of rabbinic exegesis. Once corrected, Kadushin's claim could be restated as follows. According to the interpretations of the class of aftermoderns, rabbinic exegesis conceptualizes the performative force of the scriptural word, and the value-concepts are icons or selective representations of that activity of conceptualization. According to this claim, aftermodern interpretation of rabbinic exegesis describes itself as analogous to rabbinic interpretation of the scriptural word—deep calling to deep—and it describes the scriptural "word" itself as an interpretive activity, of which aftermodern inquiry as well as rabbinic exegesis are interpretants. What Kadushin calls the "value-concept" would then represent the product of an attempt to arrest this interpretive activity—to conceptualize it, to iconize it, or to write down for a particular community at a particular time the performative force of the scriptural word, which is what the word is urging the community to do or what, therefore, God wants of it. Described this way, value-concepts are incomplete symbols. They symbolize incompletely, first, because they exhibit only selective features of the scriptural word and thus display its complete meaning only with respect to those features not yet exhibited; second, because their meaning is not independent of what it prompts the interpreting community to do in the future.

Exercising some interpretive license, it is possible to interpret Lindbeck's theory of doctrine and the aftermoderns' theories of primary words or value-concepts as context-specific applications of a common interpretive tendency.[70] Lindbeck distinguishes between first- and second-order propositions in order to distinguish the truth of doctrines from the truth of the context-specific claims we make about the world. As I interpret his argument, however, he is actually making two sorts of distinctions here, one explicit, one implicit. The explicit distinction is between two dimensions of natural language use: ordinary linguistic practice, in terms of which we make what Lindbeck calls ontological claims about the world and metalinguistic practice, through which we organize, correct, and adjust ordinary practice. In terms of this distinction, he classes doctrines among the metalinguistic practices, characterizing their truth as analytic or intrasystematic. The implicit distinction is between natural language in general and another language, which he characterizes as natural-language-like only by analogy.[71] For want of any formal term, I will label this the transformational language of the gospel text, or Scripture.[72] According to this implicit distinction, church doctrine belongs primarily to a Scripture whose purpose is to transform natural language use in the direction of another practice which we can identify only through such trans-formations. To serve this purpose, Scripture functions within natural language as a metalinguistic practice, by way of that function acquir-ing the grammatical forms of second-order propositions. Unlike an ordinary metalanguage, however, its effect is to transform ordinary language use in the interest of norms for which there is no adequate correlate in the ontologies of natural language. These norms are ar-ticulated only in the language of Scripture and, even there, only in the way scriptural language transforms ordinary language use.

In terms of this interpretation, Lindbeck's rule theory is a theory about Scripture's translational tendencies. These tendencies are de-scribed as rules insofar as they are adapted to the rule forms of natural language. In ordinary metalinguistic practice, rules appear in propo-sitional form. Functioning metalinguistically, Scripture's transforma-tional tendencies appear also in propositional form, and the resulting propositional formulations are called doctrines. Doctrines are there-fore essentially propositional, but they are so only as metalinguistic formulations of scriptural tendencies. Certain doctrines are "uncon-ditionally necessary" only to the extent that metalinguistic function is essential to Scripture's transformational purpose.

To characterize doctrines as symbols is to consider their func-tion within a transformational language. In relation to any particu-lar language as a collection of signs, doctrines function as complete symbols, indicating precisely how language use is to be organized: "virginal motherhood" is to be predicated of "Mary," and so on. In relation to any ontology, however—that is, to the objective correlate of language—doctrines function as incomplete symbols: the meanings of "virgin" and "motherhood" are context-specific. In relation, finally, to the speakers of a language as interpreters of any linguistic practice, doctrines function again as incomplete symbols, their meaning de-fined only by way of the speakers' interpretive activity. Stated more precisely, doctrines have as their interpretants the personalities of a community of interpreters, which is the life of a church. The tendency of Scripture is to transform natural ontology into the mundane life of a church rather than merely to place doctrine alongside ontology as metalanguage.

In these terms, the doctrine, as described by Lindbeck, may be contrasted with the primary word or value-concept, as described by

the aftermoderns. Doctrine is described as a context-specific propositional formulation of the transformational tendency symbolized by the
scriptural text. The tendency itself is represented only by a continuum,
or indefinite collection, of such formulations, and a value-concept is
an iconic representation of the class character of this collection. A
value-concept appears as the predicate of any propositional formulation of Scripture's transformational tendency, and a collection of
value-concepts is an abstract representation of the way some community of interpreters represents that tendency. This "way" is what
we call the religion of the community. Such a religion cannot be
defined propositionally, because there is no necessary or privileged
way to connect an icon to its object—in this case, a value-concept
to the tendency it iconizes. To teach such a religion is to offer those
characterizations of a collection of value-concepts which would stim-
ulate some particular persons to interpret Scripture as the kind of
transformational tendency a given community represents Scripture
to be. Postliberals attend, in particular, to the narrative aspects of
these characterizations, countering tendencies among both historical-
critical and philosophic interpreters to neglect narrativity in favor
of propositional definitions. For this study, only the performative attributes of the characterizations are of interest.

In these terms, a doctrine appears to be a representative instance of a community's method of interpretation: determinate and,
in that sense, unambiguous, but context-specific. It is an instance
which the community declares to be representative. A community
may offer such declarations in times of crisis, when it fears its members or descendants will fail to preserve or understand the ambiguities
and details of its normal teachings, by which we mean the ways it
normally characterizes collections of its fundamental value-concepts.
As Lindbeck suggests, doctrines are generalizable only if the conditions which stimulated their formulation are generalizable. This is,
however, to consider doctrines only with respect to their conditions
of formulation—that is, as signs of antecedent objects. In this respect,
they are complete symbols and may be represented as universal propositions, such as, "In all possible worlds, 'the dead are raised' is true."
Considered performatively, however, or with respect to their prospective interpretants, doctrines may be considered incomplete symbols. In
this respect, they may be represented as particular propositions, such

as "There is some world of meaning in which 'the dead are raised' is true." It is in this latter sense that Lindbeck describes doctrines as subject to reconciliation without capitulation.

3. WHERE DEEP CALLS: THE CONTEXT OF DISCOMFORT

If postliberals and aftermoderns offer analogous complaints, then they may take up their intellectual projects in response to a common discomfort. This working hypothesis of the pragmatic interpreter leads us to a concluding speculation. It is at best a speculation, because only a weak sort of probable inference leads from the observation of analogous effects to the supposition of a common cause or reason. Here the interpreter has no other choice than to search in his or her own experience for some rule that might connect something like these observed effects to a sought-after cause. If a source of weakness, this kind of subjectivity is also the source of dynamism in a pragmatic interpretation. It is a mark of the interpretation's own incompleteness, in the various senses discussed earlier.

As suggested by their complaints, postliberals and aftermoderns participate in the very broad movement of post-Kantian critics of what Peirce calls "Cartesian a priorism." This movement includes certain Hegelians, existentialists, phenomenologists, pragmatists, language analysts, and so on. Within the movement, postliberals and aftermoderns belong to a subgroup critical of their peers' tendencies to individualism, romanticism, antinomianism or, in general, what Lindbeck calls experiential-expressivism. Here, they join students of Peirce, Dewey, and Wittgenstein, natural language analysts, symbolists and semioticians, some process thinkers, some deconstructors, and those hermeneuts concerned to identify what K. O. Apel calls the *a priori* of intersubjective relations. Within this subgroup, finally, our critics are distinguished by their conviction that the errors of a priorism are repaired only by a hermeneutic whose premises are provided by some text-based tradition of interpretation. They argue that any alternative ontological or natural hermeneutics remains a form of a priorism, generating various doctrines of complete symbolization. They then struggle in various ways with the fact that text-based traditions are so defined by particular communities of interpreters whose

234 / *Peter Ochs*

practices are at most analogous, rather than similar or identical, to those of other communities.

The particularity of their adopted text-traditions limits the ability of postliberals and aftermoderns to argue on common terms with their philosophic peers. From the perspective of other philosophers, including other critics of "Cartesian a priorism," they may appear to have trespassed against the norms of philosophic practice, usually in favor of a religious fideism: having, *qua* philosophers, accepted membership in a community of believers, they may appear to have placed themselves at best on the margins of any community of philosophers. From the perspectives of their co-religionists, however, postliberals and aftermoderns may appear no less marginal, precisely because of their philosophic bearing. While they may argue on behalf of texts their community holds sacred and on behalf of the community's methods of interpreting them, their arguments may appear to arise in response to questions the community has no interest in asking. Their love of such terms as "incomplete symbolization" and the "cultural-linguistic approach" may place them in the category of philosophers, as opposed to that of religious practitioners.

I speculate, in other words, that postliberals and aftermoderns share the discomfort of believing themselves to be treated as at best marginal members of the two communities they love. According to the pragmatist's interpretive paradigm, the interpretive tendency they share is a method of responding to this discomfort. It is a way of analyzing religion so that the religious hermeneutic they practice may have philosophic legitimacy, and it is a way of reformulating philosophic method so that their practice of philosophy may have legitimacy in terms of their text-based religious hermeneutic. This analytic approach has performative significance, in other words, as a means of legitimating their participation in both the philosophic and religious communities. The problem is that the approach may not succeed in these terms. Despite their efforts, they may remain too religious for their philosophic peers and too philosophic for their co-religionists. In the effort to legitimate, they may only reinforce their marginality.

The postliberals' and aftermoderns' intellectual performance may succeed, however, in an unintended way. Even if failing to win them legitimacy in the eyes of others, their performance may succeed in winning them legitimacy in their own eyes, which means that it may succeed in setting the foundations of a new practice and community[73] of inquiry rather than in reforming an existent one. The postliberals' and aftermoderns' analysis of fundamental teachings—doctrines, primary words, and value-concepts—may function performatively as a means of reformulating the fundamental norms which inform their own practice and, thereby, of redesignating who and what has authority to regulate that practice. The performative force of their analysis may be to enable them to declare that they alone, as a newly designated community of interpreters, have authority to regulate their own practices. From this perspective, their analyses function semantically as criticisms of both modern or critical and premodern or uncritical norms of interpretation, and they function performatively as the potentially authoritative teachings of a new community, which they regard—in the words of Lindbeck's definition of "doctrine"—as essential to their own welfare as postliberals or aftermoderns.

The problem with this speculation is that it arises out of my work with aftermoderns, and it may, indeed, explain their behavior more readily than it explains that of the postliberals. The arguments of all the aftermoderns emerged out of their dissatisfactions with a modern philosophic practice and enabled them to retrieve some version of an ancestral hermeneutic. The postliberals, on the other hand, appear to have brought their Christianities with them to the study of philosophy;[74] some are philosophers by profession, but others are text scholars and church historians first. My speculations are, indeed, limited to the aftermodern perspective which spawns them, and I can do no more than await some confirming or disconfirming reply from the postliberal side. In the meanwhile, I offer this additional speculation to account for class differences between aftermoderns and postliberals: postliberals tend to belong to a second generation of emigrés from modern philosophy, while aftermoderns tend to be recent arrivals. This means that postliberals tend to inherit a textual hermeneutic which already displays the effects of prior confrontations between philosophic and precritical methodologies, while the aftermoderns described in this paper find themselves in the heat of battle. The aftermoderns therefore have methodological lessons to learn from the postliberals. At the same time, postliberals tend increasingly to identify aspects of rabbinic hermeneutics as prototypes of their methodology. In this regard, they may call on two subgroups of rabbinic scholars to offer them lessons in textual interpretation. The first subgroup includes text- and historical-critical scholars of rabbinic literature whose work displays many of the emergent tendencies of aftermodern interpretation.[75] These scholars examine aspects of rabbinic hermeneutics that may, indeed, serve as prototypes of some aspects of postliberal methodology. The second subgroup includes philosophic theologians whose analyses of rabbinic hermeneutical practices continue the philosophic tradition that links Cohen to Rosenzweig to Kadushin.[76]

4. A SAVING PRESENCE: POSTCRITICAL DOCTRINES

In the context of their analogous discomforts, the arguments of the postliberals and aftermoderns function performatively as incomplete symbols of potentially new practices of interpretation. They function this way, of course, only if postliberals and aftermoderns believe that they do. By way of this belief, they number themselves as members of emergent communities of interpretation for whom these symbols now represent communally authoritative teachings or, in Lindbeck's terms, doctrines. By attempting to articulate these doctrines they may identify both the distinctive characteristics and the methodological limits of their practices and thereby place them under some form of control.

In terms of the semiotic analysis of doctrines presented above in section 2, each of the postliberals' or aftermoderns' claims is a context-specific, propositional formulation of their own interpretive tendencies. Through a process of abstraction,[77] we may identify the class characters of a collection of such formulations as the value-concepts of postcritical interpretation. We may, then, characterize these value-concepts with respect to either of two correlatives. The *objective or semantic correlative* of postcritical interpretation is God's word, as displayed by way of particular kinds of scriptural interpretation. The *performative or pragmatic correlative* of postcritical interpretation is the emergent community of postcritical interpreters. We may characterize the value-concepts *objectively* as predicates of all claims about scriptural interpretation and *performatively* as indices of the postcritical interpreters' attempts to legitimate an emergent community of interpretation. The doctrines of aftermodern or postliberal interpretation are descriptions of pairs of such correlatives.

However much the performative correlatives of aftermodern and postliberal doctrines may resemble each other, the objective correlatives display the different interpretants—rabbinic and christological—through which God's word is received. Returning to the context of my own interpretations, I resume my study of rabbinic pragmatism in particular and offer a concluding, illustrative description of the emergent doctrines of aftermodern interpretation.[78] In the following section, I list, first, the label I have supplied for a given value-concept of aftermodern interpretation; then, an emblematic citation from aftermodern commentary; then, a suggestion about how the value-concept may refer, first, to its objective correlative and, second, to its performative correlative. The section as a whole is merely illustrative.

Aftermodern Doctrines

1. *The Authority of the Word*

> "God spoke." . . . The Speech of God is not less but more than literally real.[79]

a) *With Reference to Objective Correlative*: The precritical ground of all rational discourse about this world is the spoken word; the prototype of all spoken words is God's spoken word, or *dibbur*. The prototypical sign-vehicle of God's spoken word is the explicit text of Scripture and its object is the meaning of that text for its community of interpreters. For aftermoderns, this community is Israel, as the community which acknowledges the scriptural text as authority.[80] Once recognized as ground of all discourse, God's spoken word is adopted as authority over all voluntary speech.

b) *With Reference to Performative Correlative*: In affirming this value-concept, aftermoderns challenge modernist assumptions that critical inquiry does not and should not presuppose the authority of the scriptural word and of spoken words in general. Aftermoderns assert that their "absolute" empiricism exhibits the indigenous character of such words more faithfully than do other varieties of empirical or rationalizing inquiry.[81]

2. *The Incompleteness of the Word*

> Divine speech...divides while remaining one, and can do so over and over again.... The multivocality of divine speech... is not so much the product of human interpretation...as its anticipation.[82]

a) *Objective*: The scriptural text, unchanging as sign-vehicle, delivers an incomplete message about some particular object. Having acknowledged the authority of the text, the interpreter is motivated to wait for a completed message or for instructions about how to find it. The authority of the text is thus extended and the text is transformed from an authoritative sign-vehicle into an authoritative process of sign interpretation. The interpreter's own interactions with the text are an integral element of this process, which, in Peirce's terms, appears as a three-part relation among the scriptural text as sign-vehicle, the interpreter's practice as interpretant, and some as yet undesignated, context-dependent meaning as object.

b) *Performative*: The aftermoderns are asserting that God's word represents a semiotic process, not some collection of propostions, and that their empirical science of interpretation is an appropriate interpretant[83] of that process, perhaps more appropriate than what traditionalists may claim is the rabbinic tradition's indigenous hermeneutic.[84]

3. *The Word's Practical Efficacy, or Drive to Action*

> Value concepts have a drive toward concretization, endowing actions, events, lives with significance.[85]

a) *Objective*: The scriptural word's meaning is determinate with respect to its capacity to transform the meaning of some pattern of everyday conduct. The word is thus interpreted with respect to established or inherited conceptions of possible action in the world. In this sense, alone, the word may be considered a symbol of human conduct and characterized as a rule of action or law or commandment. When characterized in this way, the word may be considered the class name of a set of conditional resolutions to act, such as "if crossing the Red

Sea, act as follows; if encountering the poor of my people, act as follows, and so on." To adopt such a set of conditionals as a behavioral norm is to transform the shape of a moral character.[86]

b) *Performative*: The aftermoderns promote this value-concept against semanticist tendencies to objectify interpretive scholarship and divorce it from the pragmatic context of the scholarship itself. Since the aftermoderns define objectivity with respect to particular ontologies, or first-order systems of rules, their protests against objectification may be seen as protests also against their own marginality within the communities that would otherwise provide them such rules.[87]

4. *The Transformational Contexts of Interpretive Practice*

Objective and Performative Correlatives merge as aftermodern inquiry observes its own role in a process of scriptural interpretation.

Modern scholars of rabbinic literature tend to offer either objective or formalist readings of scriptural interpretations: according to the former, the documents of rabbinic Judaism are evidences of certain events in the lives of historically situated communities of persons; according to the latter, they are signs whose identifiable meanings are wholly reflexive, or intratextual. While recognizing the significance of each of these ways of studying the generic or nontransformational character of scriptural interpretation, aftermoderns attend in particular to its transformational character. From this perspective, references to the object or form of scriptural interpretations are ways of characterizing either of two contexts of interpretation: events in the life of a historically situated community of persons or events in some process of intellectual imagination. For the aftermodern historian, the literature of rabbinic *midrash* as well as of rabbinic *halakhah* documents the transformational influence of God's word in the life of some community, the characteristics of whose particular problems of practice must be sought "behind" that literature. For the aftermodern formalist, the literature tends to mask references to its historical context. Instead, it documents the transformational influence of God's word within some process of intellectual imagination. It offers paradigmatic judgments in the context of legal and homiletic speculations, prompted by questions which must be sought "in front of" the literature, through empathetic reading. For the aftermodern pragmatist, finally, the study of rabbinic documents is itself a performative activity. It has meaning in the context of events in some process of intellectual imagination which may be situated, in turn, in events in the life of a contemporary community of persons. The fruits of this performative activity are a transformed moral character and a transformed intellectual imagination.

As pragmatists, aftermoderns are critics of their own intellectual imaginations, vexed by what appear to be their tendencies to reason away from the concrete realities of the created world, of human community, and of text rather than toward them: in short, tendencies to turn away from God and thus to sin. Rosenzweig's absolute empiricism and Kadushin's organicism are pleas to examine the concretely given rather than the desired. Their studies suggest, however, that to examine the given is a matter of giving as well as receiving: that is, as Giambattista Vico and William James have argued in different contexts, volition and intellectual imagination have a role to play in genuine observation. For aftermoderns, the source of sin is therefore not imagination *per se*, but, rather, imagination divorced from public discourse. Perhaps, they suggest, their own sin is simply not belonging. Not unlike Peirce, the aftermoderns tend to extol the virtues of community from out of an as-yet-unreparied isolation. To which community of inquiry, after all, do they belong? According to the emergent doctrines of aftermodernism, the focal work of such a community would be to examine the documents of rabbinic Judaism with the methods of an absolute empiricism and, thereby, to articulate a descriptive theology of rabbinic Judaism. The interpretant of such a theology would remain the aftermodern community of inquiry itself. It remains to be seen if, how, or when such a community might emerge.

NOTES

Research for this paper has been supported in part by a grant from the Spencer Foundation. I am grateful to George Lindbeck, Steven Fraade, and Bruce Marshall for very helpful comments, as well as to members of the Academy for Jewish Philosophy.

1. *The Nature of Doctrine: Religion and Theology in a Postliberal Age* (Philadelphia: Westminster, 1984), 8. Hereafter cited as *Doctrine*.

2. *Doctrine*, 114, *passim*.

3. Lindbeck uses the language of instantiation to characterize the relation between what the semioticians call type and token. I prefer the term "practice" to that of "instance"; it brings with it less Platonistic baggage.

4. Substituting the term "tendency" for Lindbeck's "rule." The former fits in better with a notion of "incomplete symbol"; see below.

5. All biblical translations in this paper will be from *Tanakh, A New Translation of the Holy Scriptures according to the Traditional Hebrew Text* (Philadelphia: Jewish Publication Society, 1985).

6. The subtitle of his *Pragmatism*. See for example the edition edited by Bruce Kuklick (Indianapolis and Cambridge: Hackett, 1981).

7. "Aftermodern" is an ugly and partly jocular term which can be replaced with something meaningful only once this group is prepared to describe its own characteristics.

8. Translation from David Stern, "Midrash and Indeterminacy," *Critical Inquiry* 15 (1988): 135–36. Stern notes that "the verse from Jeremiah . . . has a meaning in its Scriptural context very different from the interpretation the sages give it. They understand Jeremiah's declaration as describing not the experience of prophecy but the substance of that experience, the content of prophetic revelation—specifically its literary product, the text of Scripture. This reading derives from what is for the Rabbis a genuine problem in the verse, the presence of two similes in it. The Rabbis always undertake their study of the Bible with the assumption that every word in Scripture is both necessary and significant. If this is so, however, why are two similes of God's word, fire *and* a hammer, employed by the prophet? The answer—in effect, the interpretation—given by the School of Rabbi Yishmael can be paraphrased as follows: My word, says God, is like fire; but what sort of fire? Like those fiery sparks produced by a hammer when it strikes rock—and like the many senses that every verse in Scripture holds ready to let fly at the strike of the interpretive hammer." Consider this different yet complementary remark on the passage by Steven Fraade: "Medieval commentators to b. Sanh. 34a. and Shab. 88b. (see Tosaphot to both passages) note the discrepancy between the biblical verse in which the *rock* is shattered by the powerful blows of the hammer, and the rabbinic interpretation in which the *hammer* itself releases fragments upon hitting the rock: the hammer, representing the act of interpretation, causes sparks to fly from the rock, representing God's word in Scripture (see Rashi to b.Shabb 88b; J. Levy, *Wörterbuch über die Talmudim und Midrashim*, rev. L. Goldschmidt, 4 vols [Berlin: B. Harz, 1924], p. 390, col. 1, S. Z. Nitzotz; and David Stern, *op. cit.*). This is not what the Talmudic texts say, in part because the proof text from Jeremiah compares God's word to the hammer. However, the Talmudic interpretation reworks Jeremiah's metaphor no less radically. Now the hammer does not

shatter (*yikhotzetz*) the rock as in Jeremiah, but emits numerous, tiny sparks (*nitzotzim*, presumably a word play), understood to be the fire of Jeremiah's preceding metaphor, upon striking the rock. In this image, multiple sparks are emitted without either the rock's or the hammer's being perceptibly diminished; divine speech (in Scripture) divides while remaining one, and can do so over and over again. . . . (Cf. *Shir Ha-Shirim Rabbah* 5:14 and parallels, and *Midrash Tehilim* 42:3.) . . . My point here is that the multivocality of divine speech (at Sinai and in Scripture) is not so much the product of human interpretation (of an otherwise univocal expression) as its anticipation. It is rabbinically conceived as being as much an aspect of divine revelation as of human interpretation, the two being conjoined." Fraade, *From Tradition to Commentary: Torah and Its Interpretation in the Midrash Sifre to Deuteronomy* (Albany: State University of New York Press, 1990), ch. 4, n. 4.

9. To add a term of John Dewey's.

10. Solomon ben Isaac of Troyes (1040–1105).

11. From the supercommentary *Metsudat David* ("Fortress of David") of the eighteenth-century exegete David Altschuler. The commentary is included in traditional editions of *Mikra'ot G'dolot*.

12. *Doctrine*, 112.

13. Ibid., 16, 24, *passim*, where the approach is exemplified by Peter Geach, G. K. Chesteron, C. S. Lewis and Malcolm Muggeridge.

14. *Doctrine*, 31, citing Bernard Lonergan, *Method in Theology* (New York: Herder and Herder, 1972), 101–24.

15. Ibid., citing Lonergan, *Method*, 120, 122.

16. *Doctrine*, 18.

17. *Doctrine*, 62, citing Clifford Geertz, *The Interpretation of Cultures* (New York: Basic Books, 1973), 90.

18. *Doctrine*, 22–23, 35–36, and *passim*.

19. Ibid., 49.

20. Ibid., 40.

21. Peirce defines "methodeutic" as "the doctrine of the general conditions of the reference of Symbols and other signs to the Interpretants which they aim to determine." *Collected Papers of Charles Sanders Peirce*, Hartshorne and Weiss, eds. (Cambridge, Mass.: Harvard University Press, 1931–1960): vol. 2, para. 93: 1902. Future references to this edition will be to volume and paragraph number, followed by probable date of writing (e.g., 2.93: 1902).

22. To use Lindbeck's term. See *Doctrine*, 80ff.

23. "An die Stelle der Methode des Denkens, wie sie alle frühere Philosophie ausgebildet hat, tritt die Methode des Sprechens" ("Das neue Denken," *Kleinere Schriften* (Berlin: Schocken Verlag, 1937), 386: translated

in excerpts from "The New Thinking," in Nahum Glatzer, *Franz Rosenzweig, His Life and Thought* (New York: Schocken, 1967), 198.

24. "Das neue Denken," 387 = "The New Thinking," 200.

25. "Die neue Philosophie tut da nicht anders, als daß sie die 'Methode' des gesunden Menschenverstandes zur Methode des wissenschaftlichen Denkens macht." "Das neue Denken," 384 = "The New Thinking," 196.

26. "Das neue Denken," 398 = "The New Thinking," 207.

27. "Das neue Denken," 395 = "The New Thinking," 206.

28. Ibid.

29. *Doctrine*, 117.

30. He cites, among others, Emile Durkheim, Lucien Lévy-Bruhl, G. A. de Laguna, displaying a general interest in studies that anticipate the ethnological theory of thick description.

31. An excessive degree, in the opinion of several critics.

32. For example, he was attracted to Whitehead's philosophy of organism, claiming that many of Whitehead's "metaphysical concepts can be taken as generalizations of the characteristics of rabbinic theology," in *Organic Thinking: A Study in Rabbinic Thought* (New York: Bloch, 1976), 247–48. Yet, he was critical of what he considered the "Platonic" aspects of Whitehead's system: among them, Whitehead's notions of "eternal objects," and of individuality in religion (ibid., 248ff.). He says that, like other philosophers of organism, Whitehead fails to distinguish the analytic concepts used in the study of organic systems from genuinely organic concepts and thus fails to attend to the individuality of each organic system (ibid., 250). Kadushin distances himself, comparably, from what, in Lindbeck's terms we may call Bergson's expressivism and Dewey's cognitivism. Among Jewish philosophers, Kadushin distances himself comparably from Maimonides' cognitivism (*The Rabbinic Mind* [New York: Jewish Theological Seminary of America: 1952], 325, and *passim*) and from the experiential-emotivism of Jewish and non-Jewish mystics (ibid., 201ff.).

33. *Organic Thinking*, 14–15.

34. See below, section 3.

35. *Doctrine*, 74.

36. Lindbeck cites Aquinas's distinction between the unchanging referent of a rule, its *significatum*, and the rule's context-specific signifier or *modus significandi* (*Doctrine*, 66; referring to Aquinas *ST* I.13.3; *CG* I.30).

37. *Doctrine*, 16.

38. Ibid.

39. Ibid., 79.

40. In his later writings, Peirce retained the *e* in *semeiotic* as a name for the science, as opposed to the adjectival *semiotic*. See, for example, 8.343 and 8.377, among his letters to Lady Welby.

41. 2.228: 1897. For a more complete introduction to Peirce's mature work on semiotics, see *Charles S. Peirce's Letters to Lady Welby*, ed. Lieb (New Haven, Conn.: Whitlock's, 1953).

42. 2.247–49: 1903.

43. 5.477.

44. 5.448nl.

45. 5.505.

46. 5.448nl: 1906.

47. 5.155: 1903.

48. 5.505.

49. 5.155.

50. According to the interpretive method which guides this study, the aftermoderns' texts, accurately read, signify neither one nor an infinity, but a family of possible meanings, each one determined with respect to some interpretant or occasion of interpretation. I am claiming for the following formulation the privilege only of belonging to this family.

51. To refer to them as "incomplete symbols" or even as "fundamental norms" is simply to add another context of interpretation.

52. From "Das soziale Ideal bei Platon und den Propheten," *Jüdische Schriften* I, Strauss, ed. (Berlin, 1924), 306–30; translation from *Reason and Hope, Selections from the Jewish Writings of Hermann Cohen*, ed. Eva Jospe (New York: W. W. Norton, 1971), 73.

53. From "Plato and Isaiah," in *The Writings of Martin Buber*, ed. Herberg (New York: New American Library, 1956), 238; translation by Olga Marx, originally appearing in *Israel and the World: Essays in a Time of Crisis* (New York: Schocken, 1948).

54. Ibid.

55. "The Love of God and the Idea of Deity: On Hermann Cohen," cited in *The Writings of Martin Buber*, 100, excerpted from *Eclipse of God: Studies in the Relation between Religion and Philosophy* (New York: Harper and Brothers, 1952), 67–84.

56. *The Writings of Martin Buber*, 101.

57. Ibid.

58. "Das Apriori der Beziehung," from *Ich und Du*, in Martin Buber, *Werke* I (Munich: Kösel-Verlag, 1962), 96. Translation from *I and Thou*, trans. Kaufmann (New York: Charles Scribner's, 1970), 78.

59. *Ich-Du, Ich-Es*: Of which word types the tokens are exemplified by such pre-grammatical forms as displayed in the Zulu sentence-word for what

we call "far away": "where one cries, 'mother I am lost'" (cf. *I and Thou*, 69–70 = *Ich und Du*, 90.).

60. "Im Anfang ist die Beziehung," *Ich und Du*, 90 ("In the beginning is relation," *I and Thou*, 68.).

61. See the "Excursus on Peirce's Semeiotic," above.

62. *Ich und Du*, 80–81 = *I and Thou*, 55–56.

63. *Rabbinic Mind*, 74–75.

64. "Haggadic statements are independent entities, containing ideas or describing situations that are complete in themselves. This does not preclude a later author or editor taking an earlier midrash and adding to it an idea of his own; the earlier midrash, the original statement, is still, of course, a complete entity in itself. On the other hand, when an editor or copyist has left us only a fragment of the midrash, that fragment, though it may make sense, seldom conveys the point of the midrash. Only when research has restored the whole passage... does the midrash yield its real meaning" (*Rabbinic Mind*, 60).

65. These have "the function of rendering object, and qualities too, separable elements in a total situation" (*Rabbinic Mind*, 69) thus "enabling us to perceive the objective relations of things and persons to each other" (p. 68). Today, a semiotician might call these indexical and iconic symbols: symbols which merely depict qualities or point to objects but do not represent definite rules of interpretive behavior.

66. "The component 'concept' tells that the values referred to are communicable ideas, that is, ideas that may be shared by the group as a whole; whilst the component 'value' tells that these ideas are nevertheless also, in a degree, personal and subjective, and that they are ideas warmly held" (ibid).

67. Ibid., 280.

68. *Organic Thinking*, 248ff. See above note 32.

69. See for example, Samuel Cohon, "The Rabbinic Mind," review of *The Rabbinic Mind* in *Jewish Quarterly Review*, 44, no. 3 (1954): 244–51; Marvin Fox, "Moral Reason," review of *Worship and Ethics* in *Commentary* 38, no. 6 (1964): 78–82; and see Richard Sarason, "Kadushin's Study of Midrash: Value Concepts and Their Literary Embodiment" and Alan Avery-Peck, "Max Kadushin as Exegete: The Commentary to Leviticus Rabbah," in *Understanding the Rabbinic Mind: Essays on the Hermeneutic of Max Kadushin*, ed. Peter Ochs (Atlanta: Scholars Press [Brown Judaic Studies], 1990).

70. I am grateful to William Elkins, who helped me clarify this interpretation of Lindbeck.

71. Thus he refers to the intratextuality of meaning in both natural languages and religious language without identifying the latter as simply an element of the former: cf. *Doctrine*, 114ff.

72. William Elkins has drawn my attention to George Tavard's semiotic analysis of this phenomenon. For example, in a discussion of Luther's concept of justice, Tavard writes that "it is in relation to the redemptive grace of Christ that sacraments have meaning and efficacy, and it is in relation to the word of God that the words of proclamation, pronounced by failing and mendacious humanity, are invested with sense. We are here at the very source of Christian semiotics: all communication and formulation of the Christian message witness to the transformation of sinner into saint. Elements belonging to this word are, in the sacraments, signifiers of divine grace. The human words of natural languages become in the kerygma— both in Scripture and in proclamation—the words of the Lord. The sinner is made, by Christ's justice, just" (*Justification: An Ecumenical Study* [New York: Paulist Press, 1983], 55). Tavard's approach is also displayed in his *La theologie parmi les sciences humaines* (Paris: Editions Beauchesne, 1975).

73. Following Peirce's usage, the term "community" refers here equiv- ocally to a community of ideas or of persons who hold them. It is thus a semiotic term which may or may not have sociological significance.

74. To sample representative work from members of this group, con- sider: Hans Frei, *The Eclipse of Biblical Narrative* (New Haven, Conn.: Yale University Press, 1974); Stanley Hauerwas, *Character and the Christian Life* (Notre Dame, Ind.: University of Notre Dame Press, 1985); Ronald Thie- mann, *Revelation and Theology: The Gospel as Narrated Promise* (University of Notre Dame Press, 1985); David Burrell, *Knowing the Unknowable God* (Uni- versity of Notre Dame Press, 1986); Bruce Marshall, *Christology in Conflict: The Identity of a Saviour in Rahner and Barth* (Oxford: Basil Blackwell, 1987); Kathryn Tanner, *God and Creation in Christian Theology* (Oxford: Blackwell, 1988); William C. Placher, *Unapologetic Theology* (Philadelphia: Westmin- ster, 1989). For a complementary approach in philosophy, see, for example, William A. Christian, Sr., *Doctrines of Religious Communities: A Philosophical Study* (New Haven, Conn.: Yale University Press, 1987). For a unique re- sponse to biblical and rabbinic Judaism, see Paul M. van Buren, *A Theology of the Jewish-Christian Reality*, Parts 1–3 (San Francisco: Harper & Row, 1980, 1983, 1988).

75. To sample work from this sizeable subgroup, see David Weiss Halivny, *Midrash, Mishnah and Gemara, The Jewish Predilection for Justified Law* (Cambridge, Mass.: Harvard University Press, 1986); Moshe Green- berg, *Understanding Exodus*, Part I (New York: Behrman House, 1969): see

"Introduction" in particular; Michael Fishbane, *Biblical Interpretation in Ancient Israel* (Oxford: Claredon Press, 1985); Steven Fraade, *From Tradition to Commentary: Torah and Its Interpretation in the Midrash Sifre to Deuteronomny* (Albany: State University of New York Press, 1990); David Stern, "Midrash and Indeterminacy," *Critical Inquiry* 15 (1988): 132–61; Richard Sarason, "Toward a New Agendum for the Study of Rabbinic Midrashic Literature," in J. Petuchowski and E. Fleischer, eds., *Studies in Aggadah, Targum and Jewish Liturgy in Memory of Joseph Heinemann* (Jerusalem: Magnes Press, 1981), English section, 55–73. See, finally, Jacob Neusner's forthcoming descriptive theology of late rabbinic midrashim, presented in a series of studies beginning with *From Literature to Theology in Formative Judaism*.

76. For sample texts from this very small subgroup, see Michael Wyschogrod, *The Body of Faith: Judaism as Corporeal Election* (New York: Seabury Press, 1983), and David Novak, *Jewish-Christian Dialogue: A Jewish Justification* (New York: Oxford University Press, 1989). For a related approach see Michael Rosenak, *Commandments and Concerns: Jewish Religious Education in Secular Society* (Philadelphia: Jewish Publication Society, 1987).

77. In terms derived from Peirce's logic, this is a process of precisive abstraction, or of identifying representative claims as tokens of a few general types. The class characters of these types, or value-concepts, are the predicates common to all possible judgments made consistent with the types. I describe and illustrate the procedure in "A Pragmatic Method of Reading Confused Philosophic Texts: The Case of Peirce's 'Illustrations,'" *Transactions of the Charles S. Peirce Society* 25, no. 3 (Summer 1989): 251–91. Transcendental and phenomenological reductions employ comparable procedures.

78. I believe the detailed work of articulating the doctrines of aftermodern Judaism would require at least two stages. The first is a pragmatic reading of rabbinic documents, which means drawing descriptive theologies of rabbinic Judaism from contemporary studies of individual rabbinic documents in their intratextual and historical contexts. This is what Kadushin called a value-conceptual study of rabbinic Judaism and what Jacob Neusner now calls a descriptive theology of the Judaism of the dual Torah (see *From Literature to Theology in Formative Judaism*). The second stage is a pragmatic interpretation of rabbinic theology from out of the immediate context of present-day postcritical inquiry: a self-consciously selective rereading of rabbinic doctrine to respond to the particular problems and questions of the aftermodern community.

79. Abraham Heschel, *Between God and Man*, ed. Fritz Rothschild (New York: Free Press, 1959), 77.

80. For the sake of comparison, I would assume that, for postliberals, this community would be the church and that, for the church, God's spoken

word would be embodied, first, in the life of Jesus Christ, which life is the *immediate object* of the scriptural text, so that all interpretations of the text are interpretations of that life. "Immediate object" refers to Peirce's concept: "we have to distinguish the Immediate Object, which is the Object as the Sign itself represents it, and whose Being is thus dependent upon the Representaion of it in the Sign, from the Dynamical Object, which is the Reality which by some means contrives to determine the Sign to its Representation" 4.536: 1906.

81. Through this assertion, the aftermoderns display their voluntarism as well as their faith, arguing on behalf of their own critical methodologies and their status within academe as well as their understanding of how we might better understand God's will.

82. Steven Fraade, *From Tradition to Commentary: Torah and Its Interpretation in the Midrash Sifre to Deuteronomy* (Albany: State University of New York Press, 1990): ch. 4, n. 4.

83. In Peirce's usage, a process of performative representation.

84. At the same time, the concept of incompleteness also recommends a methodological pluralism at odds with some of the aftermoderns' tendencies to promote their doctrine dogmatically. If the Word has many interpretants, then the truth of the aftermodern interpretant will be displayed only with respect to its own premises.

85. Paraphrased from Kadushin, *Worship and Ethics* (Evanston, Ill.: Northwestern University Press, 1964), 21ff.

86. A certain kind of human character, defined as the possession of a certain set of conditional resolutions to act, is the practical interpretant of the word as law. The literature of rabbinic *halakhah*, for example, records interpretations of the scriptural word with respect to particular patterns of conduct.

87. Their critical inquiry may have accompanied their alienation from traditional, first-order practices without at the same time providing an alternative. Now they ask a reformulated inquiry to provide some method for redefining communal relations *for them* as well as redefining methods of studying the rabbinic community of inquiry. In the tradition of the *Wissenschaft des Judentums* they inherited, some aftermoderns may tend to repress this practical concern; the repression adds tensions and ironies to their work and their rhetoric.

VARIETIES OF RELIGIOUS AIMS: BEYOND EXCLUSIVISM, INCLUSIVISM, AND PLURALISM

J. A. DiNoia, O.P.

Can non-Christians attain salvation? Do other religions aim at salvation? Some form of the first question has been traditional in Christian theology of religions. The second question has a more contemporary ring. Both questions bulk large in current theology of religions. So much is this the case that contrasting positions in the field are classified as exclusivist, inclusivist, or pluralist—according to the prevailing typology—chiefly on the basis of the responses their proponents give to these questions.[1]

I

The prominence of these two questions and the intensity of the debate they have engendered are readily understandable. Questions about the chances outsiders have of attaining salvation take on a special urgency today as renewed esteem for other religions blossoms everywhere in the Christian community. Dismissing the formula *extra ecclesiam nulla salus* as offensive to other communities, many Christian theologians seek to express their esteem for them by fielding optimistic accounts both of non-Christians' prospects of attaining salvation and of the salvific bent of their religions.[2] Thus inclusivist and pluralist theologians are united in their rejection of the exclusivist position that salvation is attainable only within the embrace of explicit Christian faith. Broadly speaking, inclusivists are those who espouse some version of the view that all religious communities implicitly aim at the salvation which the Christian community most adequately commends, while pluralists contend that all religious communities aim at salvation under the variety of descriptions enshrined by their traditions.

Although pluralists and inclusivists converge in their opposition to exclusivism, their descriptions of the nature of the salvation available to non-Christians do not coincide.

When inclusivist theologians assert that non-Christian persons can attain salvation, or that their communities aim at salvation, "salvation" seems to refer to all or much of what Christians understand it to comprise: complete well-being in the life to come in eternal fellowship with the divine Trinity and with other human beings, won for us by Jesus Christ, through whom grace is given in the present life to nurture the beginnings of this fellowship and to overcome obstacles to its flourishing that arise from creaturely limitations and from sin. Christian doctrines about the universal scope of the divine salvific will and the unlimited applicability of Christ's redemption are understood to entail that every human being is given the opportunity to attain to the fullness of salvation. Inclusivist theologians advance a variety of theories to explain not only how non-Christian persons can receive the grace necessary to make this possibility actual in particular instances, but also how the religions which these persons practice can be salvific for them.[3]

In comparison with inclusivists, pluralist theologians seem to mean something less specific by salvation when they assert that non-Christian persons and communities aim at attaining it. According to pluralist theology of religions, every religious community can be understood to mean by "salvation" at least minimally a state of being that transcends the limitations of present existence and that is attainable through the form of life prescribed in the community's teachings. Aiming at salvation under its various descriptions (mokṣa, nibbāna, najāt, and so on) is one of the main functions that religious communities fulfill. For pluralists, the soteriological core discernible in the teachings of different religious communities warrants a Christian assertion of the availability of salvation beyond the boundaries of the Christian community.[4]

Both inclusivist and pluralist positions broadly invoke the empirical study of religions to support their contention that non-Christians and their communities aim to attain salvation in some form. It can be observed that many religious communities teach something about the human need for some kind of liberation from states of insufficiency variously described as suffering, ignorance, bondage, or sin. In addition, religious communities summon their current and potential members to strive for a higher state of being in which this liberation will be experienced in combination with many other material and spiritual benefits.

As Grace Jantzen has noted, however, "salvation" even in its nonreligious senses is a "slippery notion." She cautions theologians confronted with the rustling world of religions to avoid the unexamined assumption that "all religions have a concept of salvation at all, let alone that they all mean the same thing by it or offer the same way to obtain it: it is misleading to assume that there is some one thing that is obtained when salvation is obtained."[5] For, while many religious communities can be observed to teach that a certain present condition of human existence must be escaped or transcended, they differ profoundly in their descriptions of the nature of that condition, of the higher state of being to be sought, and of the means to reach it.

Inclusivist and pluralist theologians do not overlook these variations. Indeed, they have developed subtle strategies to encompass them. Pluralist positions, it might be supposed, would have the advantage here, since they frankly acknowledge the luxuriance of the religious landscape, so to speak. The various soteriological doctrines of the major religious communities are to be valued for the exalted conceptions of human life and destiny they embody and for the ways they complement and enrich each other. Pluralists interpret these doctrines as partial expressions of a commonly sought goal designated by such terms as "Reality-centeredness" (in a currently influential formulation).[6] Inclusivist theologians take a different tack. Rather than view cross-religious variations as representative of parallel or complementary soteriological programs, inclusivist theologians tend to regard such variations as subsumable into the all-embracing Christian scheme of salvation. The soteriological programs of other communities pursue hiddenly or partially what the Christian community pursues explicitly and fully.

But there is reason to doubt that the soteriological doctrines of other religious communities survive their transposition to pluralist and inclusivist theological contexts with their distinctive features intact.

Generally speaking, pluralist theology of religions tends to homogenize cross-religious variations in concepts of salvation in the direction of an indeterminate common goal, nonspecific conditions of insufficiency and limitation, and an undefined program for transcending them. Pluralism's "principle of soteriological equality," as Philip Almond has called it,[7] yields an undifferentiated concept of salvation to which no religious community could finally lay claim. Christian doctrines about salvation, no less than those of other communities, are interpreted by pluralist theologians in ways that narrow their scope or blur their distinctive features.[8] Thus, to take but one example, the christological minimalism typical of pluralist accounts of Christian soteriology tends to be paralleled in their treatment of other religious communities' particularistic claims to universality as well.[9]

In comparison with pluralist positions, inclusivist theology of religions has the advantage of combining a favorable account of other religious communities with a strong avowal of the universal scope of salvation in Christ. But inclusivist positions imply that a non-Christian who is a Buddhist, a Hindu, a Jew, or a Muslim can hiddenly attain salvation in Christ while overtly pursuing the soteriological program commended by his or her own community. This program may or may not be fully compatible with attaining and enjoying salvation as Christians conceive it, and in any case possesses a finality of its own. In addition, inclusivists want to extend traditional doctrine by affirming not only that non-Christian persons can attain salvation, but also that their communities aim, though haltingly, at salvation as Christians understand it. This view of other religious communities has the effect of sublating their distinctive soteriological doctrines to the Christian scheme of salvation.[10]

It may be that these inclusivist and pluralist strategies for dealing with variations in soteriological concepts are necessitated by the way the project of theology of religions has come to be conceived. Given the prominence of questions about the salvation of non-Christians and the salvific value of their religions, pluralists and inclusivists are in effect committed from the outset to demonstrating that Hindu, Buddhist, Muslim, Judaic, and other religious communities join the

Christian community in the quest for salvation. The dual specters of exclusivism and relativism presumably exert some pressure on the soteriocentrism of inclusivist and pluralist positions. If other religions cannot be shown to aim at salvation, then it would seem to follow either that it can only be sought and attained in the Christian community (exclusivism), or, more remotely, that the world's religions are so disparate in their conceptions and purposes as to be without any sort of common ground (relativism). In any case, Christian theology of religions conceived in this vein seems bound to equalize or absorb the ineffaceably particular soteriological programs of other religious communities.

It would be desirable for Christian theology of religions to take better account of such variations than inclusivist and pluralist positions are equipped to do. Although the differences in soteriological doctrines from one community to the next should not be exaggerated, they are not unimportant. It may be taken as an indication of their significance that internal debate about this range of issues has sometimes generated disagreements within the communities themselves, to the point of giving rise to the formation of subcommunities divided along the lines mapped by these disagreements. (Consider, for example, intra-Christian debates about the doctrines of grace and justification.) Cross-religious variations in soteriological concepts and doctrines are likely to prove no less significant than strongly felt internal ones.

It should be possible for the soteriological programs of Judaic, Muslim, Hindu, Buddhist, and other religious communities to retain more of their internal significance when transposed to Christian contexts of discussion. This possibility is at least worth exploring. Such an approach—were it feasible—would have certain advantages in the present climate of religious interaction. Respect for other religious communities seems to require that their distinctive doctrinal claims be taken seriously by Christian theology of religions. In addition, Christian participation in interreligious dialogue seems to suppose a readiness to grasp the whole scheme of practice and belief that another religious community presents to the world. There is an understandable tendency for Christians to want to voice their esteem for other religious communities by saying that they, after all, set out to accomplish just what we set out to accomplish, though they express things

differently. But a more appropriate strategy might be to try to determine whether the different modes of expression do not in fact signal
importantly different aims. It would be basic to such a strategy to take
what Kenneth Surin has called the "intractable otherness" of other
religions more at face value.[11]

One way to begin would be to try to place a religious community's soteriological program within the total framework of its body
of doctrines. Rather than ask whether non-Christians can attain salvation or whether their religions aim at salvation, Christian theology
of religions would ask: How do the soteriological programs of other
religious communities promote the pursuit and enjoyment of the distinctive overall goals they propose for human life? Questions about
salvation would continue on the menu, so to speak, but they would
take second place to questions about the varieties of aims proposed
by religious communities, and the patterns of dispositions and actions
they call forth.

II

Each of the world's great religious traditions directs its adherents
to some ultimate aim of life and proposes some pattern which life as
a whole ought to take in view of that aim. As William A. Christian
has observed, "there seems to be a deep-seated tendency in the major
religious communities to develop a comprehensive pattern of life . . .
which bears on all human interests . . . and on all situations in which
human beings find themselves."[12] Deploying the analogy of a cultural-
linguistic scheme, George A. Lindbeck has made a similar point by
drawing attention to the ways that religious traditions mold the whole
of the life and experience of their adherents.[13]

Thus, the entire outlook of pious Christians has come to be
shaped by the fundamental conviction that a good life is one lived in
seeking to be in fellowship with God and with other human beings
in him. In effect, the whole message of the Scriptures as these have
come to be interpreted in the traditions of their community is to foster
this aim across all the interests and occasions of life. The prayers and
stories, customs and rites, beliefs and ethical teachings of the Christian
community have God the Blessed Trinity as their focus and aim.

The Christian theologian can notice that something like this is true of the Judaic community as well. Rabbi Hayim Halevy Donin has written that "the overall reason given by the Torah for demanding of the Jew that he follow all its laws and regulations" is that Israel will become holy. "Speak to the whole Israelite community and say to them: you shall be holy for I the Lord your God am holy" (Lev. 19:2). The detail and scope of the law is such as to suffuse every part of human life, to penetrate all its crevices, with holiness.[14]

Torah, gospel, dharma—these terms designate patterns of thinking and acting through which religious communities shape the personal and communal existence of their members, and equip them for engagement in the whole range of life's interests and occasions. One way for the Christian theologian to grasp what another religious community undertakes to accomplish is by studying the comprehensive pattern of life it commends in its practical doctrines. In its doctrines and institutions, a religious community fosters not only ways of thinking and belief, but also ways of being and acting which encompass the whole of life. The community's soteriological program, should it possess one, will have its point within this overall pattern.

The Christian theologian can notice that implicit in the proposal of comprehensive patterns of life are proposals about the aim life ought to have as a whole. Each of the world's religious communities seems to propose an aim of life which is worth seeking above other aims—and usually above all other aims as well, though not necessarily to their exclusion. Union with the Blessed Trinity, holiness in all aspects of life, surrender to Allah, the cessation of desire: these are some of the expressions by which the Christian, Judaic, Muslim and Buddhist communities can be understood respectively to designate that which should be sought above all else.

There is a dual sense to the "ultimacy" of the aims religious communities commend to their members (and to potential members as well). Ultimate aims elicit comprehensive courses of action which in turn shape specific courses of action. In this way ultimate aims are in the first place ingredient in particular courses of action. The finality is intentional rather than temporal. The courses of action— specific and comprehensive—which a community recommends in its practical doctrines derive their character and point from the objects they pursue. Thus in the form of Judaism described by Rabbi Donin,

256 / J. A. DiNoia, O.P.

holiness is ultimate in the sense that, whatever else may be sought, it has primacy. But ultimate aims can also be final in a temporal sense. A religious community may project to its members the enjoyment of a future, and possibly permanent state, in which what is sought through the course of earthly existence can be fully realized. We may suppose, for example, that the holiness which is ultimate for the Judaic community should characterize not only each individual occasion of action in life, but also the cumulative activity of a completed lifetime.[15]

If the specific and comprehensive courses of action recommended by a community's practical doctrines get their point from the ultimate aim they envisage, the character of the agents for whom these aims are ultimate are also molded by this activity. The pursuit of overarching religious aims is formative of character. Inculcation of patterns of skills, conduct, and experience seems to be a central feature of the practical programs of most religious communities. The point of this cultivation of a range of "virtues" seems to be that it insures not only the attainment but also the enjoyment of the end commended by the community. In their practical doctrines, religious communities thus not only commend the means to attain the ultimate end of life (intentionally and temporally), but also the dispositions to enjoy it.

Thus, the patterns of life commended by religious communities may be understood as comprehensive in the sense that they give shape to life as a whole in the light of an ultimate aim of life. In this way, they may be said to foster a web of cognitive and affective dispositions, many of which perdure in that they permit the enjoyment of a temporally final end of life beyond earthly life.

The soteriological program of a religious community arises from its complex of teachings about the aim of life, the shape life ought to take in light of this aim, and the dispositions which will foster its uninterrupted (earthly or transworldly) enjoyment. Clearly, the goal of salvation can be understood only in terms of this complex of teachings. In addition, the community's understanding of the ultimate aim of life in part determines its conception of the potentialities of human beings to attain and enjoy it. No aim can have meaning for agents who are not—or cannot become—in some sense fit to seek and obtain it. It is evident, then, that another segment of a community's soteriological doctrines—conceptions of human nature and the limitations which beset it—link with the overall aim of life a community proposes. Finally, the means by which these limitations are to be transcended are defined by the whole ensemble of the community's practical doctrines.

It seems correct to conclude that the person whom the community could pronounce to be "saved" (to employ a Christian locution) would be a person whose life had been shaped according to the distinctive pattern which it fosters. Whether it could judge someone to be saved whose life had not been shaped in this way would be an issue of considerable complexity for most religious communities. Some, like Christianity, have addressed themselves to it. The issue will be of concern precisely because the pursuit of a particular form of life and the attainment of the aim it promises are linked so inextricably in the ethos and idiom of most religious communities. It is refreshing to note in passing that the Christian community is not alone in facing this kind of issue.[16]

More to the point, however, it is clear that both pluralist and inclusivist positions fail to account for this inextricable connection between the particular aims of life commended by religious communities and the specific sets of dispositions they foster to promote the attainment and enjoyment of those aims. Thus, in different ways, both inclusivism and pluralism tend to divorce what in most religious traditions are understood to be inseparable—as the foregoing more purely conceptual analysis of the link between aims and patterns of life also suggests. Inclusivist positions imply that the affective and intellectual dispositions fostered by different religious communities in fact promote the attainment and enjoyment not of the aims of life they commend to their members but the aim of life commended by the Christian community. Since for pluralist positions the true aim of life always eludes anything but partial conceptualization and thus can never in itself specify the formation of the dispositions to attain and enjoy it, the particular aims commended by religious communities beckon their members not finally to the ends they commend, but to the enjoyment of an unnameable reality which transcends them all.

The preceding analysis lends support to the theological endeavor to find an alternative to the inclusivist and pluralist assimilation of the soteriological programs of other religious communities. This line of inquiry can be pursued further by making the foregoing analysis more concrete through consideration of some illustrations of the connections between soteriological programs and the comprehensive patterns of life communities commend.

III

Consider the following description of the Christian pattern of life. Its formulation is influenced by the Roman Catholic tradition, particularly in its articulation by Thomas Aquinas. Presumably, other Christian traditions could develop a comparable description for similarly illustrative purposes. It is presented in order to exhibit more clearly the potential significance, for theology of religions, of the truth that other religious communities propose distinct (though not necessarily opposed) patterns of life in view of particular definitions of the overall aim of life.

The Christian community can be understood to propose that the most important thing in life is to enjoy a relationship of love, or *caritas*, with the Blessed Trinity—a relationship initiated by God himself in the sacrament of baptism and fostered through the other sacraments, a relationship flowing into all dealings with other human beings and culminating in beatific vision in the life to come. Beatific vision involves not the static contemplation of the divine essence but a direct knowledge and experience of God's personal life that bursts forth in love. The term "vision" describes the degree of intimacy fundamental to the culmination of the life of charity (unmediated, unobstructed, direct love); "beatific," its blissfulness. It could be said that the claim that interpersonal relationships in *caritas* are fundamental to human existence is warranted for Christians by the doctrine that relation is found in God himself. The disposition to be drawn into relation with the Blessed Trinity and with others in God is itself God's gift, the infused theological virtue of charity. Everything in Christianity is geared to the cultivation of these relationships in *caritas*.

The formative character of these convictions is clear in the annual observance of the liturgical season of Lent-Easter, from Ash Wednesday through Easter and Pentecost, and (by extension) to the feast of the Blessed Trinity. Perhaps more explicitly than any other in the liturgical year, this sequence of weeks is devoted to the cultivation of Christian life and virtue, with the primacy of charity at the center. The practices of penance and the cultivation of virtue are not primarily self-directed activities, but oriented to the enablement and enhancement of love for God and others. The more human beings are drawn away from sinful patterns of life through the grace of conversion, the more they are drawn into communion with others and with God.

In Lent the commitment to the struggle against sin is firmly located in "taking up the cross" with Christ. Here, soteriology becomes concrete, so to speak. Through the Lectionary sequencing and pairing of readings from the Scriptures, as well as through the prayers, prefaces, and hymns, and the developing liturgical "moods" of this season, the Christian's struggle is continually linked with crucial moments in the narrative of Christ: temptation, transfiguration, cross-bearing, death, resurrection, and glory. The action which once and for all accomplished our salvation now transforms our lives in grace. Our appropriation of the benefits of this action takes many forms over the course of our lifetimes. There is an important sense in which this transformation entails a "conformation." The pattern of the uniquely specifying actions which won our redemption is replicated in the faithful following of Christ by each Christian disciple. When Christ warns his disciples at Caesarea Philippi (Matt. 16:13–28)—a passage that plays an important role in linking Christian identity with the narrative of Christ's *passio*—that through him is the way to find one's true identity, he in effect links their transformation with a conformation to him. The *"imago dei"* is brought to perfection in his disciples by his Holy Spirit, who assimilates them to the perfect image, the Son. Thus the community can pray that the Father, according to one of the eucharistic prefaces, "might see and love in us what he sees and loves in Christ."

But conformity to Christ does not involve a finally anonymous uniformity. Rather, Christ's grace unlocks the potential for the realization of the unique personal identities of each disciple. The victory of Easter wins for Christ's disciples the resurrection of the body: the transfigured but perduring personal identities of an indefinite number of uniquely specified, "named," persons, in the perfect union of *caritas*

with each other and the Blessed Trinity—itself personally "Named"—
in the life to come. "And we all, with unveiled face, beholding the
glory of the Lord, are being changed into his likeness from one degree
of glory to another" (2 Cor. 3:18).

It is worthwhile to linger over this description in order to make
clear how concretely Christian soteriological doctrines are set into
the whole Christian pattern of life. If some such description of the
Christian pattern of life—with prominence given to soteriological
doctrines—is persuasive, it suggests that the dispositions to attain
and enjoy the true aim of life develop over the course of a lifetime of
divinely engendered and sustained "cultivation." Christian salvation
means, finally, becoming a certain kind of person, one who can enjoy
the end of life that the Christian community commends. It makes
no difference to the specificity of this aim that Christians believe it
to be identical with the aim all human beings should seek. The single, divinely willed order of grace and salvation—according to Christian doctrines under the construal which informs this discussion—
embraces the entire human race. It remains true, nonetheless, that the
salvation to which, by God's design for the human race, the Christian community bears witness and affords access comprises a highly
specified aim, range of dispositions, and pattern of transformation.

The soteriological programs of other religious communities are
likewise embedded in larger contexts of belief and practice. Hence,
it is misleading to extract soteriological fragments from the various
comprehensive patterns of life commended by other communities in
order to show that all aim at salvation, because either salvation in
some form, or Christian salvation implicitly, is what all religions seek
in their doctrines and life.

Suppose that there were a religious community which aimed at a
state—let us call it "enlightenment"—in which the impermanence of
personal identity would be "realized" and with it the cessation of desire
"enjoyed." This community would presumably set out to cultivate in
its members dispositions which would foster this realization and enjoyment. Also, presumably, these would be different from dispositions—
such as those fostered by the Christian community—which have in
view the fulfillment of personal identity and the perfection of personal relations. There is reason to suppose that the dispositions to
attain and enjoy the perfect fellowship of charity would be different

from those to attain and enjoy a state of being that might be called "enlightenment." Clearly, furthermore, the soteriological program of such a community would be likely to differ from that of Christianity on such issues as the conditions of human existence and the means by which they are to be transcended or transformed.[17]

A possible pluralist objection to this whole line of argument is germane at this point. It might be objected that neither "Blessed Trinity" nor "enlightenment" properly describes the essentially indescribable "transcendent," but could only aim at describing it. This objection misses the mark. Experientially, it matters little that the expressed objectives do not adequately describe the "transcendent." Whatever the character of the religious conceptions about the aim of life, just as such they function to specify the dispositions and activities cultivated in view of their present or eventual attainment and enjoyment. To say that religions aim at "ultimacy" or at "reality" is to state an aim of such generality as to fail entirely to describe what actually transpires in religious communities. To be sure, Christians, Jews, Muslims, Hindus, Buddhists, and others not only disagree on how to describe the "ultimate": they disagree profoundly about what the "ultimate" is in itself.[18] But even if it were conceded that these were disagreements only about descriptions of something in itself utterly indescribable, the argument here would still stand. Conceptions of the end of life function as objectives which specify dispositions, activities, and patterns of activity nonetheless.

Do the practical doctrines of the hypothetical religious community described above commend an aim of life which in addition to being different from the one proposed by Christianity is also opposed to it, such that seeking and attaining the one would exclude seeking and attaining the other?[19]

There are at least two ways in which it could be shown that aims of life were opposed: if the courses of action which they recommended were incapable of joint fulfillment, or if the dispositions they undertook to cultivate ruled out or neglected the cultivation of some others. Two aims of action, each having primacy, would be opposed to each other. But distinct aims can be interrelated with, or subordinated to, or independent of one another. In that case, the pursuit of one aim would not necessarily exclude another. These connections might not be apparent at first. Sometimes, in the pursuit of one aim, an agent unknowingly promotes his attainment of another. One might discover that one had unintentionally developed the potential to be a baseball pitcher by throwing stones often while growing up.[20] Practicing the violin would not contribute directly to developing a marathon runner, but neither would it exclude such an aim. On the other hand, the type of physical conditioning needed to produce a sumo wrestler would presumably rule out a career in ballet dancing.

Just as in these ordinary human endeavors, there are likewise many possibilities in the religious realm. Extensive comparative analysis and dialogue would be required before doctrinal differences about the true aim of life between Christianity and other religious communities could be identified as true oppositions.[21] After such study and reflection, a Christian theologian might be led to propose, for example, that the pursuit of "enlightenment" was subordinate and not opposed to the pursuit of fellowship with the Blessed Trinity. But the argument here does not hinge on a specification of the nature of the differences that might come to be identified. Rather, it makes a case for the significance of precisely the kinds of analysis which the foregoing illustrations merely hint at. Venturing beyond the conversation which currently engages inclusivists and pluralists, Christian theology of religions would endeavor to frame its confidence in the availability of salvation beyond the confines of the Christian community in a manner consistent with an acknowledgment of the varieties of aims pursued by other religious communities.

IV

Can non-Christians attain salvation? Do other religions aim at salvation? In order to make some headway in charting the territory beyond the boundaries of current debate, one task of Christian theology of religions would be to distinguish and rethink these two questions.

Consider the latter question first: Do other religions aim at salvation? Since much of the present essay up to this point has been devoted to an analysis of this question, it can be treated more briefly now. For reasons that should be plain, no blanket affirmative response to the question of whether other religious communities aim at salvation is either possible or appropriate. In Christian theology of religions, judgments about the matter would depend on knowing something rather specific about the doctrines of the religious communities in question—especially their doctrines about life's overall aim and shape. Furthermore, it would have to be clear not only what is meant by "salvation," but also how soteriology fits into the larger context of the body of doctrines of a community. In the terms of the analysis offered above, if this question cannot be avoided, it would need to be framed differently: Do other religious communities, while pursuing their distinctive aims, foster rather than obstruct the development in their members of the dispositions to attain and enjoy the true end of life, fellowship with the Blessed Trinity? The Second Vatican Council's Declaration on Non-Christian Religions can be construed to be offering a qualified affirmative response to this question, though without framing it in these terms.[22]

But, if Christians cannot state unconditionally that other religious communities aim at salvation, it by no means follows that they can say nothing positive about these communities. The argument of this essay implies that other ways of expressing an appreciative valuation of non-Christian religious communities might even be preferable in present circumstances. There are alternatives to asserting that other religions are partially equipped to attain that to which Christianity affords surer access (inclusivism), or that all religions are more or less equally equipped to attain something that finally eludes them all (less satisfactorily, pluralism). Christian theology of religions might investigate the "unsubstitutable uniqueness of the God-willed missions of non-Christian religions," writes George Lindbeck, "within which potentialities can be actualized and realities explored that are not within the direct purview of the peoples of Messianic witness, but are nevertheless God-willed and God-approved anticipations of aspects of the coming kingdom."[23] Elsewhere, it has been suggested that "the providential diversity of religions" might encompass an as yet unforeseen and unspecifiable role for other religions in the divine plan for the human race.[24] Once freed of the assumption that other religious communities aim to accomplish the same things that Christianity does, Christian theologians will have much to learn from the study of their literatures as well as from the debate which such study is likely to engender.[25] Given the profundity and range of these literatures, not to mention their sheer volume, the potential for further inquiry and theological construction is virtually unlimited.[26]

V

But our first question is still outstanding: Can non-Christians attain salvation? The conviction that they can remains an unexpungeable feature of Christian confession. Mainstream Christian communities have for the most part been confident that, through the grace of God, persons can receive and develop the dispositions conducive to and necessary for the enjoyment of the true end of life even independently of membership in the Christian community which devotes itself explicitly to their cultivation. This confidence is based upon the doctrines of the unrestricted scope of the divine salvific will and the universality of the redemption won for humankind by Jesus Christ.[27]

Once the well-trodden paths of inclusivism and pluralism are left behind, can this confidence find any satisfactory theological formulation? Is it possible, in other words, to account theologically for the availability of salvation to non-Christians without ascribing to them the pursuit of an aim of life which they either explicitly reject or could not recognize as their own? Can Christian theology of religions express confidence that the members of Judaic, Muslim, Hindu, Buddhist, and other religious communities can (now or eventually) attain and enjoy fellowship with the Blessed Trinity while possessing alternative conceptions of the aim of life and cultivating dispositions consistent with these conceptions?

To gain a perspective on this issue, consider the situation of a person who belongs to what Christians would regard as a thoroughly corrupt religion—one, let us say, which centers upon a demonic deity worshiped by rites of human sacrifice. Suppose further that, responsive to the prompting of divine grace, such a person has recognized and distanced herself from the corrupt elements of her religion. Clearly, although Christians might find nothing in this religious community they could judge to be conducive to salvation, a person who was a member of this community could still attain salvation.

The point of this illustration is certainly not that most other religions are in some way corrupt. Rather, it suggests in the first place that the question of whether non-Christians can attain salvation is at least distinguishable from the question of whether their religions aim at salvation as Christians mean it. Christian confidence in the salvation of other religious people is logically independent of judgments about the aims of life commended by their communities. A blanket affirmation that other religions aim at salvation (in some way or other) is not required to sustain Christian confidence in the availability of salvation to outsiders. Theological expression of such confidence is consistent with a systematic acknowledgment of the varieties of aims religious communities pursue.

Secondly, once drawn, this distinction has the advantage of steering Christian theology of religions toward the desired affirmation of the possibility of salvation for non-Christians but framed with their explicit religious aims in view.

Echoing the first chapter of Paul's Letter to the Romans, a traditional approach to the issue invokes the ubiquity and significance of the conditions for moral choice. Thus, throughout his writings Aquinas advanced a cumulatively compelling case for the view that every occasion of action poses for each human being the possibility of choosing the moral good and thereby orienting oneself to the ultimate good. Indeed, the consequences of the failure to do so can on occasion be reversed by subsequent good actions. This is the case not primarily because of virtualities present in the conditions of moral action—and not despite them, either—but because of God's gift in grace. Without reviewing here all the premises upon which Aquinas could draw in support of this contention, the point is that he articulates the unrestricted range of the divine action in prompting and rewarding the uprightness of moral choices made by human beings, Christian and non-Christian alike. The choice of the particular, real human good—namely, for Aquinas, the choice of the moral good—is always a confirmation of the human orientation toward enjoyment of the fullness of goodness in God. In the concrete order of salvation, there is no such thing as moral goodness—or moral defect, for that matter—as an ingredient of a purely natural order of things apart from grace.[28] Whether grace is given in baptism or in the "desire" for it, human beings stand equally in the sight of God before their moral choices, despite the many variables (cultural or religious) which may characterize their particular situation and condition. Plainly, the moral good that beckons human choice in every instance need not be framed in the terms of explicitly religious conceptualities.

It is significant that elsewhere, when addressing the question of the faith needed for salvation, Aquinas can be construed as being more cautious in his assessment of the possibilities of salvation for non-Christians whose explicit knowledge of the faith would of necessity be deficient.[29] It is not important for our purposes what explicit content Aquinas identifies as necessary for salvation (in fact, at least implicit knowledge of the Trinity). What is significant is that Aquinas's overall position on these issues is typically both cautious and confident: cautious in stating an explicit cognitive content necessary for salvation, confident in stating the ubiquity of grace in moral choices.

Aquinas's restraint in describing the present states of non-Christians is instructive. It implies that Christian theology of religions should limit itself to a confident affirmation of the general possibility of salvation as something present or underway in the lives of non-Christians. But the endeavor to field an overly detailed account of how this can be the case for particular non-Christians who are Hindus, Buddhists, Muslims, or Jews inevitably risks underestimating the significance of the distinctive religious aims which they intentionally pursue.

The conceptual tools to do more than this are simply lacking. About the most that could be said would be that a particular religious community may foster dispositions which advanced its members partly along the way to fellowship with the Blessed Trinity. Aims can occur in ordered sequences and priorities assigned to "higher" aims do not negate or exclude subordinate aims. It was observed above that a person could develop dispositions with a view to a certain aim without the awareness that the attainment of this aim afforded access to another. It might turn out that religious aims pursued as ultimate were themselves encompassed by an end yet more ultimate. Thus, Muslims or Buddhists could be said to develop dispositions conducive to the enjoyment of the true aim of life—fellowship with the Blessed Trinity—even if they did so in the light of conceptions which ruled out personal relation either in God himself or in the ultimate state of enlightenment. The upshot would be that such persons could reach to the threshold of the enjoyment of the true aim of life not only despite but also because of dispositions fostered in their communities, even though some of their doctrines are regarded as mistaken or incomplete from the Christian point of view.

But it is clear that this line of reflection veers perilously close to the very difficulties which this essay has been concerned to avoid.

The expressed finalities of Buddhist and Muslim patterns of life certainly do not envisage subordination to the finality commended by the Christian community. There is perhaps less danger of downplaying these distinctive finalities if judgments framed with this degree of detail were thought of as appropriate only in an eschatological perspective. This is the light in which to understand the attraction of what can be termed prospective accounts of the salvation of non-Christians, such as that proposed by George Lindbeck and others.[30] By projecting the moment of experienced salvation into the time of death or beyond, Christian theology of religions in a prospective vein combines a confident affirmation of the possibility of salvation for non-Christians with a respect for their distinctive doctrines about the true aim of life and for the finality of the dispositions they foster in their communities.

Recent prospective accounts of the salvation of non-Christians can be usefully amplified by appeal to the doctrine of purgatory. At first, it may strike the reader as foolhardy to invoke the doctrine of purgatory at this juncture—in effect, trying to resolve one set of difficulties with a proposal infinitely more problematic. Vexing problems beset the doctrine, notably: the nature of the intermediate state it assumes; the time, place, and imagery of purgatory; the range of intra-Christian disagreements about the doctrine. In fact, however, the doctrine has been well defended of late.[31] If it is granted for the sake of discussion that the chief difficulties can be satisfactorily dealt with and resolved, then Christian theology of religions may be able to tap the potential of this neglected doctrine.

The doctrine of purgatory is formulated with a view to the enjoyment of the life to come by believers who die in the state of unrepented minor sin or with the lingering dispositional consequences of repented and forgiven patterns of sin. The doctrine envisages an intermediate state (between death and the Last Judgment) in which any personal obstacles (what Rahner calls a lack of integration) to the full enjoyment of the true end of life—fellowship with the Blessed Trinity—are eliminated.[32] According to standard Catholic doctrine, purgatory does not provide an opportunity to reverse life-shaping decisions taken prior to death. This is the sense of saying that one's eternal fate is settled at death; individual judgment by Christ occurs immediately after death. Hence, the interval between individual judgment and the general judgment cannot be considered as one in which conversion could now occur when none had taken place prior to death, or that the fundamental orientation of one's life could be altered. The decisions taken in life cannot turn out to have been irrelevant to the shape of the life to come.[33]

The point of the doctrine is that a certain kind of life may render one unfit for the *immediate* enjoyment of fellowship with the Blessed Trinity, even though one is destined for it. The dispositions to enjoy fellowship with the Blessed Trinity have not developed fully, though of course no contrary ("hellish") dispositions remain ineradicably entrenched. On this interpretation of the doctrine, it is not so much that God cannot abide imperfection as that in an unpurified state a human being could not fully enjoy God's company. An interval or experience of additional transformation—gained for us by Christ—is needed. It is not essential to the doctrine that purgatory be thought of as a place or duration, and certainly not a punishment by fire. What is crucial is that it allows for an interval (which may be thought of as instantaneous and coterminous with death) the essential feature of which is the experience of a necessary purification or transformation in view of the assured prospect of eternal bliss.[34]

If this possibility is open to Christians, then surely there is no reason in principle to rule it out for non-Christians. According to Catholic doctrine, purgatory provides for an interval for the rectification of whatever is lacking in any human being who dies justified or in the state of grace, but unprepared for the full enjoyment of bliss.

The doctrine of purgatory permits Christian theology a wide measure of confidence about the salvation of non-Christians (just as much as it does for many imperfect Christians who are, for that matter, in the greater peril) without underestimating the distinctive aims they have pursued in life. Whatever transformation purgatory will entail for non-Christians, its purely cognitive side should not be exaggerated. The transformation of purgatory will not involve simply a disruptive "reeducation" about the nature of the "transcendent" which—having been discovered to be radically other than one had supposed it to be—now demands a radical revision of one's beliefs. As we have noted, the pursuit of religious aims and the cultivation of religious dispositions not directly opposed to the enjoyment of fellowship with the Blessed Trinity can be viewed as in some sense preparatory for it. The doctrine of purgatory derives its force from convictions about the continuity between the earthly and postmortem life of those who die in the state of grace. Presumably, for non-Christians purgatory would involve the realization of the continuities, as well as the discontinuities between what they had practiced and believed and what is indeed the case about the true aim of life.[35]

But theology of religions strays beyond its limits here. Except that it must allow for this possibility and can broadly sketch its structure, theological analysis is not competent to specify in detail what this purifying interval will involve for individual human beings—rollicking religious imagination to the contrary notwithstanding. Proposals with an eschatological ring to them should be advanced in a judiciously restrained tone.[36] The contribution which the doctrine of purgatory makes here is that it allows respect for the varieties of aims which religious people pursue in this life without ruling on the question of their bearing on the life to come.

The argument of this paper is intended to be exploratory. It has pressed here and there at the boundaries of current debate in order to point the way to promising avenues of study and reflection in Christian theology of religions. No attempt has been made exhaustively to canvass the enormous literature in the field. A great deal more work is needed to test the viability of key elements in the approach suggested in this paper. To offset possible misunderstandings of what has been proposed here, it should be noted that it is no part of the argument of this paper that having an "aim of life"—whether ultimate or intermediary—is a defining feature of "religion." Nor has it been argued that, within large worldwide communities, a single, invariant conception of the true aim of life prevails. The argument here does entail the observation that "aims of life" figure prominently in existing religious communities, and the supposition that, if they exhibit roughly the structure sketched here, then Christian theology of religions should take them into account in advancing proposals about the availability of salvation beyond the confines of the Christian community. If the reader has been struck by the plausibility of this argument, then the debate has already moved beyond the confines set for it by the soteriocentrism of inclusivist and pluralist positions.

NOTES

1. This typology figures prominently in representative recent surveys of the field: Alan Race, *Christians and Religious Pluralism* (Maryknoll, N.Y.: Orbis, 1982); Gavin D'Costa, *Theology and Religious Pluralism* (Oxford: Basil Blackwell, 1986) and "Theology of Religions," in *The Modern Theologians*, ed. David F. Ford (Oxford: Basil Blackwell, 1989), vol. 2: 274–90.

2. Although in recent literature the formula *extra ecclesiam nulla salus* has been construed as bearing on the salvation of non-Christians, Gavin D'Costa has shown that it has a more properly intra-Christian force. In its origins and for most of its history, the formula has been directed against Christians who break away from the main body of the church (apostates, heretics, and schismatics); attempts to apply it to the situation of non-Christians have been resisted by doctrinal authorities. For details, see D'Costa's important paper, "*Extra Ecclesiam Nulla Salus* Revisited," *Religious Pluralism: Colston Symposium Proceedings 1987*, ed. Ian Hannett (London: Routledge, forthcoming). The writings of Hendrik Kraemer—notably his *The Christian Message in a Non-Christian World* (London: Edinburgh House Press, 1938)—are commonly taken to exemplify the exclusivist approach. The present essay focuses primarily on inclusivist and pluralist approaches.

3. Some form of inclusivism is espoused by a wide range of authors: for examples see Race, *Christians and Religious Pluralism*, 38–69, and Paul F. Knitter, who describes inclusivism as the "catholic model" in *No Other Name?* (Maryknoll, N.Y.: Orbis, 1985), 120–44. The inclusivist approach is perhaps best represented by Karl Rahner's influential essays in *Theological Investigations* (London: Darton, Longman & Todd, 1961–), notably "Christianity and World Religions," vol. 5: 115–34; "Anonymous Christians," 6: 390–98; "Observations on the Problem of the Anonymous Christian," 14: 280–94; "Jesus Christ in the Non-Christian Religions," 17: 38–50. For a spirited defense and reconstruction of a broadly Rahnerian inclusivism, see Gavin D'Costa, *Theology and Religious Pluralism*, 81–139. As the title suggests, Kenneth Cragg's *The Christ and the Faiths* (Philadelphia: Westminster, 1986) represents a form of inclusivism in which "Christ" is taken to symbolize the fundamental aspirations common to all major religious traditions.

4. As employed in this essay, the term "pluralism" refers not to the fact of religious diversity, but to a family of theological positions developed to take account of religious diversity. Decisive in the formation of most of these positions have been the writings of John Hick—most recently, *An Interpretation of Religion* (New Haven, Conn.: Yale University Press, 1989)—and Wilfred Cantwell Smith—notably, *Towards a World Theology* (Philadelphia: Westminster Press, 1981). Recent books espousing pluralist positions are Knitter, *No Other Name?* (where pluralism is termed the "theocentric model"); John

Hick and Paul F. Knitter, *The Myth of Christian Uniqueness* (Maryknoll, N.Y.: Orbis Books, 1987); Eugene Hillman, *Many Paths* (Maryknoll, N.Y.: Orbis Books, 1989).

5. Grace M. Jantzen, "Human Diversity and Salvation in Christ," *Religious Studies* 20 (1984): 579–80.

6. The term is John Hick's. See, for example, his *Problems of Religious Pluralism* (New York: St. Martin's Press, 1985), 34–45.

7. Philip Almond, "John Hick's Copernican Theology," *Theology* 86 (1983): 36–41, and "Wilfred Cantwell Smith as a Theologian of Religions," *Harvard Theological Review* 76 (1983): 335–42.

8. See Kenneth Surin, "Towards a Materialist Critique of Religious Pluralism : A Polemical Examination of the Discourse of John Hick and Wilfred Cantwell Smith," *The Thomist* 53 (1989): 655–73; also forthcoming in Hannett, ed., *Religious Pluralism.*

9. See, for example, Knitter, *No Other Name?*, 171–204. Although he does not discuss other religions in these pages, the logic of Knitter's christological minimalism suggests a parallel minimalism in the treatment of other religions.

10. For an analysis and critique of Rahnerian inclusivism, see J. A. Di-Noia, "Implicit Faith, General Revelation and the State of Non-Christians," *The Thomist* 47 (1983): 209–41.

11. Surin, "Towards a Materialist Critique," 673.

12. William A. Christian, Sr., *Doctrines of Religious Communities* (New Haven, Conn.: Yale University Press, 1987), 186.

13. George A. Lindbeck, *The Nature of Doctrine* (Philadelphia: Westminster, 1984), 32–41.

14. Hayim H. Donin, *To Be a Jew* (New York: Basic Books, 1972), 35.

15. This discussion combines claims in philosophical ethics drawn from Thomas Aquinas, *Summa Theologiae* la2ae, 1–5, with William A. Christian's philosophical analysis of the logic of practical doctrines. My reading of Aquinas on these issues has been influenced by Ralph McInerny, *Ethica Thomistica* (Washington, D.C.: Catholic University Press of America, 1982); John Finnis, "Practical Reasoning, Human Goods and the End of Man," *New Blackfriars* 66 (1985): 438–51; and Romanus Cessario, *The Moral Virtues and Theological Ethics* (Notre Dame, Ind.: University of Notre Dame Press, 1990). The discussion of practical doctrines presupposes William A. Christian, Sr., *Meaning and Truth in Religion* (Princeton, N.J.: Princeton University Press, 1964), 60–77; *Oppositions of Religious Doctrines* (New York: Herder & Herder, 1972), 43–59; *Doctrines of Religious Communities*, 5–11, 176–92. In an important recent book, John P. Reeder, Jr., has attempted to show how ethics and

soteriology are related in religious traditions: *Source, Sanction and Salvation* (Englewood Cliffs, N.J.: Prentice Hall, 1988).

16. For a general philosophical account of religious doctrines addressing this issue, see J. A. DiNoia, "The Doctrines of a Religious Community about Other Religions," *Religious Studies* 18 (1982): 293–307.

17. This hypothetical description was suggested by the doctrines of Theravada Buddhism. The illustration is offered as hypothetical since it is no part of the argument of this essay to present an account of the doctrines of this community that would be acceptable to its own scholars or to non-Buddhist students of its traditions. The illustration implies that the realization of the state of enlightenment involves recognition of the impermanence of the self and with it, presumably, the impossibility of interpersonal relations in the "post-earthly" state. The extent to which the doctrines of Theravada Buddhism (especially that of the "no-self") imply this extinction is a matter of considerable dispute. See, for example, Donald Swearer, "Bhikkhu Buddhadasa on Ethics and Society," *Journal of Religious Ethics* 7 (1979): 54–64, and G. L. Doore, "Religion Within the Limits of the Quest for the Highest Good," *Religious Studies* 19 (1983): 345–59.

18. For a preliminary discussion of this issue see J. A. DiNoia, "Philosophical Theology in the Perspective of Religious Diversity," *Theological Studies* 49 (1988): 401–16. My forthcoming essay, "Pluralist Theology of Religions: Pluralistic or Non-Pluralistic?" (in *The Myth of Religious Pluralism*, ed. Gavin D'Costa [Maryknoll, N.Y.: Orbis Books, 1990]), defends the possibility and seriousness of interreligious disagreements about the nature of the ultimate. See also William P. Alston, "Religious Diversity and Perceptual Knowledge of God," *Faith and Philosophy* 5 (1988): 433–48.

19. My understanding and formulation of this question owes much to Christian's discussion of oppositions of religious doctrines in *Doctrines of Religious Communities*, 125–44, and to Thomas F. Tracy's summary of recent philosophy of action in *God, Action and Embodiment* (Grand Rapids, Mich.: Eerdmans, 1984), chs. 1 and 5.

20. I am indebted to Louis Pressman for this example.

21. For a wide-ranging analysis of this issue, see Christian, *Oppositions of Religious Doctrines*.

22. "Declaration on the Relation of the Church to Non-Christian Religions," *Vatican Council II: Conciliar and Post Conciliar Documents*, ed. Austin Flannery (Northport, N.Y.: Costello Publishing Company, 1975), 1: 738–42. For recent commentary on this declaration, see the essays composed for *Vatican II: Assessment and Perspectives*, ed. René Latourelle (New York: Paulist Press, 1988–), 3: 160–336.

23. Lindbeck, *The Nature of Doctrine*, 54.

24. J. A. DiNoia, "The Universality of Salvation and the Diversity of Religious Aims," *Worldmission* 32 (1981–82): 4–15.

25. See Paul J. Griffiths, "An Apology for Apologetics," *Faith and Philosophy* 5 (1988): 400–420.

26. See William C. Placher, *Unapologetic Theology: A Christian Voice in a Pluralistic Conversation* (Louisville, Ky.: Westminster/John Knox Press, 1989), 143–49.

27. For a reliable historical survey of Christian theology of religions, see Louis Capéran, *Le Problème du salut des infidèles* (Toulouse: Grand Séminaire, 1934), vol. 1.

28. Thomas Aquinas, *Summa Theologiae*, Ia2ae, 89, 6. See Thomas C. O'Brien, "Question 89, 6: A Commentary," in Blackfriars *Summa Theologiae* (New York: McGraw-Hill, and London, Eyre & Spottiswoode, 1974), vol. 27: 125–33.

29. Thomas Aquinas, *Summa Theologiae*, Ia2ae, 7–8; *De Veritate*, 14, 11.

30. Lindbeck, *The Nature of Doctrine*, 55–63, and "Fides ex auditu and the Salvation of non-Christians," *The Gospel and the Ambiguity of the Church*, ed. Vilmos Vajta (Philadelphia: Fortress Press, 1973), 91–123; DiNoia, "The Universality of Salvation and the Diversity of Religious Aims." It is confusing to find a prospective account like Lindbeck's characterized as exclusivist by Gavin D'Costa in "Theology of Religions," 276–78, when in fact such accounts are advanced precisely to do justice to the full range of empirical, philosophical, and doctrinal factors which standard exclusivist accounts deal with even less well than inclusivist and pluralist ones.

31. Notably by Karl Rahner, "Purgatory," *Theological Investigations* 19: 181–91, and by Joseph Ratzinger, *Eschatology: Death and Eternal Life*, trans. Michael Waldstein (Washington, D.C.: Catholic University of America Press, 1988), 218–33. Reliable surveys of the doctrine are presented by A. Piolante, "Il Dogma del Purgatorio," *Euntes Docete* 6 (1953), 287–311, and, more accessibly, by R. J. Bastian, "Purgatory," *New Catholic Encyclopedia* 11: 1034–39. A fascinating study of the development of the doctrine from the patristic through the medieval periods is presented by Jacques LeGoff, *The Birth of Purgatory*, trans. Arthur Goldhammer (Chicago: University of Chicago Press, 1984).

32. See Peter C. Phan's fine summary of Rahner's essays bearing on the topic in *Eternity in Time: A Study of Karl Rahner's Eschatology* (Selinsgrove, Pa.: Susquehanna University Press, 1988), 122–34.

33. Ratzinger, 205–9. See also Germain Grisez, *The Way of the Lord Jesus: Christian Moral Principles* (Chicago: Franciscan Herald Press, 1983), 445–46.

34. Thomas Aquinas, *Summa Theologiae*, Suppl. 69–70.

35. Jantzen, 590, objects to prospective or eschatological accounts of the salvation of non-Christians on the grounds that they posit an implausible—because utterly discontinuous—transformation of persons in the life to come. This is an important objection. But it does not seem fatal to the approach being suggested here, since the doctrine of purgatory envisages the possibility that, even for Christians, the transition to bliss will be "revolutionary," so to speak, and not merely in a cognitive sense. On the other hand, in response to Kenneth Surin's complaints about the "subsequence theory" that prospective accounts seem to involve (see " 'Many Religions and the One True Faith': on Lindbeck's Chapter Three," *Modern Theology* 4 [1988]: 187–209), it can be said that the doctrine of purgatory does not envisage a sharp, temporal disjunction between earthly life and the life to come: a link obtains between purgation in this life and purgation in the next, although (according to Aquinas) the former is willingly undertaken or embraced and the latter is more passively endured.

36. See Karl Rahner, "The Hermeneutics of Eschatological Assertions," *Theological Investigations* 4: 323–46.

EPILOGUE: GEORGE LINDBECK AND *THE NATURE OF DOCTRINE*

HANS W. FREI

When I first knew George Lindbeck, some thirty-seven years ago, we were both graduate students living on campus, and we would talk together earnestly from time to time, after the eternal fashion of graduate students—studiously, perhaps a bit solemnly and usually about very large topics, but above all very much like two people with very different ways of thinking who were always surprised at the end of the day at how much they shared when it came to the things that mattered to them both. It has been like that ever since for me. There was a period in the sixties when Professor Lindbeck seemed forever to be in Rome or other non-American parts of the compass, and conversation between us went into the freezer for a while; but the more important thing is that when we picked up again on a regular basis (it was, as he may not remember, one day over the exquisite lunch cuisine of Ezra Stiles College), it was as though we had never stopped; we simply picked up where we had left off. Now that, I submit to you, is a platitude. But it is also one—though certainly not the only— good test for the way friendships work, especially friendships among academic people: Do you pick up naturally after a long interval?

I say these things by way of asking you to agree with me, silently of course, that I surely can't be expected to give a balanced critical analysis of Professor Lindbeck's book. The association has been too long for that, my own stake in that slim volume too great.

I want to make three points about the book, one of them with three subpoints.

275

1. Two people have said to me on separate occasions that what
startled them about this book is that it states what they had really believed all along but had never been able to articulate properly. That's
a common experience, and it's one of the crucial ways in which a
book demonstrates its importance. It's also a dangerous quality. Very
often, especially in theology, scholars start off from shared convictions, a "common sense" in the best sense of that term, shared views
and a shared sensibility, and then relentlessly press some element in
that amalgam, untying one knot after another, until at some psychological point a common vocabulary and a shared sensibility turn into
a technical, often esoteric special-school outlook.

That's not the case with this book. The author invites you to
share a common vocabulary and sensibility. It's his cultural-linguistic
proposal for thinking about religion as a cultural or symbolic medium
in which we are enabled to live a common life and learn a common
language, in contrast to those who think of religion as an internal
experience which is shared with others only in the second place and
also in contrast to those who think of it as a true and unvarying
proposition about objective states of affairs. This basic part of the
book is an invitation to accept the superiority of a certain theory
of religion for certain purposes, but also an invitation to share the
sensibility it articulates or of which it is the grammar. But the invitation never outstrips the common sense it outlines. The *skill* in
Lindbeck's book is to offer another paradigm for common sensibility and theory simply, imaginatively, persuasively. The *self-discipline*
in Lindbeck's book is that in describing the sense and evoking the
sensibility of how cultures and persons are related, the author never
pushes the common sense beyond its limits, into that realm where
sensibility is constrained because aid to reflection has imperceptibly
turned instead into guidance by a technical guru or therapist. The
art in Lindbeck's book is the superb way in which he handles the
illustrations and analogies which are indispensable in the service of
the skill and the self-discipline. Those cogent and apt illustrations
that strike home every time should make any Germanic Thinker turn
blue with envy. All this is what may have persuaded my two friends
to say what they did about the book; and to be able to say what they
did is to mark the book as important.

2. The *point* about the invitation to share this new "common sense" is not the "common sense" itself. To be sure, Lindbeck thinks of it in its own right as a better theory for the general academic study of religion than its nearest rivals, but that's not its point in *this* book: The cultural-linguistic theory or approach to religion is there solely for the service it can render to the ongoing description or self-description of the Christian community and, by extension, to conversation in which members of various religions would be making grammatical remarks to each other about living, believing, and ritually enacting what their religion is about. I only have time to draw attention to one feature of this general point. Despite the fact that chapter 1 very clearly starts with the ecumenical matrix of reflection on doctrine, it only dawned on me gradually how central that really is to the book. Doctrinal reconciliation without doctrinal change is what Lindbeck reports from his large ecumenical experience: How to understand or account for "the intertwining of variability and invariability in matters of faith" (p. 17)? The whole book is governed by that question. Neither those who see doctrines as true and unvarying information nor those who see them as secondary and historically varying expressions of non- or pre-cognitive religious experience can answer that question or provide the logic enabling one to understand it. Lindbeck's answer is that in order to account for ecumenical agreement among formerly opposed parties who insist that they are nonetheless remaining faithful to their own traditional views—say, on justification by faith alone—one has to say that church doctrines function first of all "not as expressive symbols or as truth claims, but as communally authoritative rules of discourse, attitude and action." "Rules, unlike propositions or expressive symbols, retain an invariant meaning under changing conditions of compatibility and conflict" (p. 18). The whole book is an inquiry into how to explain that reality through the possibility immanent in it. It is a modest transcendental inquiry. The given reality is the agreement among adherents of formerly mutually opposed doctrines who insist that their doctrines are normative and abiding and not secondary and varying expressions of more basic religious outlooks. If that's the reality, how do you account for it? What is its internal logic? Lindbeck's answer is: by understanding doctrines as the

second-order rules, the grammar of the Christian community understood as a cultural symbol system—one in which *we* live and move
and have at least part of our being. And what in turn enables you
to understand doctrines that way? That's the function of the analysis of and invitation to the particular common sense about religion
which he (and others, both philosophers and social scientists) offers as "cultural-linguistic" theory. *Without the absolute priority of that
Christian-ecumenical reality, without its reality, forget the "rule" or regulative approach, forget the cultural-linguistic theory—forget the book.* In
that shape of the book's logic, three things are implied to my mind
(among many others).

A. First, and I hope I'm not here simply subverting Lindbeck's
agenda and substituting my own, Christian theology is a discipline
both in the non-ecclesiastical academy and in the church. Certainly
that constantly dual vocation has been its great strength at Yale Divinity School. Lindbeck stands foursquare in that tradition, and in
effect says that to do that duality justice one has to order one's priorities about it: Both vocations are best served when theology is seen
to be in service to the church first, to the academy second. Academic
theology is that second-order reflection which is an appropriate, albeit very modest instrument in aid of the critical description and
self-description of specific, religious-cultural communities, in our case
the Christian church.

B. Second, there will be plenty of flak for the book because of
the question that governs it: What is the logic inherent in the given
fact of ecumenical agreement? It will come, as Professor Lindbeck
knows, from the people he classifies as propositionalists in doctrine
more than from the others whom he calls experiential-expressivists,
although those who combine experiential-expressive and cognitive
categories will also want to make their rejoinders. There will be moderate propositionalists who will tell him that what he says about doctrines as second-order rules is sufficiently kin to doctrines as first-order
propositional statements that he could allow second-order doctrines
about the Trinity, atonement, etc., to have the character not only
of intra-systematic but ontological truth statements. Would he please
say more on that score? More traditional propositionalists will simply
ignore the question that sets the rule for the logic of the book, and
in effect rule it out of order. In effect they will say there is no such

thing as the ecumenical reality you report; it is appearance rather than reality and your business should have been to show how people could fool themselves into thinking it: If you take doctrines to be *normative*, you must take them to be unvarying or perhaps slightly varying statements about recognizably unvarying truth.

On the other side from the moderate propositionalists will be those who will say: Go on, show people how to use Christian language properly and that will take care of the question of its truth. There is no *special* question of that kind.

Now it's obvious that there are some things about the truth status of Christian discourse that puzzle Professor Lindbeck, to the extent that he agrees they need sorting out. Witness the fact that when in the slim index of the book you come to the word "truth," there are no fewer than eight subheadings under the rubric itself. A simple exhortation to you, George, at that point, a plea, if it's not too presumptuous: No matter from which quarter they needle you under the heading of that term, stick to your own agenda. You will have to say more about this general topic—and half under my breath, I will confess to some *qualified* sympathy for the moderate propositionalists—but no matter how complex or ambiguous your response, it must not abandon the priority of the agenda you have set in the book, the ecumenical reality which governs not only your theology but also the communal sensibility in which you have articulated it. Stick to your guns; treat the truth question also under the auspices of your theme, otherwise you will point us back to the theological past rather than to the future of which this book is such an encouraging earnest.

C. More briefly, another technical point in the form of a question: In our day Karl Barth is famous for telling us that prolegomena to dogmatic theology are part of dogmatic theology itself. Schleiermacher, by contrast, had suggested that prolegomena are distinct from theology, and when they are done properly they serve not as rigid presuppositions, axioms for arguments, or the assignment of theology to a more general logical class, but as mobile, connected thoughts helping to transport the reader's mind, mayhap her heart, into the communal context in which dogmatics is done. Am I right in thinking that in this respect, though certainly not in others, Professor Lindbeck's cultural-linguistic theory of religion functions in a way that is closer to Schleiermacher? But that the dogmatics to which these prolegomena help introduce the reader are closer to Barth, for whom dogmatics is second-order redescription of the normative text of the church, in effect the gospel narratives, the church's paradigmatic story and the paradigm of its life and language?

3. Now a final point about the book. I have recently reread some material by and about one of the most troubled, learned, and respectable academic figures hovering in the vicinity of the church in modern academic theology—Ernst Troeltsch. He was perhaps the most poignant of the religious liberals. First the church's tradition of unvarying normative belief gave way under his feet, indeed according to him *had* to give way, and then the relative superiority of the Christian over other religions; and yet, said he, in the West we're stuck with Christianity; no other religion can be inside us, and on the other hand neither can no religion at all. Not much of a religion that, you will say, with its affirmation of something called "cultures" as the location of proximity to the unknown divine, each in its own distinct way, and the better ones with that high ideal of humanity and that respect for persons which comes with the sense of a hidden purpose to all things historical. You're right, of course—not much of a religion either in religious beliefs or affections: But don't knock it; Troeltsch saw barbarism, cruel and enslaving intolerance, and a steadily increasing loss of humanity in human intercourse looming ahead among his fellow Germans, and there weren't enough like him who detested polarization as inhuman from the bottom of their hearts. There was for Troeltsch, unhappily, no effective norm to authorize restraint and humaneness in the chaos where one normative cultural symbol for the divine after another appears, makes its claims and then declines and disappears. Within 'Christianity' alone this was so true that that religion was in his eyes nothing more than a series of loosely connected but really disparate cultural constructs side by side and one after another in drastically changing historical contexts. Troeltsch referred the religious meaning of Christianity to the hidden religious significance of each of its many cultural contexts or epochs. He was a deeply devout, barely theistic liberal humanist of very high political standards and Christian sympathies. Cultural change was real for him, basic and permanent: the language of the church was various, changing, and not basic.

At least one theme in Professor Lindbeck's book is very close to and very understanding of troubled visions like this one, except that Lindbeck simply, ever so gently, and almost imperceptibly stands Troeltsch on his head. Especially in a day when young church people, especially in the "first" world, often keenly feel a loss of immediate relevance to their cultural context, there is religious strength and cultural confidence in a reminder of the church's mission in the name of Jesus of Nazareth, which reverses Troeltsch's cultural-religious fears into Christian hope in the midst and even in behalf of changing cultures. For example:

> It need not be the religion that is primarily reinterpreted as world views change, but rather the reverse: changing world views may be reinterpreted by one and same religion. . . . Jesus Christ, for instance, is in one setting affirmed primarily as the Messiah; in another as the incarnate Logos; and in a third, perhaps, as Bonhoeffer's "Man for Others" or Barth's "Humanity of God." Yet amid these shifts in Christological affirmations and in the corresponding experiences of Jesus Christ, the story of passion and resurrection and the basic rule for its use remain the same. Theological and religious transformations that lead to relativistic denials of an abiding identity (when one assumes constancy must be propositional, or symbolic, or experiential) can be seen, if one adopts rule theory, as the fusion of a self-identical story with the new worlds within which it is told and retold. (pp. 82–83)

In a powerful essay written quite a few years ago, "Ecumenism and the Future of Belief," Lindbeck amplified on the vocation of the Christian community and Christian individuals to live Christianly—in a sociological rather than theological sense 'sectarianly'—in desacralized societies. The theme is often implied, though not explicitly unfolded in this book. The half-invisible presence in the book is the paradigmatic Christian person whose experience is authorized by the reconciliation enacted in our world through Jesus of Nazareth, whose community is the community founded on that reconciliation. Under this impetus and authorization, such a person becomes a reconciling presence wherever bitter enmity threatens to pit human individuals and groups against each other. In a reversal of Troeltsch's vision, let us call this kind of person *the orthodox Christian as liberal humanist*. In saying that there *is* such a person—and that, all appearances to the contrary, (s)he is not a contradiction in terms but fits naturally into our world, we honor one aim of the book, we honor the rightly teaching academic theologian—as well as many a courageous, affectionate, and loyal pastor and lay person—and we honor the person of the author of this remarkable volume.

WRITINGS OF GEORGE A. LINDBECK

BOOKS

The Future of Roman Catholic Theology, Philadelphia: Fortress; London: S.P.C.K., 1970; also as *Le catholicisme a-t-il un avenir?* Paris: Casterman, 1971.

Infallibility (The Pere Marquette Theology Lecture), Milwaukee: Marquette University Press, 1972.

University Divinity Schools: A Report on Ecclesiastically Independent Theological Education (in association with Karl Deutsch and Nathan Glazer), New York: The Rockefeller Foundation, 1976.

The Nature of Doctrine: Religion and Theology in a Postliberal Age, Philadelphia: Westminster, 1984.

ARTICLES

"N.A.M. Organizes Church and Industry Conferences," *Social Action* 11/6 (1945): 4–20.

"Catholicisme Américain," *Le Semeur* (organ of the Fédération Française des Associations Chrétiennes d'Etudiants) 46 (1947): 274–81.

"A Note on Aristotle's Discussion of God and the World," *Review of Metaphysics* 2 (1948): 99–106.

"Should the U.S. Send Ambassador to Vatican?" *Foreign Policy Bulletin* 31/7 (1951): 4, 6.

"Philosophy and 'Existenz' in Early Christianity," *Review of Metaphysics* 10 (1957): 428–40.

"Participation and Existence in the Interpretation of St. Thomas Aquinas," *Franciscan Studies* 17 (1957): 1–22, 107–25.

"Thomism," in *Handbook of Christian Theology*, ed. Marvin Halverson and Arthur A. Cohen, New York: Meridian, 1958, 361–63.

"Roman Catholic Reactions to the Third Assembly of the L.W.F.," *Lutheran World* 5 (1958–59): 70–73; also in *Lutherische Rundschau* 8 (1958): 78–81.

Translation of Martin Luther, *Contra Latomus*; *Luther's Works*, American Edition, vol. 32, Philadelphia: Muhlenberg, 1958, 133–266.

"Nominalism and the Problem of Meaning as Illustrated by Pierre d'Ailly on Predestination and Justification," *Harvard Theological Review* 52 (1959): 43–60.

"Revelation, Natural Law and the Thought of Reinhold Niebuhr," *Natural Law Forum* 4 (1959): 146–51.

"A New Roman Catholic View of Justification," *Ecumenical Review* 11 (1959): 334–40.

"Interconfessional Studies," *Lutheran World* 6 (1959–60): 315–20; also in *Lutherische Rundschau* 9 (1959): 376–82.

Contribution to "Symposium on a Roman Catholic President," *American Lutheran* 43 (1960): 190–92.

"Thomism—Barrier or Bridge?" *Our Sunday Visitor*, Nov. 20, 1960, 2A–3A.

"The Evangelical Possibilities of Roman Catholic Theology," *Lutheran World* 7 (1960–61), 142–52; also in *Lutherische Rundschau* 10 (1960): 197–209.

"The Confessions as Ideology and Witness in the History of Lutheranism," *Lutheran World* 7 (1960–61): 388–401; also in *Lutherische Rundschau* 10 (1960): 456–67.

"Roman Catholicism on the Eve of the Council," in *The Papal Council and the Gospel*, ed. Kristen E. Skydsgaard, Minneapolis: Augsburg, 1961, 61–92; also in *Konzil und Evangelium*, ed. Kristen E. Skydsgaard, Göttingen: Vandenhoeck & Ruprecht, 1961, 63–94; and as "El catolicismo Romano on Visperas del Concilio," *Cuadernos Teologicos* 11 (1962): 101–29.

"John Courtney Murray, S.J.: An Evaluation," *Christianity and Crisis* 21 (1961): 213–16.

"Reform and Infallibility," *Cross Currents* 11 (1961): 345–56.

"Conversation of the Faithful," *Saturday Review* 44 (March 4, 1961): 24–25.

"Natural Law in the Thought of Paul Tillich," *Natural Law Forum* 7 (1962): 84–96.

"Reform and the Council," *Lutheran World* 9 (1962): 303–17; also in *Lutherische Rundschau* 12 (1962): 389–405.

"The Second Vatican Council," *Christianity and Crisis* 22 (1962): 164–68, and *Concordia Theological Monthly* 34 (1963): 19–24.

"The Thrust of 'Progressive' Catholicism," *Commonweal* 79 (1963): 105–7.

"Liturgical Reform in the Second Vatican Council," *Lutheran World* 10 (1963): 161–71; also in *Lutherische Rundschau* 13 (1963):

191–204; and (in part) in *Ende des Gegen-Reformation?* ed. J. C. Hampe, Berlin-Stuttgart: Krenz Verlag, 1964, 90–101.

"The Future of Roman Catholic Theology in the Light of the First Session of the Second Vatican Council," *Dialog* 2 (1963): 245–53.

"A Letter from Rome," *Yale Divinity News*, 1963, 3–6.

"So Far, Surprisingly Good," *The National Lutheran* 31/3 (March 1963): 12–14, 19.

"On Councils: Impressions from Helsinki, Rome and Montreal," *Lutheran World* 11 (1964): 37–48; also in *Lutherische Rundschau* 14 (1964): 45–60; also (in part) in Hampe, ed. (see above), 359–63, and in *Catholic World* 193 (1964): 272–81.

"Reform, But Slow and Cautious," *Concordia Theological Monthly* 35 (1964): 284–86.

"A Protestant View of the Ecclesiological Status of the Roman Catholic Church," *Journal of Ecumenical Studies* 1 (1964): 243–70; also as "Eine protestantische Ansicht über den ekklesiologischen Status der römisch-katholischen Kirche," *Una Sancta* (Meitingen) 19 (1964): 101–24.

"Theologische Begründing der Stiftung für ökumenische Forschung" and "Dialog mit Rom," in *Helsinki 1963: Beiträge zum theologischen Gespräch des lutherischen Weltbundes*, ed. Erwin Wilkens, Berlin: Lutherisches Verlagshaus, 1964, 233–39, 240–53.

"Ecclesiology and Roman Catholic Renewal," *Religion in Life* 33 (1964): 383–94.

"Pierre Abelard," *The American Peoples Encyclopedia*, 20 vols., New York: Grolier, 1964.

"Ecumenism and Liturgical Renewal," *Una Sancta* (New York) 21/3–4 (1964): 7–11.

"The *A Priori* in St. Thomas's Theory of Knowledge," in *The Heritage of Christian Thought*, ed. Robert E. Cushman and Egil Grislis, New York: Harper, 1965, 41–63.

"The Status of the Nicene Creed as Dogma of the Church: Some Questions from Lutherans to Roman Catholics," in *The Status of the Nicene Creed as Dogma of the Church* (*Lutherans and Catholics in Dialogue* 1), ed. Paul C. Empie and T. Austin Murphy, Minneapolis: Augsburg, 1965, 11–15.

"Preface," "Pope John's Council: First Session," "Paul VI Becomes Pope: Second Session" (with Warren A. Quanbeck), and "Church and World: Schema 13," in *Dialogue on the Way: Protestants Report from Rome on the Vatican Council*, ed. George A. Lindbeck, Minneapolis: Augsburg, 1965, v–ix, 18–71, 231–52 (also as *Dialog Unterwegs*, Göttingen: Vandenhoeck & Ruprecht, 1965; *Le dialogue est ouvert*, Neuchatel: Delachaux & Niestlé, 1965; *El Dialogo esta abierto*, Barcelona: Ediciones de Cultura Popular, 1967).

"The Jews, Renewal, and Ecumenism," *Journal of Ecumenical Studies* 2 (1965): 471–73.

"The Thought of Karl Rahner, S.J.," *Christianity and Crisis* 25 (1965): 211–15.

"Medieval Theology," *The Encyclopedia of the Lutheran Church*, Minneapolis: Augsburg, 1965, vol. 2, 1510–16.

"The Constitution on the Church: A Protestant Point of View," in *Vatican II: An Interfaith Appraisal*, ed. John H. Hiller, Notre Dame, Ind.: University of Notre Dame Press, 1966, 219–30; also as "Die Kirchenlehre des Konzils ist ein Übergang," in *Die Autorität der Freiheit*, ed. J. C. Hampe, vol. 1, Munich: Kösel, 1967, 359–72.

"The Framework of Protestant-Catholic Disagreement," in *The Word in History: The St. Xavier Symposium*, ed. T. Patrick Burke, New York: Sheed & Ward, 1966, 102–19.

"Church in the Modern World," *Saturday Review* 49 (July 30, 1966): 36.

"Jewish Christian Dialogue," *Journal of Ecumenical Studies* 3 (1966): 146–47.

"A Definitive Look at Vatican II," *Christianity and Crisis* 26 (1966): 291–95.

"There Is No Protestant Church," *Una Sancta* (New York) 23/1 (1966): 91–100.

"Karl Rahner and a Protestant View of the Sacramentality of the Ministry," *Proceedings of the Catholic Theological Society of America* 21 (1966): 262–88; also as "The Sacramentality of the Ministry: Karl Rahner and a Protestant View," in *Oecumenica 1967: Jahrbuch für ökumenische Forschung*, ed. Friedrich W. Kantzenbach and Vilmos Vajta, Strasbourg: Centre d'Etudes Oecumeniques, 1967, 282–301.

"Reply to J. M. Oesterreicher," *Christianity and Crisis* 26 (1966): 133–34.

"The Declaration on Religious Liberty," in *Challenge and Response*, ed. Warren A. Quanbeck, Minneapolis: Augsburg, 1966, 145–60; also as "Die Erklärung über die Religionsfreiheit," in *Wir sind gefragt*, ed. Friedrich W. Kantzenbach and Vilmos Vajta, Göttingen: Vandenhoeck & Ruprecht, 1966, 145–60.

"The Reformation in an Ecumenical Age," *Princeton Seminary Bulletin* 61/1 (1967): 21–28.

"Secular Ecumenism in Action," *Catholic World* 205 (1967): 7–13.

"Ottaviani's Counterpart," *Christian Century* 84 (1967): 15–16.

"The Problem of Doctrinal Development and Contemporary Protestant Theology," in *Man as Man and Believer*, ed. Edward Schillebeeckx and Boniface Willems, *Concilium* 21, New York: Paulist Press, 1967, 133–49.

"Ecumenism, Cosmic Redemption and the Council," in *Ecumenism, the Spirit and Worship*, ed. Leonard Swidler, Pittsburgh: Dusquesne University Press, 1967, 62–79.

"Discovering Thomas: (1) The Classical Statement of Christian Theism," *Una Sancta* (New York), 24/1 (1967): 45–52; "(2) Tentative Language about the Trinity," 24/3, 44–48; "(3) The Origin of Man," 24/4, 67–75; "(4) Hope and the Sola Fide," 25/1, 66–73.

"The New Vision of the World and the Ecumenical Revolution," *Religious Education* 62 (1967): 83–90.

"Ecumenism and the Future of Belief," *Una Sancta* (New York) 25/3 (1968): 3–17.

"The Lutheran Doctrine of the Ministry: Catholic and Reformed," *Theological Studies* 30 (1969): 588–612; also as "Doctrinal Standards, Theological Theories and Practical Aspects of the Ministry in the Lutheran Churches," in *Evangelium-Welt-Kirche*, ed. Harding Meyer, Frankfurt am Main, 1975, 263–84.

"The Present Ecumenical and Church Situation in West Malaysia and Singapore," *South East Asia Journal of Theology* 11 (1969): 72–80.

"Ecumenism and World Mission: Foundations, Principles and Policies," *Lutheran World* 17 (1970): 69–77.

290 / Writings of George A. Lindbeck

The Future of the Dialogue: Pluralism or an Eventual Synthesis of
Doctrine?" in *Christian Action and Openness*, ed. Joseph Papin,
Villanova, Pa.: Villanova University Press, 1970, 37–51.

"The Sectarian Future of the Church," in *The God Experience*, ed.
J. P. Whelan, S.J., New York: Newman, 1971, 226–43.

"Protestant Problems with Lonergan on Development of Dogma," in
Foundations of Theology, ed. Philip McShane, S.J., Dublin: Gill
& Macmillan, 1971, 115–23.

"The Infallibility Debate," in *The Infallibility Debate*, ed. John J. Kir-
van, New York: Paulist Press, 1971, 35–65.

"Unbelievers and the 'Sola Christi,'" *Dialog* 12 (1973): 182–89.

"Papacy and *ius divinum*: A Lutheran View," in *Papal Primacy and the
Universal Church* (*Lutherans and Catholics in Dialogue 5*), ed. Paul
C. Empie and T. Austin Murphy, Minneapolis: Augsburg, 1974,
193–207.

"*Fides ex auditu* and the Salvation of non-Christians," in *The Gospel
and the Ambiguity of the Church*, ed. Vilmos Vajta, Philadelphia:
Fortress, 1974, 91–123; also in *Das Evangelium und die Zwei-
deutigkeit der Kirche*, ed. Vilmos Vajta, Göttingen: Vandenhoeck
& Ruprecht, 1973, 122–57.

"The Crisis in American Catholicism," in *Our Common History as
Christians*, ed. J. Deschner et al., New York: Oxford, 1975,
47–66.

"Papal Infallibility: A Protestant Response," *Commonweal* 102 (1975):
145–46.

"Theological Revolutions and the Present Crisis," *Theology Digest* 23
(1975): 307–19 (The Twentieth Annual Robert Cardinal Bel-
larmine Lecture, St. Louis University).

"What I Think about the Roman Catholic Church: The Catholic Crisis," *Commonweal* 103 (1976): 107–10.

"A Lutheran View of Intercommunion with Roman Catholics," *Journal of Ecumenical Studies* 13 (1976): 242–48; also in *The Eucharist in Ecumenical Dialogue*, ed. Leonard Swidler, New York: Paulist Press, 1976, 52–58.

"Lutheran Response" (to Avery Dulles, "Intercommunion between Lutherans and Roman Catholics"), *Journal of Ecumenical Studies* 13 (1976): 257–59.

"Lutherans and the Papacy," *Journal of Ecumenical Studies* 13 (1976): 358–68.

"Two Types of Ecumenism," in *The Papin Festschrift*, vol. 2, ed. J. Armenti, Villanova, Pa.: Villanova University Press, 1976, 371–75.

"Der Zusammenhang von Kirchenkritik und Rechtfertigungslehre," in *Luther damals und heute*, ed. Walter Kasper and Hans Küng, *Concilium* 12, Zürich and Mainz, 1976, 481–86.

"A Battle for Theology: Hartford in Historical Perspective," in *Against the World, for the World: The Hartford Appeal and the Future of American Religion*, ed. Peter L. Berger and Richard J. Neuhaus, New York: Seabury, 1976, 20–43.

"Critical Reflections," in *Religious Freedom: 1965 and 1975*, ed. Walter J. Burghardt, New York: Paulist Press, 1977, 52–54.

"Theological Education in North America Today," *Bulletin of the Council on the Study of Religion* 8/4 (1977): 85, 87–89.

"Problems on the Road to Unity: Infallibility," *Unitatis Redintegratio: 1964–1974: Eine Bilanz der Auswirkungen des Ökumenismusdekrets*, ed. Gerard Békés and Vilmos Vajta (*Studia Anselmiana*

71), Frankfurt: Verlag Otto Lembeck; Verlag Josef Knecht, 1977, 98–109.

"Theologische Methode und Wissenschaftstheorie," *Theologische Revue* 74 (1978): 266–80.

"Reception and Method: Reflections on the Ecumenical Role of the LWF," in *Ecumenical Methodology*, ed. Peder Nørgaard-Højen, Geneva: Lutheran World Federation, 1978, 33–48.

"Christians between Arabs and Jews," *Worldview* 22/9 (1979): 25–26, 35–39.

"The Reformation and the Infallibility Debate," in *Teaching Authority and Infallibility in the Church* (*Lutherans and Catholics in Dialogue* 6), ed. Paul C. Empie, T. Austin Murphy and Joseph A. Burgess, Minneapolis: Augsburg, 1980, 101–19.

"Report on the Roman Catholic/Lutheran Dialogue," in *LWF Documentation* no. 4, Geneva: Lutheran World Federation, 1980, 18–23; also as "Bericht über den römisch-katholisch/evangelisch-lutherischen Dialog," *LWB-Dokumentation* 4: 19–24.

"The Bible as Realistic Narrative," *Consensus in Theology? A Dialogue with Hans Küng and Edward Schillebeeckx*, ed. Leonard Swidler; identical with *Journal of Ecumenical Studies* 17/1 (1980), Philadelphia: Westminster, 1980, 81–85.

"The Augsburg Confession in the Light of Contemporary Catholic-Lutheran Dialogue" (with Vilmos Vajta), in *The Role of the Augsburg Confession: Catholic and Lutheran Views*, Philadelphia: Fortress, 1980, 81–95.

"Lutheran Churches," *Ministry in America*, ed. David S. Schuller, Merton P. Strommen, Milo L. Brekke, New York: Harper & Row, 1980, 414–45.

"Rite Vocatus: Der theologische Hintergrund zu CA 14," in *Confessio Augustana und Confutatio*, ed. Erwin Iserloh, Münster: Aschendorff, 1980, 454–67.

"Hesychastic Prayer and the Christianizing of Platonism: Some Protestant Reflections," in *Prayer in Late Antiquity and in Early Christianity: Yearbook 1978–1979 of the Ecumenical Institute for Advanced Theological Studies*, ed. P. Benoit, Tantur/Jerusalem, 1981, 71–88.

"The Limits of Diversity in the Understanding of Justification," *Lutheran Theological Seminary Bulletin* (Gettysburg, Pa.) 61/1 (1981): 3–16.

"The Divided Church," in *Call to Global Mission* (Background Papers, Convention of the Lutheran Church in America, Sept. 3–10, 1982), New York: LCA Division for World Mission and Ecumenism, 313–24.

"Bishops and the Ministry of the Gospel" (with Avery Dulles), in *Confessing One Faith*, ed. George Forell and James McCue, Minneapolis: Augsburg, 1982, 147–72; also as "Die Bischöfe und der Dienst des Evangeliums: Ein Kommentar zu CA 5, 14, 28" (with Avery Dulles), in *Confessio Augustana: Bekenntnis des einen Glaubens*, ed. Harding Meyer and Heinz Schütte, Paderborn: Bonifacius; Frankfurt am Main: Lembeck, 1980, 139–68.

"An Assessment Re-Assessed: Paul Tillich on the Reformation," *The Journal of Religion* 63 (1983): 376–93.

"Reflections on the New York Forum: From Academy to Church," *Theological Education* 19 (1983): 65–70.

"Historiskt uttalande om Luther" (with Lars Thunberg and Hans Martinsen), *Svenisk Teologisk Kvartalskrift* 59 (1983): 139–43.

"Luther on Law in Ecumenical Context," *Dialog* 22 (1983), 270–74.

"Vatican II and Protestant Self-Understanding," in *Vatican II: Open Questions and New Horizons*, ed. Gerald M. Fagin, Wilmington: M. Glazier, 1984, 58–74.

"Letter from Budapest: Bitter Taste," *Forum Letter* (New York), 13/9 (Sept. 28, 1984): 1–4.

"Modernity and Luther's Understanding of the Freedom of the Christian," in *Martin Luther and the Modern Mind*, ed. Manfred Hoffman, *Toronto Studies in Theology* 22, Toronto and New York: Edwin Mellen Press, 1985, 1–22.

"The Ratzinger File: But If One Despairs. . .," *Commonweal* 112 (1985): 635–36.

"A Question of Compatibility: A Lutheran Reflects on Trent," *Justification by Faith* (*Lutherans and Catholics in Dialogue* 7), ed. H. George Anderson, et al., Minneapolis: Augsburg, 1985, 230–40.

"Justification by Faith: An Analysis of the 1983 Report," *LCA Partners* 6 (1985): 7–12, 30.

"Barth and Textuality," *Theology Today* 43 (1986): 361–76.

"The Story-Shaped Church: Critical Exegesis and Theological Interpretation," in *Scriptural Authority and Narrative Interpretation*, ed. Garrett Green, Philadelphia: Fortress, 1987, 161–78.

"The Search for Habitable Texts," *Daedalus* 117/2 (1988): 153–56.

"The Church," in *Keeping the Faith: Essays to Mark the Centenary of Lux Mundi*, ed. Geoffrey Wainwright, Philadelphia: Fortress, 1988, 179–208.

"Non-Theological Factors and Structures of Unity," in *Einheit der Kirche: Neue Entwicklungen und Perspektiven*, ed. Günther Gassmann and Peder Nørgaard-Højen, Frankfurt: Verlag Otto Lembeck, 1988, 133–45.

"Scripture, Consensus, and Community," *This World* 23 (Fall 1988): 5–24; also in *The Crisis of Biblical Authority: The Ratzinger Conference on Bible and Church*, ed. Richard John Neuhaus, Grand Rapids: Eerdmans, 1989, 74–101.

"The Reformation Heritage and Christian Unity," *Lutheran Quarterly* (n.s.) 2 (1988): 477–502.

"Spiritual Formation and Theological Education," *Theological Education* 24, Suppl. 1 (1988): 10–32.

"Ecumenical Theology," *The Modern Theologians*, vol. 2, ed. David F. Ford, Oxford: Blackwell, 1989, 255–73.

"Episcopacy and the Unification of the Churches: Two Approaches," in *Promoting Unity: Themes in Lutheran-Catholic Dialogue*, ed. H. George Anderson and James R. Crumley, Jr., Minneapolis: Augsburg, 1989, 51–65.

"The Church's Mission to a Postmodern Culture," in *Postmodern Theology: Christian Faith in a Pluralist World*, ed. Frederic B. Burnham, New York: Harper & Row, 1989, 37–55.

"Response to Bruce Marshall," *The Thomist* 53 (1989), 403–6.

"Education for Lutheran Ministry in Non-Denominational Settings," *Dialog* 28 (1989): 114–16.

"Theologians, Theological Faculties, and the ELCA Study of Ministry," *Dialog* 28 (1989): 198–205.

"Martin Luther and the Rabbinic Mind," in *Understanding the Rabbinic Mind: Essays on the Hermeneutic of Max Kadushin*, ed. Peter Ochs, Atlanta: Scholars Press (Brown Judaic Studies), 1990.

SELECTED REVIEWS

"A Great Scotist Study" (review of Etienne Gilson's *Jean Duns Scot*) *Review of Metaphysics* 7 (1954): 422–35.

Review of Jaroslav Pelikan's *The Riddle of Roman Catholicism*, *Lutheran World* 7 (1960–61): 103–4; also in *Lutherische Rundschau* 10: 116–18.

"Erikson's *Young Man Luther*: A Historical and Theological Reappraisal," *Soundings* 56 (1973): 210–27; also in *Encounter with Erickson*, ed. D. Capps et al., Missoula, Mont.: Scholars Press, 1977, 7–27.

Review of Marina Warner's *Alone of All Her Sex: The Myth and Cult of the Virgin Mary*, *Commonweal* 104 (1977): 23–25.

Review of Gordan D. Kaufman's *An Essay on Theological Method*, *Religious Studies Review* 5 (1979): 262–64.

Review of John Hick, ed., *The Myth of God Incarnate*, *The Journal of Religion* 59 (1979): 248–50.

"Ebeling: Climax of a Great Tradition" (reviewing Gerhard Ebeling, *Dogmatik des christlichen Glaubens*, vol. 1), *The Journal of Religion* 61 (1981): 309–14.

Review of Jeffrey Stout's *Ethics after Babel: The Languages of Morals and Their Discontents*, *Theology Today* 46 (1989): 59–61.

ECUMENICAL DIALOGUES

International Lutheran-Roman Catholic Dialogues

George Lindbeck was participant in and signatory to:

Roman Catholic/Lutheran Study Commission, "The Gospel and the Church," *Lutheran World* 19 (1972): 259–72; also in *Lutherische Rundschau* 22 (1972): 344–62; reprinted in *Growth in Agreement: Reports and Agreed Statements of Ecumenical Conversations on a World Level*, ed. Harding Meyer and Lukas Vischer, New York: Paulist Press; Geneva: World Council of Churches, 1984, 168–89.

George Lindbeck was co-chair of the following Roman Catholic/Lutheran Joint Commissions, and signatory to the agreed statements they produced:

The Eucharist, Geneva: Lutheran World Federation, 1980; reprinted in *Growth in Agreement*, 190–214; also as *Das Herrenmahl*, Paderborn: Verlag Bonifatius; Frankfurt: Verlag Otto Lembeck, 1978.

Ways to Community, Geneva: Lutheran World Federation, 1981; reprinted in *Growth in Agreement*, 215–40; also as *Wege zur Gemeinschaft*, Paderborn: Verlag Bonifatius; Frankfurt: Verlag Otto Lembeck, 1981.

"All Under One Christ: Statement on the Augsburg Confession"; also printed as "Alle unter einem Christus: Stellungmahme zum Augsburgischen Bekenntnis," English and German published in same volume with *Ways to Community* or *Wege zur Gemeinschaft*, also in *Growth in Agreement*, 241–47.

The Ministry in the Church, Geneva: Lutheran World Federation: 1982; reprinted in *Growth in Agreement*, 248–75; also printed as *Das Geistliche Amt in der Kirche*, Paderborn: Verlag Bonifatius; Frankfurt: Verlag Otto Lembeck, 1982.

Facing Unity: Models, Forms and Phases of Catholic-Lutheran Church Fellowship, Geneva: Lutheran World Federation, 1985; also printed as *Einheit Vor Uns: Modelle, Formen und Phasen katholisch/ lutherischer Kirchengemeinschaft*, Paderborn: Verlag Bonifatius; Frankfurt: Verlag Otto Lembeck, 1985.

"Martin Luther—Witness to Jesus Christ: Statement on the Occasion of Martin Luther's 500th Birthday"; also printed as "Martin Luther—Zeuge Jesu Christi: Wort anlasslich des 500. Geburtstages Martin Luthers," English and German published in same volume with *Facing Unity* or *Einheit Vor Uns*.

American Lutheran-Roman Catholic Dialogues

Lutherans and Catholics in Dialogue (USA). George Lindbeck was participant in the following Dialogues, and signatory to the agreed statements they produced (all published by Augsburg, Minneapolis):

The Status of the Nicene Creed as Dogma of the Church (1965).
One Baptism for the Remission of Sin (1966).
The Eucharist as Sacrifice (1967).
Eucharist and Ministry (1970).
Papal Primacy and the Universal Church (1974).
Teaching Authority and Infallibility in the Church (1979).
Justification by Faith (1985).

Index of Names

Adolfs, Robert, 211 n. 14
Almond, Philip, 252
Alston, William P., 272 n. 18
Alter, Robert, 61 n. 24, 125 n. 2
Altschuler, David, 242 n. 11
Anselm, 76, 142
Apel, Karl Otto, 233
Aquinas. *See* Thomas Aquinas
Arendt, Hannah, 33 n. 65
Aristotle, 22, 77, 90–91, 95–96,
    109–11, 113–14, 116, 121
Aron, Raymond, 197
Auerbach, Erich, 40, 59 n. 16, 162 n. 7
Augustine, 50, 55, 76–77, 92, 109, 123
Avery-Peck, Alan, 245 n. 69

Balthasar, Hans Urs von, 53, 67 n. 75,
    99 n. 19, 100 n. 24
Barrett, Lee C., 144 n. 2, 187 n. 28,
    188 n. 30
Barth, Gerhard, 63 n. 40
Barth, Karl, 40, 77, 85, 152, 281–82
Barthes, Roland, 162 n. 8
Barton, John, 62 n. 37, 64 n. 46
Bastian, R. J., 273 n. 31
Beinert, Wolfgang, 190 n. 40
Beker, J. Christian, 67 n. 72
Bell, Daniel, 15
Bellah, Robert N., 20
Bendix, Reinhard, 212 n. 22
Berger, Peter, 172
Bergson, Henri, 243 n. 32
Bettenhausen, Elizabeth, 190 n. 44
Betz, Hans Dieter, 60 n. 22
Bonaventure, 96
Bornkamm, Günther, 63 n. 40

Brahe, Tycho, 137
Breidert, M., 211 n. 15
Buber, Martin, 214–15, 218, 225–27
Buckley, Michael, 131–32, 134–40,
    143–44
Bultmann, Rudolf, 46, 55
Burrell, David B., 3, 246 n. 74
Butterfield, Herbert, 137

Calvin, John, 131
Capéran, Louis, 273 n. 27
Cessario, Romanus, 271 n. 15
Chenu, M.-D., 145 n. 21
Chesterton, G. K., 243 n. 13
Christian, William A., Sr., 74, 100 n.
    25, 172–74, 246 n. 74, 254, 271 n.
    15, 272 nn. 19, 21
Clark, Mary T., 129 n. 51
Clarke, Samuel, 134
Cohen, Hermann, 214–15, 218,
    225–27, 236
Cohon, Samuel, 245 n. 69
Collins, John, 67 n. 73
Comstock, Gary, 59 n. 16
Cone, James, 48
Cousins, Ewert, 67 n. 75
Cragg, Kenneth, 270 n. 3
Crossan, John Dominic, 47, 64 n. 51
Crowe, Frederick, 129 nn. 50, 53
Crump, Eric, 58 n. 13

Davidson, Donald, 74–75, 88
Davies, W. D., 50
D'Costa, Gavin, 270 nn. 1–3; 273 n. 30
de Laguna, G. A., 243 n. 30
de Lubac, Henri, 66 n. 64

299